PRAISE FOR *GLOBAL MIGRATION AND CHRISTIAN FAITH*

"This volume utilizes a multidisciplinary approach and diverse perspectives to assess human migration as it intersects with Christian life, impacts faith, and shapes the church's mission. The treatment is probing and provocative. The essays tackle some of the most pressing issues around migration and religion in ways that make the collection a valuable source for both academic teaching and serious Christian reflection. Readers will find their thinking challenged and their understanding deepened."

—JEHU J. HANCILES, Candler School of Theology, Emory University

"In the midst of an unprecedented global refugee crisis, Christian scholars, pastors, and lay people alike are asking how their faith should inform their views on the topic of migration. While many discussions on immigration begin and end with politics, *Global Migration and Christian Faith* brings thoughtful perspectives rooted in the Bible, theology, church history, and missiology to Christians seeking to understand and respond faithfully to the challenges and opportunities of migration."

—MATTHEW SOERENS, US Director of Church Mobilization and Advocacy, World Relief

"In this evocative collection, Carroll and Bacote bring together biblical, theological, historical, and practical reflections for addressing today's migration questions. Christians need urgently to draw out the riches of the past for ministering to migrants today, and these essays are a model of how to go about that task."

—MYLES WERNTZ, Abilene Christian University

"This book . . . does much to provide clarity by reading the signs of our times in the light of the breadth and depth of our history, our sacred texts and traditions. The authors—who offer insights from across the spectrum of Christianity—challenge us to consider how the complex and urgent realities of people on the move must make us rethink who we are as Christians and what we are called to do."

—JEAN-PIERRE M. RUIZ, St. John's University

"Migration is global and so is the church. But is your faith? *Global Migration and Christian Faith* gives an unequivocal *yes*! These scholars show us that a Christian faith rooted in biblical truth and standing firmly on theological principles can (and must!) respond to the crises of migrants and refugee neighbors at our borders. Here's how: rev up your theological imagination, hear the prophetic invitations in these pages, open your heart, and let's get started."

—JULIA LAMBERT FOGG, author of *Finding Jesus at the Border: Opening Our Hearts to the Stories of Our Immigrant Neighbors*

Global Migration and Christian Faith

Global Migration and Christian Faith

Implications for Identity and Mission

EDITED BY

M. DANIEL CARROLL R.
VINCENT E. BACOTE

WIPF & STOCK · Eugene, Oregon

GLOBAL MIGRATION AND CHRISTIAN FAITH
Implications for Identity and Mission

Cascade Books
An Imprint of Wipf and Stock Publishers
199 W. 8th Ave., Suite 3
Eugene, OR 97401

www.wipfandstock.com

PAPERBACK ISBN: 978-1-7252-8148-6
HARDCOVER ISBN: 978-1-7252-8147-9
EBOOK ISBN: 978-1-7252-8149-3

Cataloguing-in-Publication data:

Names: Carroll R., M. Daniel, editor. | Bacote, Vincent E., editor.

Title: Global migration and Christian faith : implications for identity and
mission / M. Daniel Carroll R. and Vincent E. Bacote, editors.

Description: Eugene, OR: Cascade Books, 2021 | Includes bibliographical
references and index.

Identifiers: ISBN 978-1-7252-8148-6 (paperback) | ISBN 978-1-7252-8147-9
(hardcover) | ISBN 978-1-7252-8149-3 (ebook)

Subjects: LCSH: Emigration and immigration in the Bible. | Emigration and
immigration—Religious aspects—Christianity. | Refugees—Government
policy.

Classification: BS680.E38 .G150 2021 (paperback) | BS680.E38 (ebook)

12/13/21

Contents

THEOLOGICAL REFLECTIONS

ECCLESIOLOGICAL AND MISSIOLOGICAL CHALLENGES

Preface

Go. Move. Relocate. Migrate. These are examples of the "motion" words we encounter as we follow the narrative of the Bible and the history of the church. We cannot escape the centrality of movement in the history of Israel and God's mission in the world. There are multiple circumstances that lead to the geographic transitions of the people we encounter in the Bible and in the church. Some are nomadic, some are sent, some are summoned, and some seek survival. These various migrations have included complications in trajectory, duration, and ultimate destination, along with conflicts within and without. Of course, these experiences are not limited to the people of God. It is a story shared by many millions in the history of the world and today.

Issues revolving around migration are becoming particularly acute. It is a time of great distress and perplexity, a time in which multiple cultural and political factors have many Christians confused about how to think about questions of mission, migration, and certainly immigration. These were some of the concerns behind the planning of the 2020 Wheaton Theology Conference. Unfortunately, what could have been an excellent space for reflection and discussion had to be cancelled due to the COVID-19 pandemic. In spite of that setback, we solicited essays from the invited presenters for this volume. The aim of the conference had been to provide broad exposure to various dimensions of migration from several disciplines and from different Christian traditions. It is important to consider perspectives historical (migration is not something new; how did the church and some of its iconic leaders respond in the past?), biblical (migration is central to both Old and New Testaments), ecumenical–theological (the spectrum of traditions), and ecclesiological–missiological (realities on the ground that challenge the identity and role of the church). This diversity of perspectives helps unveil the complexity of matters related to migration.

The scope of the topic is also important for perspective. Questions of migration are global in nature, not just in terms of migration to Western Hemisphere countries. The promises of globalization ring hollow for many, and multiple crises have led to many relocations birthed from desperation. How are we to understand and respond to these circumstances? What obligations do we have as Christians in the face of these circumstances? Our hope is that these essays will help equip the church to convey God's concerns for these issues to the broader public, and that this be expressed by various constituencies and across different traditions.

This volume begins with potential insights from the past. Looking back is vital not merely for information, but more importantly for ways to discover emphases often overlooked when considering historical figures and movements. Leopoldo A. Sánchez M. looks at two writings of the German reformer Martin Luther, one early in his career and one later. Sánchez invites us to consider whether it is time to add an additional "sola" to the those typically associated with the Protestant Reformation (*sola scriptura, sola fide, sola gratia, solus Christus,* and *soli Deo Gloria*). He directs our attention to Luther's distinction between two types of "love" in his last thesis of the *Heidelberg Disputation* (1518) and his discussion of Abraham's hospitality in Genesis 18 in his *Lectures on Genesis* (1535–1545). Sánchez argues that they offer a hermeneutical lens for dealing with migrant neighbors today in ways that move beyond a utilitarian ethic of love on the basis of affinity; they could suggest a way to account for hospitality as a mark of the church in the world. While many tend to think of Luther in terms of justification by faith or a distinction between two kingdoms, here we are prompted to consider how our perspective and practice toward migrant neighbors is framed by regarding them as those loved by God, not because of any merit but because of God's generosity. What if *sola hospitalitate dei* were to be added to the Reformation's legacy?

We live in an era in which we take for granted the availability of Bible in many languages and numerous translations. In a novel approach, Jennifer Powell McNutt explores how the process of getting the Bible into "the language of the people" could inform the way we think about migration and refugees: the Bible in the vernacular was itself a refugee. The Bible was "on the run," as it was carried by adherents of the Reformation as they made their way to Geneva. Those involved in translating the Bible into the vernacular settled in or passed through this "safe harbor." McNutt is our guide to learning about the refugee experiences of those producing Bibles in English, Italian, Spanish, and French. It is easy to forget the dangers involved in that era. Many involved with the transportation and translation of Bibles into the vernacular suffered greatly or were killed. The stakes for the persons and for the Bible were very high. In a time when many migrants take treacherous journeys in search of a better life, it is helpful to recognize the analogous experience of Reformation refugees and refugee Bibles. An appreciation of that Reformation "refugee heritage" might broaden perspectives and cultivate greater empathy.

The second section of this volume turns to biblical studies. M. Daniel Carroll R. takes us to the very beginning, to Genesis, in order to consider how that book could provide new insights into matters of migration and mission. He first looks at the three approaches to the meaning of the image of God (essentialist, relational, and functional), opting for the last. One of the most important features of the functional emphasis is that it would regard all humans as not only given a fundamental dignity by God but also as embued with the capacity to contribute to the good of society. This interpretation would question the tendency to look at migrants as unwelcome or parasitic interlopers in "our space." The second half of the chapter considers the migrations we find in Genesis and connects this to the role of Abram's mission to bless the earth (Gen 12:1–3). Migration is central to the patriarchs and their families and to how they live out that mission in their engagements with other people and places. Migration was then, always has been, and today is integral to the history of God's global mission.

Involuntary migration is not new to human history. It also was a reality in the ancient world. C. L. Crouch focuses on the prophetic books, specifically Jeremiah and Ezekiel, examining theological and ideological concerns resulting from the involuntary migration of God's people after the fall of Jerusalem to the Babylonians. She highlights that these sort of geographic transitions have traumatic effects. These experiences raise questions about the experience of the people of God in great duress, irrespective of cause (though largely due in this case to covenant infidelity). What does it mean to acknowledge such suffering as the people of God? How do God's people respond to and view him when, as in Ezekiel, their involuntary migration lands them in something akin to refugee camps? Crouch uses the phrase "emergency theology" to refer to the reflections on God that emerge from these crises. This theology will not be comprehensive and neat, but it offers what might be called "concrete words from God as we go." Not surprisingly, it may be incomplete or ambigious amid the messiness and uncertainty of a people in diaspora, who earlier had held a neat understanding of God. Today we might ask, "How do we understand and communicate God's promises and commitments to his people and his world to so many whose lives are turned upside down?" And, "how do those who of us are more settled learn from contemporary emergency theologies?"

The phrase "theological imagination" can make some nervous. In this case "imagination" does not mean "fake" or "fantastical." Instead it refers to what we often do already when considering how apply Scripture to life. Joshua Jipp invites us to consider how three threads throughout Luke and Acts help us envision how to respond to current immigration crises with compassion, hospitality, and humility. He first discusses Jesus as *stranger-guest*. This way of thinking about Jesus should not be a surprise in light of the annunciation, the announcement of the coming of the Messiah who is coming from another place, from heaven to earth. Jesus comes to visit and save, and he experiences hospitality from some and hostility from others. He is the king of strangers, who identifies with the lowly and vulnerable. Second, Jipp emphasizes the mandate to cross borders to build new and suprising friendships. This is particularly evident in the book of Acts, where the outpouring of the Holy Spirit at Pentecost crosses borders of language (speaking in tongues) and ethnicity (the gospel goes to Samaritans, an Ethiopian, and Gentiles). The gospel is not intended to be cloistered but spread to all *peoples* of the earth. Crossing borders and transgressing stigmas is central to Christian mission. The third emphasis underscores the ethnic reasoning of Luke-Acts that subverts popular belief that ethnic differences are to be set aside. While some believe that unity in Christ requires cleansing ethnic particularity, Jipp provides counter-examples. For instance, Jipp demonstrates how Jesus and Paul reveal that God welcomes all, not by demanding sameness but by subverting false ethnic assumptions through the parable of the Good Samaritan and an account of the hospitality shown by the Maltese to those shipwrecked with Paul.

Diaspora is the term applied to those displaced by upheavals due to war, disease, ethnic strife, and more. Nelson Morales considers how the books of James and 1 Peter can inform a global theology of migration. Having lived outside his home country for twenty-seven years, Morales approaches these books from the perspective of a migrant. He considers the reasons for dispersion, relationships with one's homeland and the hostland, interrelationships within diasporic communities, and the end of exile. Nelson reveals the presence of a disapora mentality that has also been present through the history of the church: the early church and those in Reformation era experienced displacement many times and even Vatican II has spoken of the church as a pilgrim in a strange land. A diaspora perspective should make the church sensitive to the lives and circumstances of those who have been displaced from their homelands today.

Moving to contributions from the field of theology, Peter Phan discusses a theology of place by examining the role and significance of land in migration and in the lives of migrants. The three expressions in the chapter title, "home land," "foreign land," and "our land," are taken literally and figuratively. Literally, "land" designates an area of ground, which today is often, albeit not always, identified with a country and, more narrowly, a nation-state with demarcated borders. Metaphorically, "land" is a metonymy for all the things that constitute the basic elements of human existence, including but not limited to material and non-material artifacts, economics, politics, culture, society, and religion. The qualifiers "home," "foreign," and "our" represent roughly the three stages that most migrants normally go through: their departure from their "home land" (country of origin), their arrival at and life in a "foreign land" (country of destination), and the transformation of the land of the receiving country into "our land." Phan discusses the complexities of the migrant experience as they move through these stages. He urges readers to ultimately derive their understanding of "land" from the book of Hebrews. There it is understood as a gift and not as permanent or assured possession. Land was to be distributed to all Israelites, as well as to the sojourners among them. For land to move from "home" land to "our" land requires the inclusion of migrants along with the native born, a participation in the trajectory that leads to the universal and all-inclusive kingdom of God.

Daniel Groody considers the question of "illegal" border crossings by reflection on the incarnation. Groody regards Jesus as the migrant Son of God who came to earth as a human, who returned in his ascension after his death and resurrection and makes possible our return migration to our homeland in heaven. In his view, salvation history is understood as the great migration, one that crosses borders of many kinds (the cosmos, human flesh, geography, life and death). Considering Adam and Eve as the first illegal aliens because they violated God's command to not eat of the tree, Groody observes that Christ's incarnation is God's provision of a second Adam, who makes possible our migration to our true home. One of the most intriguing ideas in this chapter is the observation that Christ's miraculous conception into the womb of Mary, a betrothed but not yet married virgin, was in a sense an illegal border crossing, because it was a violation of Jewish law. In this sense, Jesus was an illegal alien chosen to save the world. Jesus truly identifies with all of us, who have been "illegal" since the fall.

The final section of this volume considers missiological and ecclesiological challenges. The first essay deals with one of the great challenges of our time: climate change. Mark Douglas provides a vivid picture of how climate changes have led to migration and multiple conflicts. How should we regard these displaced, and who should take responsibility for addressing their plight? Douglas exposes gaps in modern understandings of the non-human natural world, the shape of human agency, and even what it means to be human. Turning to the work of Hugo Grotius, not only as a theologian but also as the father of modern international law, Douglas observes that, though the Dutch jurist himself was at times a refugee, his work gives little attention to the status of migrants. One result was the creation of a tradition of international law that has not taken into account matters connected to the rights of migrants (their existence is in tension with modern conceptions of the self and the state) and lacks a properly complex understanding of the relationship of humans to the non-human world. Consequently, the non-human world has been regarded as a tool or stage to be used by humans, certainly part of the reason for the climate crisis. The challenge we face, contends Douglas, is that climate refugees also are adrift in that they do not have much of a place through the lens of international law. A new vision that understands persons and their relationship to the non-human world within an environmental social imaginary is imperative.

George Kalantzis takes us to Lesbos, Europe's largest refugee camp, and unveils the gritty realities of that place of great distress, conflict, poor conditions, and considerable despair. How do we think about those in Lesbos and many other refugee camps? What will enable us to conceive of theologies that can rehumanize those in these desperate straits? Labels like "refugee" and "migrant" can leads to considering those is places like Lesbos in terms of status rather than as persons; even terms like "survivor" are safe but insufficient. Heavily dependent upon others and largely stripped of personal agency, these persons need to regain their sense of humanity. NGOs and similar organizations are not equipped to do this. This should be the work of communities of faith, who regard persons as being made in the image of God. It is the church's responsibility to restore and bring hope to others. Central to this task is replacing unhelpful narratives with the life-giving gospel story that prompts the church to feed the hungry, tend the sick, and shelter the homeless. This work can be overwhelming, especially if the goal is to be rewarded for these expressions of care. Christians should leave the *telos* to God and perform merciful actions simply because it is what Christians do. This may require new ecclesiologies that envision cultivating relationships with those who think of themselves as merely refugees, helping them learn (or relearn) that they too can be hosts who contribute to others.

The final chapter proposes a theology of mission that emerges from the conviction that "God is on the move." Samuel George beckons us to consider the concept of *Motus Dei*, to think about God as continually moving and at work in the world. Mission, then, is about following God and participating in a perpetual discernment process to be sure our steps are aligned with his. George spans various domains of systematic theology, from creation to soteriology to pneumatology and eschatology. Examples include the hovering of God's spirit at the dawn of creation to Christ's descent in the incarnation to an eschatology where we anticipate a kingdom that is coming. Motion is everywhere. A significant implication for mission is George's observation that the gospel cannot be captive to any people, geography, or culture. Such limitations would alter the faith and deprive it of its innate dynamism. The mission of the church should emerge from an understanding of a God who is on the move, a mission that conveys a faith that is transportable and translatable, one that crosses borders all the time.

These eleven chapters cross disciplines and Christian traditions. Every one, each its own way, argues that faithful Christianity requires generous engagements that dignify these persons, appreciates their realities, and welcomes their contributions. The challenges of a world with overwhelming voluntary and involuntary migration are daunting. Those who are reconciled to God through Christ cannot resort to forms of provincialism and protectionism and so resist our charge to be those who seek God's grace and wisdom to respond properly to the millions on the move today.

M. Daniel Carroll R.
Vincent Bacote

Abbreviations

Am Hist Rev	*American Historical Review*
ANEM	Ancient Near East Monographs
BECNT	Baker Exegetical Commentary on the New Testament
BBR	*Bulletin of Biblical Research*
BibInt	*Biblical Interpretation*
BZNW	Beihefte zur Zeitschrift für die neutestamentliche Wissenschaft
CEB	Common English Bible
CHRC	*Church History and Religious Culture*
CJ	*Concordia Journal*
CUSAS	Cornell University Studies in Assyriology and Sumerology
EcRev	*Ecumenical Review*
EMQ	*Evangelical Missions Quarterly*
ERT	*Evangelical Review of Theology*
ESV	English Standard Version
FAT	Forschungen zum Alten Testament
HBAI	*Hebrew Bible and Ancient Israel*
Herm	Hermeneia
HS	*Hebrew Studies*

HTR	Harvard Theological Review
ICC	International Critical Commentary
Int	Interpretation
Int Hist Rev	International History Review
Int J Refug Law	International Journal of Refugee Law
IntStQ	International Studies Quarterly
Int Mig Rev	International Migration Review
JBL	Journal of Biblical Literature
JCST	Journal of Catholic Social Thought
J Hum Rights Pract	Journal of Human Rights Practice
J Refug Stud	Journal of Refugee Studies
JSOT	Journal for the Study of the Old Testament
JTS	Journal of Theological Studies
JTI	Journal of Theological Interpretation
JTISup	Journal of Theological Interpretation, Supplements
LHBOTS	Library of Hebrew Bible/Old Testament Studies
LW	Luther's Works
LXX	Septuagint
MS	Medieval Studies
Mod Theol	Modern Theology
MT	Masoretic Text
NABRE	New American Bible, Revised Edition
NAC	New American Commentary
NIGTC	The New International Greek Testament Commentary
NIV	New International Version
NIVAC	The New International Version Application Commentary
NLT	New Living Translation
NovTSup	Supplements to Novum Testamentum
NRSV	New Revised Standard Version

NSBT	New Studies in Biblical Theology
OTM	Old Testament Message
PNTC	Pillar New Testament Commentary
Polit Theolog	*Political Theology*
PRS	*Perspectives in Religious Studies*
Proc Natl Acad Sci	*Proceedings of the National Academy of Sciences*
Ref Rev	*Refugee Review*
RSV	Revised Standard Version
SBET	*Scottish Bulletin of Evangelical Theology*
SemeiaSt	Semeia Studies
SOTSMS	Society for Old Testament Studies Monograph Series
TS	*Theological Studies*
VTSup	Supplements to Vetus Testamentum
WBC	Word Biblical Commentary
WUNT	Wissenschaftliche Untersuchungen zum Neuen Testament
WW	*Word and World*
ZECNT	Zondervan Exegetical Commentary on the New Testament

List of Contributors

VINCENT BACOTE is Associate Professor of Theology and Director of The Center for Applied Christian Ethics at Wheaton College (IL).

M. DANIEL CARROLL R. (RODAS) is Scripture Press Ministries Professor of Biblical Studies and Pedagogy at Wheaton College (IL).

C. L. CROUCH is Professor of Hebrew Bible/Old Testament and Ancient Judaism at Radboud University Nijmegen and Research Associate in the Department of Old Testament and Hebrew Scriptures at the University of Pretoria.

MARK DOUGLAS is Professor of Christian Ethics and Director of the ThM Program at Columbia Theological Seminary.

SAM GEORGE is Director of the Global Diaspora Institute of The Global Diaspora Network and the Lausanne Catalyst for Diasporas of the Lausanne Movement.

DANIEL G. GROODY, CSC is Vice President and Associate Provost and Associate Professor of Theology and Global Affairs at the University of Notre Dame.

JOSHUA JIPP is Associate Professor of New Testament at Trinity Evangelical Divinity School.

GEORGE KALANTZIS is Professor of Theology and Director of The Wheaton Center for Early Christian Studies at Wheaton College (IL).

JENNIFER POWELL McNUTT is Franklin S. Dyrness Associate Professor of Biblical and Theological Studies at Wheaton College (IL).

NELSON MORALES is Dean and Professor of New Testament at El Seminario Teológico Centroamericano in Guatemala City, Guatemala.

PETER C. PHAN is Ignacio Ellacuría Chair of Catholic Social Thought at Georgetown University.

LEOPOLDO A. SÁNCHEZ M. is Werner R.H. Krause and Elizabeth Ringger Krause Professor of Hispanic Ministries, Professor of Systematic Theology, and Director of The Center for Hispanic Studies at Concordia Seminary, St. Louis.

Historical Perspectives

Is It Time for Another Reformation *Sola*?

Luther's Two Kinds of Love and the Immigrant Other

Leopoldo A. Sánchez M.

ACROSS THE GLOBE, QUESTIONS dealing with the status of refugees and immigrants are among the most hotly debated. Pew Research Center studies consistently show how North Americans are more or less evenly split along party lines on policy issues such as refugee admissions, border security and deportations, and paths to citizenship for unauthorized immigrants.[1] With some exceptions, attitudes and opinions concerning the immigrant other in the United States reflect the political polarization of our times. At times, these political divisions and allegiances trickle into our churches, arguably dressed in theological language, calling for an either-or position on complex issues that require more nuance: "What about *illegal* do you not understand?" some say. Others respond, "What about *loving the neighbor as yourself* do you not understand?" These questions are often asked by Christians as if they were absolute contrasting political and theological options, rather than starting points for rich conversations that foster productive dialogue and action. In a Facebook world where people typically "like" those with whom they already agree, we can easily fall prey to framing theological questions on debated social issues in terms of allegiance to or affinity with one's tribe. The drive for social acceptance or justification in one's group

---

1. See Pew Research Center, "Republicans Turn More Negative toward Refugees," and "Americans' Immigration Policy Priorities."

gets in the way of thinking generously with others.[2] Tribal thinking prevents dialogue with others who may think differently from us, drawing each side into its own corner and club. We miss an opportunity to come together for the sake of understanding issues that affect many neighbors, and possibly working together on them.

In the shuffle of identity politics and tribally framed responses to complex social issues such as immigration law and reform, an interesting thing takes place: The refugee and immigrant neighbor, her struggles and hopes, becomes invisible. Worse yet, such neighbors are placed or subsumed under the preferred categories of this or that tribe, that is to say, under polarities such as legality-illegality ("What about *illegal* do you not understand?") or hostility-hospitality ("What about *loving your neighbor as yourself* do you not understand?"). The stranger neighbor, the immigrant other, is not approached on his or her own terms, but rather in terms of a prior ethic whereby people "like" those with whom they have some affinity or perhaps can benefit from, and "unlike" those whom they see as undesirable, unattractive, or a burden to our way of life. The church *should* do better.

In this essay, I argue that Luther's *Heidelberg Disputation*'s distinction between human love and divine love (or the love of the cross) offers a way to form persons with the capacity to deal with neighbors beyond what a utilitarian ethic of affinity (Facebook love, so to speak) allows, fostering a Christlike ethic that tends toward that which is unattractive or unlikable. Indeed, Luther's distinction reveals that discourses on the refugee and immigrant other in contemporary immigration debates, on both sides of the political divide, are often based on a utilitarian ethic grounded in and reduced to human love. Although there is a place for human love when discussing the immigration politics in a secular society (such as the love of fellow citizens), Christians must also move beyond it by embodying ways of engaging the refugee and immigrant other through a cruciform ethic of divine love that does not only point out the bad in people but bestows the good on them. Through a brief comparison between Luther's earlier *Heidelberg Disputation* (1518) and his reflections on Abraham's hospitality written later in his *Lectures on Genesis* (1535–1545), I show how his principle that the love of the cross bestows good upon the poor and needy person is consistent throughout his career. Furthermore, at a time when we have the largest number of neighbors on the move in history, I propose that Luther's cruciform principle can best be articulated by adding another Reformation

---

2. "Why would people ever think, when thinking deprives them of 'the pleasure or sharing an attitude one knows is socially approved'—especially in an online environment where the social approval of one's attitudes is so much easier to acquire, in the currency of likes, faves, followers, and friends?" Jacobs, *How to Think*, 21.

sola to the marks of the church in the world, namely, a *sola hospitalitate dei* (God's hospitality alone). Finally, I note that despite contrasting approaches to immigration, Luther's heirs writing on the issue today are remarkably able to exercise an ethic of divine love in their dialogue with others with whom we disagree, in a way that the immigrant other affected by such dialogue does not fall between the cracks but is properly accounted for.

LOVING LIKE A THEOLOGIAN OF THE CROSS: TWO KINDS OF LOVE IN LUTHER'S *HEIDELBERG DISPUTATION* (1518)

Toumo Mannermaa makes the bold claim that Luther's distinction between "God's Love" (*Jumalan rakkaus*) and "Human Love" (*Ihmisen rakkaus*) provides the fundamental framework that "determines the basic structure of Luther's theology."[3] Although Luther's distinction between two kinds of love appears early on in his career in the last thesis of the *Heidelberg Disputation*, the author observes that such distinction does not only lay out the interpretative key for the rest of the *Disputation* but is the theological presupposition in Luther's whole outlook on God, humanity, faith, the word, worship, and ethics. In thesis twenty-eight, Luther writes: "The love of God does not find, but creates, that which is pleasing to it. The love of man comes into being through that which is pleasing to it."[4] We can restate the second half of this thesis as follows: Humans love people with whom they share attributes they see (or want to see) in themselves—attributes they are already naturally attracted to and thus see as pleasing. In his explanation of this thesis, Luther elaborates on the type of pleasing attributes natural human reason or intellect seeks in others. According to many theologians of his day, those attributes are "the true and good" in people.

> The intellect cannot by nature comprehend an object which does not exist, that is the poor and needy person, but only a thing which does exist, that is the true and good. Therefore it judges according to appearances, is a respecter of persons, and judges according to that which can be seen, etc.[5]

In this statement Luther attacks what he sees as "the argument held by... 'all' philosophers and theologians that the cause of love is always in its object."[6]

3. Mannermaa, *Two Kinds of Love*, 9.
4. *LW* 31:41.
5. *LW* 31:57–58.
6. Mannermaa, *Two Kinds of Love*, 2.

The object the natural human intellect seeks after is, as Luther notes, "the true and good." But by looking for "the true and good" in people, human love paradoxically misses and dismisses "the poor and needy person." According to scholastic theology, humans are naturally inclined and driven to love others with whom they have in common the goodness they see (or want to realize more fully) in themselves.[7] We may call this love by affinity. Even Thomas Aquinas's notion of "friendship love," by which one loves another without self-interest, is still oriented toward mutually sharing with friends things one has in common with them, or things one likes in them.[8] In other words, when it comes to human love, like is attracted to like. Like likes like. Facebook love!

In a teaching with roots in Augustine's Trinitarian theology, medieval scholastics like Thomas taught that humans are naturally disposed toward goodness because they are created in their own essence after the image of God in whom all the perfections of goodness exist. There is a similarity between God and humans in that humans possess attributes of the Creator, though in a creaturely way—attributes such as wisdom, justice, and goodness. Therefore, human love ideally reflects God's love, and vice versa, which means that God too loves people because they have something in common with him; in Thomas's words, "God loves the object in proportion to the degree to which its proper goodness has become actualized."[9] God loves you to the extent that you reflect his goodness, his likeness in you. God may initiate this work in you, and work with you to get you there, but the same principle of affinity applies.

According to Mannermaa, "Luther concludes that in scholastic theology, which follows the logic of Aristotle, the image of God has been changed into the likeness of the human image and human beings, and thus in accordance with Human Love."[10] The overall picture one gets from the theology Luther reacts against is the idea that human love reflects or images divine love (or more precisely, divine attributes), so that both types of love seek after the true and good they are naturally attracted to. In the case of humans, they strive to do so constantly; in the case of God, he does so perfectly. In either case, the implication is that, by loving people as objects of goodness who best reflect divine attributes in a creaturely way, both God and humans seek to love others to the degree that their righteousness, works, free will, or reason are deemed good.

7. Mannermaa, *Two Kinds of Love*, 10–11.
8. Mannermaa, *Two Kinds of Love*, 16.
9. Mannermaa, *Two Kinds of Love*, 19.
10. Mannermaa, *Two Kinds of Love*, 19.

In thesis nineteen of the *Heidelberg Disputation*, Luther states: "That person does not deserve to be called a theologian who looks upon the invisible things of God as though they were clearly perceptible in those things which have actually happened [Rom 1:20]."[11] In his explanation of this thesis, Luther uses the term "the invisible things of God" to refer to divine attributes such as "virtue, godliness, wisdom, justice, goodness, and so forth."[12] These are precisely the type of attributes that humans—or as Luther would call them, theologians of glory!—naturally seek in themselves or in others as objects of love. Theologians of glory seek after those "invisible qualities" of God that they find or perceive to be visible, apparent, or reflected in themselves or others, which in turn justifies their being loved by God or their loving others in God's name.

How then is natural human love overcome with God's love in humans? It does not happen naturally, or by human initiative. For Luther, loving according to God's love requires nothing less than an act of God's Spirit to create out of nothing a new person with a new heart or disposition—a person who will not only love those whom he naturally likes, but more importantly, those who are not easy to like. But this change of heart means the old person (sinner) in us must come to an end. Reflecting on the *Disputation*, Gerhard Forde observes that the point of Luther's theological theses is to show how God forms theologians of the cross who die in order to be raised with Christ.[13] Forde's claim that the cross is above all an attack on "our *spiritual aspirations*,"[14] on "*the sinner's theology* . . . the *best* we have to offer, not the worst,"[15] aligns well with Luther's critique of human love as a natural inclination toward finding the invisible, spiritual, and good qualities of God in ourselves and others. As Mannermaa puts it, "the theology of glory is based on Human Love."[16] Accordingly, theologians of glory focus on the beauty of their works to make them righteous before God, their free will (or right choices) to avoid sin, and their rational ability to know God's invisible attributes through what (or who) they observe in creation. Therefore, they also love those with whom they share such a high view of their spiritual capacity. When used to establish one's or others' worthiness to be loved by God, gifts from God which are "good" in themselves (that is, good works, will, and reason) become "mortal sins" or "evil" in that they drive us toward

11. *LW* 31:52.

12. *LW* 31:52.

13. Forde, *On Being a Theologian of the Cross*, 3–4.

14. Forde, *On Being a Theologian of the Cross*, 1.

15. Forde, *On Being a Theologian of the Cross*, 4.

16. Mannermaa, *Two Kinds of Love*, 28.

that self-realizing love which looks for what is attractive in us and others, and away from God's creative love in Christ toward us and in us.[17]

Theologians of the cross, on the other hand, receive by faith the beauty of God's works, will, and revelation (reason) in the crucified Christ—that is, they receive what appears "evil" in the eyes of the world but is ultimately "good" for us.[18] They die to their human attempts to earn the love of God so that they can be raised anew as receivers of God's unmerited love in Christ. Otherwise stated, human love, which naturally looks for "that which is pleasing to it," must be put to death in us, so that God's love "which does not find, but creates, that which is pleasing to it" might shape us to love that which is not naturally attractive to us. This means moving from a view of divine love based on imaging divine attributes to a view of divine love based on imaging Christ's love for the marginal neighbor, that is, sinners, the poor, and the needy. In his explanation to thesis twenty-eight, Luther defines "the love of the cross" as follows:

> Rather than seeking its own good, the love of God flows forth and bestows good. Therefore sinners are attractive because they are loved; they are not loved because they are attractive. For this reason the love of man avoids sinners and evil persons. Thus Christ says: "For I came not to call the righteous, but sinners" [Matt 9:13]. This is the love of the cross, born of the cross, which turns in the direction where it does not find good which it may enjoy, but where it may confer good upon the bad and needy person. "It is more blessed to give than to receive" [Acts 20:35], says the Apostle.[19]

---

17. "Although the works of man always seem attractive and good, they are nevertheless likely to be mortal sins" (thesis three). *LW* 31:39. "A theologian of glory calls evil good and good evil" (thesis twenty-one). *LW* 31:40.

18. "Although the works of God always seem unattractive and appear evil, they are nevertheless really eternal merits" (thesis four). *LW* 31:39. In his explanation of thesis twenty-one, Luther notes that "the friends of the cross say that the cross is good and [human] works are evil, for through the cross works are destroyed and the old Adam, who is especially edified by works, is crucified." *LW* 31:53.

19. *LW* 31:57. C. S. Lewis distinguishes between Divine Gift-Love in humans and natural Gift-love: "But Divine Gift-Love—Love Himself working in a man—is wholly disinterested and desires what is simply best for the beloved. Again, natural Gift-love is always directed to objects which the lover finds in some way intrinsically lovable—objects to which Affection or Eros or a shared point of view attracts him, or, failing that, to the grateful and the deserving, or perhaps to those whose helplessness is of a winning and appealing kind. But Divine Gift-Love in the man enables him to love what is not naturally lovable; lepers, criminals, enemies, morons, the sulky, the superior and the sneering." Lewis, *Four Loves*, 177.

The love of God in Christ is not like natural human love. God's love is not naturally oriented toward a person possessing goodness, but rather toward persons who are deemed unrighteous. When God's love flows in and through humans, their love too is oriented toward people who are seen as bad, sinful, or poor. Being made a theologian of the cross through death and resurrection, humans image in their lives the type of divine love they have received in Christ. Luther calls such imaging "the love of the cross, born of the cross." Sinners are not loved by God because he finds some attractive qualities ("the true and good") in them. Instead, God creates the object of his love from scratch, and thus "sinners are attractive because they are loved" by God in Christ. So also, God's people do not love neighbors because they are attractive or beautiful, or because they have something they "may enjoy," but rather confer on them God's spiritual and material blessings to restore them as God's good and beautiful creation amid the brokenness of creation. As Mannermaa puts it: "God gives Godself to . . . that which is bad or evil, and this is also the task of Christians in their relationship with their neighbors. This is why Luther calls Christians 'Christ(s),' and this is what Luther means with the expression of being 'Christ to one's neighbors.'"[20]

BUT WHAT'S IN IT FOR ME? TWO KINDS OF LOVE AND THE IMMIGRANT OTHER

In an essay subtitled "God's Mercy for a Culture of Violence and Death," Alberto L. García calls for the addition of a *sola caritate dei* (God's love alone) to Lutheran Reformation language as a way to clarify and proclaim the witness of the gospel in a North American culture of increasing exclusion and violence toward immigrants.[21] He sees such life-denying culture as resulting from an idolatrous view of the nation-state. When the nation-state is seen as a sacralized institution whose leaders can do no wrong, such an uncritical attitude encourages an ethic of excluding people in society who are seen as potential enemies of the state or, more generally, the American way of life.[22] In the aftermath of 9/11 and in the current political climate, refugees from predominantly Muslim countries and immigrants (particularly from Mexico and Central America), perhaps more than any other group, are seen with suspicion as such potential enemies. When North Americans, including Christians, uncritically adopt a form of civil religion grounded

20. Mannermaa, *Two Kinds of Love*, 64–65.

21. García and Nunes, *Wittenberg Meets the World*, 59–62; for what is good and bad in a person's love of country, see Lewis, *Four Loves*, 39–49.

22. García and Nunes, *Wittenberg Meets the World*, 56–57.

in a sacralized absolute distinction between "us" (citizens) and "them" (migrants), they tend to make refugees and immigrants scapegoats for the ills of the nation; strip them of their dignity by reducing them to criminals; take advantage of their labors and bodies; and fail to reach out to them with the gospel and works of love.[23]

As a tool to unmask what García sees as the idolatry of civil religion and offer a gospel witness in the midst of its culture of exclusion and violence, he deploys Luther's contrast between the love of humans and the love of God in humans.[24] As a reminder, human love is driven, even if benignly so, by self-interest, and thus seeks that which it likes and is naturally attracted to; by contrast, the Christlike love of God in humans moves in the direction of what is not good or naturally attractive, but rather toward what is sinful, bad, poor, and unattractive. In North America today, García observes that migrants are seen as the most unattractive of neighbors, becoming the objects of rhetoric that justifies their dehumanization. In this climate, he challenges the church to embody God's radical love in Christ toward the excluded other. The church is called to live her faith through the love of God alone, which flows through humans to others, by embodying a life of *sola caritate dei* or *sola agape dei*, that is to say, by embodying a love that is unmerited and unconditional.[25] García's argument raises an important question for Lutherans and other Christians who hold to the *solas* (that is, *sola scriptura, sola gratia,* and *sola fide*) as part of their Reformation heritage and identity. How does Luther's distinction between two kinds of love help us to reflect on immigrants today, particularly on attitudes toward them, in a context where the love of affinity among people of a common nation is politicized in such a way that outsiders tend to be seen with suspicion and labeled as potential enemies, or to put it less negatively, in a way that outsiders are valued according to the benefits or lack thereof they bring to the host nation?

If we consider how refugees and immigrants are often portrayed in the national media, they are seen through the lens of what Luther would call a theology of glory grounded in and reduced to natural human love. Since such love always has an ideal object one looks up to, it finally "comes into being through what is pleasing to it" and "seeks its own good." Humans naturally tend to love others "because they are attractive," that is, because such people reflect attributes like those of the Creator humans also seek

23. García and Nunes, *Wittenberg Meets the World*, 57–58.
24. García and Nunes, *Wittenberg Meets the World*, 61–62.
25. García and Nunes, *Wittenberg Meets the World*, 60.

to realize in themselves. That someone typically becomes attractive if and when that someone is of benefit to us.

When attractive attributes such as holiness, truth, justice, wisdom, beauty, goodness, and so on are judged to be lacking in migrants—particularly those who offend people the most, like the Muslim refugee or the undocumented immigrant—they are seen with suspicion and portrayed in the worst possible light. While it is true that undocumented immigrants have broken a law, and their status needs resolution before the law, there is often in the public discourse an emotionally charged and dehumanizing response against them. They are reduced to convenient one-size-fits-all categories such as "criminals," "rapists," or "bad hombres." In some church circles, these immigrants are not only seen as sinners, but often as paragons of sin and thus the worst of sinners. In response to this approach, advocates of migrants ironically operate from the same framework when they argue for their acceptance on the basis of attractive qualities such as their work ethic, love of family, and spirituality. The discussion turns to the need for the law to take into consideration the contributions immigrants, including the unauthorized, make to the economy, the community, and the church. Here conservatives and liberals, closed and open borders folks, become strange bedfellows. For both, loving or acceptance of migrants is ultimately conditional upon their capacity to reflect in their lives what is most attractive, pleasing, and beneficial to us.

Luther describes the love of the theologian of the cross in a non-utilitarian way, namely, as a love "which turns in the direction where it does not find good which it may enjoy, but where it may confer good upon the bad and needy person." Such love does not seek a likeable object to love, but rather loves the unlikable. What if Christians learned to love the refugee and immigrant other with such Christlike love? Such love would surely "call a thing what it is," acknowledge their sins, as with any sinner, without romanticizing them, denying them moral agency, or reducing them to victims. But such love would also acknowledge their humanity, needs, struggles, and hopes. Such a love would not merely point to that which is bad in people as an end in itself, but move toward thinking creatively about appropriate ways to bestow that which is good in them. Indeed, the love of the cross that moves Christians toward that which is not attractive may lead them to enter the world of the refugee and immigrant other more deeply, listen to these neighbors' stories of migration, visit them in detention centers, pray for them and their families, accompany them to immigration court, assist with the payment of legal fees, advocate for them before elected government officials, or partner with pro-bono immigration services and other social agencies to offer them legal counsel and humanitarian assistance.

IS IT TIME FOR ANOTHER REFORMATION SOLA? ABRAHAM'S HOSPITALITY IN THE *LECTURES ON GENESIS* (1535–1545)

Written later in his life, Luther's teachings on Abraham's hospitality toward the three strangers at Mamre in the *Lectures on Genesis* (1535–1545) are consistent with thesis twenty-eight of his earlier *Heidelberg Disputation* (1518). Both call for a cruciform love toward outsiders. In his commentary on Genesis 18, Luther argues that hospitality toward exiles rises to the level of an external mark of the church that flows from the gospel, so that the church becomes the house of Abraham in a world filled with people on the move.[26] Whether Luther discusses brotherly love toward Christians or general goodness toward other strangers, or whether he speaks of the responsibilities of the state toward their own residents vis-à-vis people coming from other lands, the same principle holds true, namely, the love of God in humans tends in the direction of the needy. Luther asks Christians, which in his day would have included church authorities and godly princes acting as government authorities, to act toward strangers persecuted on account of the word ("true strangers") or fleeing their lands for other reasons ("strangers of the state"), in a way that they would do their best to bestow good upon the needy. Hospitality toward strangers is not finally predicated on human love, such as the love people of a state share for one another (though this is not excluded), but rather on the principle of God's love in humans whereby sinful, bad, and needy persons are attractive because they are loved.

In his day, Luther could appeal to a Christian prince's morality and praise the kind of Christlike hospitality and mercy flowing through him in his compassion to exiles. In the case of a godly prince, Luther saw his hospitality as an instance of a calling through which not merely human love but God's love shown through his civil servant bestows good upon strangers. The situation today is different. In post-Christendom, we may or not be able to appeal to a prince's morality, and perhaps even less a ruler's Christian ethos. Public discourse on refugees and immigrants will do no better than the human love of the philosophers, and various sectors of society will debate public policies on immigration on the basis of the perceived liabilities or benefits of refugees and immigrants to the nation. Decisions on their status will be made on whether they have desirable and pleasant qualities that we share in common with them. That is as far as human love discourses can take us, and that might be good enough for getting along in a society with competing views of the good.

26. For a fuller treatment, see Sánchez, "The Church Is the House."

There is a place in immigration debates for arguments based on the love of affinity, particularly the common bond citizens and residents of a nation have together. Yet this type of love and hospitable love do not have to be seen as mutually exclusive. Solidarity with the immigrant other does not exclude hard thinking about complex issues that aim at consensus or compromise in a divided society—compromise that is often based on a utilitarian ethic.[27] For instance, Lutheran political theorist Peter Meilaender argues that in the context of modern nation-states' rights to regulate their borders, public policy must understandably give priority to the needs of their fellow citizens and their visions of what constitutes community. But even though the author takes as his point of departure a preferential option for fellow citizens, he also notes two "exceptions" that can justify placing limits on the nation-state's priority to look out for the needs of those within its borders, namely, the situation of desperate refugees and keeping families together.[28] Arguments based on human love toward fellow citizens and residents are taken seriously, but do not forbid making room for arguments based on an ethic of hospitality that also takes proper account of the plight of foreigners.

Luther accounts for human love in affirming the responsibility of nations to take care of their own citizens, but at the same time calls Christians to a certain higher standard when dealing with exiles—a more radical love and hospitality than the one available to the philosophers and theologians of his day. Thus Luther can acknowledge the priority the state should give to its "needy citizens . . . ahead of the others,"[29] and also praise his head of state for extending hospitality and protection to "miserable exiles, who flee for refuge."[30] The natural human love of countrymen and women remains, but does not exclude the love of the stranger.[31] Even though Christians will need to engage like-minded people in society to reach consensus or compromise on civil matters, Christians cannot simply stop with human love when they think about unpopular or unlikable neighbors. When they appeal to human

27. Jacobs argues that, whereas a generous "solidarity" toward neighbors who are "unlike you" at times may trump "critical reflection," there is also a "public policy" space in which "solidarity is not enough" but "must be supplemented by a colder-eyed look at what particular strategies and tactics are most likely to realize the desired end" on issues that concern people with competing views of the common good. Jacobs, *How to Think*, 68–69.

28. Meilaender, *Toward a Theory*, 174–83.

29. *LW* 7:338.

30. *LW* 3:181–82.

31. C. S. Lewis argues that "Charity does not dwindle into merely natural love but natural love is taken up into, made the tuned and obedient instrument of, Love Himself." Lewis, *Four Loves*, 184. Turning natural love into charitable love includes dispositions toward the unlovable such as "forbearance, tolerance, forgiveness" (186).

love as an end in itself, they become theologians of glory. They only begin to love those whom they see as reflecting the glory of God (in a creaturely way) in their lives, and disregard those whom they see as lacking such divine-like qualities. To avoid a utilitarian approach to neighbors that ends with human love, Christians must also ask how they can embody both as citizens of heaven and citizens of the state the love of the cross and Abraham's hospitality in their callings to attend to neighbors who are marginalized by church and society.

Sadly, Christians have too often stopped at human love when it comes to refugees and immigrants, especially those who offend them the most. Lutherans have done so when they point to or name their sinful or bad acts, or their lack of attractive or beneficial qualities, but are unwilling to bestow any good upon them. Pointing to the bad *and* bestowing the good is what a theologian of the cross does, but pointing to the bad *without* bestowing the good bears all the marks of a theologian of glory. This requires a different way of thinking than the one available to natural human reason. In his commentary on Genesis 18, Luther reminds us that when we look at strangers through the "eyes of the flesh," their "bodily appearance is a hindrance to us," but when we look at them with the "inner eyes of faith" we see that "God is coming" to us in his saints.[32] Here Luther has in mind fellow Christians with whom we share the common bond of fellowship in Christ, but he also extends such hospitality to other strangers who are not among the "saints" but nevertheless require our general kindness.[33]

What if we were to look at strangers, especially those who offend us the most, through the eyes of Abraham (*Lectures on Genesis*), or through the eyes of the cross (*Heidelberg Disputation*)? Embodying such hospitality is a high call, a difficult one to practice today, at a time when public and even Christian discourse on refugees and immigrants is highly politicized, tribal, and divisive. In his own day, Luther complained about hospitality toward exiles being a rare thing to see even among Christians![34] Not much has changed, since human nature in and of itself operates on the basis of the love of affinity. At a time when a disposition toward hospitality for those who are unlike us is in short demand, I propose it is time for another Reformation *sola*. Inspired by Luther's *Heidelberg Disputation*, García proposes *sola agape dei*, "God's love alone." I pitch my tent with him, but would also like to communicate another dimension of "the love of God in humans" (*amor dei in*

32. *LW* 3:196.

33. Luther points out that if a "Turk or Tartar" (i.e., a Muslim) came to us as a "stranger" and "in distress," we should not disregard him "even though he is not suffering because of the Word." *LW* 3:183–84.

34. *LW* 3:196.

homines) in thesis twenty-eight of the *Disputation* by using the language of the *Lectures on Genesis*, chapter 18. What about another *sola* that highlights hospitality, which we are in dire need of today, as a mark of the church? Such hospitality is the fruit of God's grace alone (*sola gratia*), received by faith alone (*sola fide*), as it is spoken to us in Scripture alone (*sola scriptura*). Such hospitality norms our lives in the world, but has its origin in God's own love for us in Christ, and thus in God's own hospitality toward outsiders. What about a *sola hospitalitate dei*, "God's hospitality alone," as another way to clarify what the love of God in humans—the *sola agape dei* (that is, the divine love alone) of the *Heidelberg Disputation*—might look like at a time such as this when we have the largest number of people on the move? *Sola hospitalitate dei*. When we, like Abraham, embody God's hospitality alone, like does not merely find like it may enjoy but creates a space to welcome the unlikely and unlikable other into God's life and ours. We move from human love to Christlike love.

NUANCE AND SOLIDARITY: LESSONS FROM LUTHER'S HEIRS IN DIVISIVE TIMES

In our current cultural situation, national opinions and attitudes toward refugees and immigrants do not merely illustrate that we live in divisive times, but tend to reduce these neighbors to one-sided categories advanced by opposing bands. They are either romanticized as victims without moral agency, or perhaps more often than not, demonized and dehumanized as societal burdens. Is there a way to move beyond such simplistic thinking toward a more balanced approach that moves beyond one-sided views of immigration reform and the immigrant other? I have argued that even when Luther's heirs disagree significantly on the starting point for approaching questions concerning immigration, they still yield remarkably similar fruit in the careful attention they give to the situation of strangers, including both refugees and the undocumented, in their proposals for comprehensive US immigration law and reform.[35]

In their book *They Are Us*, Stephen Bouman and Ralston Deffenbaugh enter the immigration debate with a commitment to hospitality toward strangers as a fundamental and guiding biblical value, which in turn leads them to take as their point of departure a preferential option for the stranger in their assessment of immigration laws.[36] Significantly, their preferential option for immigrants on the basis of divine love does not get in the way

35. Sánchez, "Bearing So Much."
36. Bouman and Deffenbaugh, *They Are Us*, 10.

of their dealing with the need to think about the laws of the land in terms of the love of affinity. The authors conclude that the immigration system is broken in three ways, namely, the backlog in visa applications keeps families apart, a number of visas for unskilled workers do not meet labor demand and this leads to unfair labor practices, and prison-like detention centers for low-risk immigrants (including children) is an unnecessary and harsh form of punishment.[37] The priority of solidarity with the stranger does not evade thinking about questions concerning immigration law and reform. The authors' concern for making laws better may be seen as a way of showing their respect for the very rule of law such laws seek to uphold (and thus their respect for fellow citizens), as well as their respect for the immigrant other with whom they want to deal adequately and with fairness.

On the other hand, Peter Meilaender deploys the concept of "special relationships" to support a preferential option for fellow citizens and residents of the nation in immigration laws.[38] Yet despite beginning with a preferential option for fellow countrymen and women on the basis of the love of affinity, Meilaender also proposes, for instance, that undocumented immigrants "who have lived in this country for an extended period, starting families and putting down roots, at some point can no longer reasonably be regarded as outsiders. *De facto*, if not *de jure*, they are one of us."[39] So Meilaender ends up, at least in the case of some undocumented immigrants, in the same place where Bouman and Deffenbaugh started, namely, with the assertion that at least in some significant cases, *They Are Us*! Love based on commonality or affinity does not exclude a complementary ethic of solidarity with the immigrant other.

Although Bouman/Deffenbaugh and Meilaender reflect on immigration issues from different starting points, one from a preferential option for the stranger and another from a preferential option for citizens and other residents in close proximity to one another, they both have ways of accounting for hospitality and law in their arguments. Their positions are not ultimately one-sided, but nuanced. They neither romanticize nor demonize immigrants. Despite the different and even contrasting rhetorical entry points into the moral dilemma of immigration by these heirs of Luther, it is remarkable—especially in our politically divisive times—that both take

37. Bouman and Deffenbaugh, *They Are Us*, 59–69.

38. "The world, after all, contains countless needy people who require assistance. How are we to know whom to help? So we begin with those to whom we stand in special relationships. . . . Immigration regulations are a way of embodying in policy a preferential love for our own fellow citizens and the way of life that we share. Such a preference can be overridden, but it is not inherently suspect." Meilaender, "Immigration."

39. Meilaender, "Immigration."

into serious consideration Luther's concern for Christians to embody a Christlike way of loving poor, needy, and unattractive neighbors, that does not merely point out the bad but is willing to bestow the good upon them. They give us an example of the way forward, one in which Christians do not merely mirror the culture's way of doing things. They embody a more hospitable way, one in which we move beyond Facebook love to the love of the cross the Spirit of Christ works in and through us, that is, God's love revealed in the Face of Christ.

BIBLIOGRAPHY

Bouman, Stephen, and Ralston Deffenbaugh. *They Are Us: Lutherans and Immigration*. Minneapolis: Fortress, 2009.

Forde, Gerhard O. *On Being a Theologian of the Cross: Reflections on Luther's Heidelberg Disputation, 1518*. Grand Rapids: Eerdmans, 1997.

García, Alberto L., and John A. Nunes. *Wittenberg Meets the World: Reimagining the Reformation at the Margins*. Grand Rapids: Eerdmans, 2017.

Jacobs, Alan. *How to Think: A Survival Guide for a World at Odds*. New York: Currency, 2017.

Lewis, C. S. *The Four Loves*. New York: Harcourt, Bruce & World, 1960.

Luther, Martin. *Heidelberg Disputation*. In *Luther's Works: Career of the Reformer I*, vol. 31, edited by Harold J. Grimm and Helmut T. Lehmann. Philadelphia: Fortress, 1957.

———. *Lectures on Genesis: Chapters 15–20*. In *Luther's Works*, vol. 3, edited by J. J. Pelikan et al. St. Louis: Concordia, 1961.

Mannermaa, Tuomo. *Two Kinds of Love: Martin Luther's Religious World*. Minneapolis: Fortress, 2010.

Meilaender, Peter C. "Immigration: Citizens and Strangers." *First Things* (May 2007). https://www.firstthings.com/article/2007/05/immigration-citizens-strangers.

———. *Toward a Theory of Immigration*. New York: Palgrave, 2001.

Pew Research Center. "Americans' Immigration Policy Priorities: Divisions Between—and Within—the Two Parties." November 12, 2019. https://www.pewresearch.org/fact-tank/2019/11/12/americans-immigration-policy-priorities-divisions-between-and-within-the-two-parties.

———. "Republicans Turn More Negative toward Refugees as Number Admitted to U.S. Plummets." May 14, 2018. https://www.pewresearch.org/fact-tank/2018/05/24/republicans-turn-more-negative-toward-refugees-as-number-admitted-to-u-s-plummets.

Sánchez M., Leopoldo A. "Bearing So Much Similar Fruit: Lutheran Theology and Comprehensive Immigration Reform." In *Secular Governance: Lutheran Perspectives on Contemporary Legal Issues*, edited by Ronald W. Duty and Marie A. Failinger, 184–205. Grand Rapids: Eerdmans, 2016.

———. "The Church Is the House of Abraham: Reflections on Martin Luther's Teaching on Hospitality toward Exiles." *Concordia Journal* 44 (2018) 23–39.

The Bible for Refugees in Calvin's Geneva

Jennifer Powell McNutt

THE REFUGEE PLIGHT NOW AND THEN

IN OCTOBER 2015, PHOTOGRAPHER Antonio Masiello captured a harrowing moment of refugees and migrants disembarking a rugged boat.[1] They had just completed the precarious journey across the Aegean Sea from Turkey to the Greek island of Lesbos, but any relief they might have felt from survival is sorely absent from their faces. In place of consolation remained the ongoing trauma of displacement. The knowledge that their journey had only just begun weighs heavily on their expressions. This is not a journey home. Strikingly, at the center of the image are arms reaching over the water as a child is passed from boat to rock and into an unknown future. They are moving because they must. They are moving to stay alive for themselves and for the next generation.

Out of the nearly 80 million people experiencing displacement in our world today, an astounding 26 million are navigating a refugee's life.[2] Sadly,

1. "Refugees and Migrants Get Off a Fishing Boat at the Greek Island of Lesbos after Crossing the Aegean Sea from Turkey in October 2015. Antonio Masiello/NurPhoto via ZUMA Press," https://www.cnn.com/2015/09/03/world/gallery/europes-refugee-crisis/index.html.

2. According to the UN Refugee Agency, 1 percent of the world's population faces displacement today due to persecution and conflict, which represents nearly 80 million

though the scope and longevity of the crisis today are unprecedented, the contours of their story are not new: the daunting journey undertaken to seek out refuge; the ongoing grief for what has been lost; and the fear and hope for what awaits. These experiences and more were also shared by those forcibly displaced and persecuted during the Reformation over five hundred years ago. Centuries before the advent of photojournalism, the plight of the refugee was presented through the lens of various early modern artistic and literary mediums from paintings to martyrologies. Protestant artist François Dubois, for example, fled France for Geneva (1572–1584) after likely experiencing firsthand the St. Bartholomew's Day massacre, where thousands of Protestants were shockingly butchered in the streets of Paris. Dubois's painting of that moment is valued as a rarity for depicting such a recent event from his own time.[3] In Dubois's case and for many thousands of others, the city of Geneva provided safe harbor for regrouping in the midst of crisis, and under her care, another kind of record of the refugee plight took form, namely, the Bible in common languages.

CALVIN'S CITY OF REFUGE

As migration and religious exile escalated during the second wave of the Reformation,[4] the city of Geneva offered a place of refuge for an array of displaced Protestants—including the Frenchman John Calvin. Calvin's arrival in the summer of 1536 had been spurred by persecution that resulted from the Affair of the Placards (October to November 1534), when placards denouncing the mass were posted in Paris and beyond.[5] Calvin fled to Basel where further study of biblical languages and deepening friendships with a network of Reformation leaders awaited him.[6] There Calvin's writing bore fruit with the completion of the first edition of his *Institutes* (1536) as well as the preface and introduction to his cousin Pierre Olivétan's French translation of the Bible (1535). Passing through Geneva only three months after

people, 40 percent of whom are children: https://www.unhcr.org/figures-at-a-glance.html.

3. The struggles of the Huguenots and their Desert Churches would continue to be represented in art through the work of artists including Max Leenhardt and Jeanne Lombard, who depicted the stories of Huguenots reading the Bible in prison, fleeing with their families through the fields, and worshipping under cover of the mountainous landscape. Paintings are housed at the Musée du Désert in Mialet, France.

4. For an overview, see Terpstra, *Religious Refugees*.

5. Europe was also dealing with the fallout from the Munster Rebellion (February 1534–June 1535).

6. A summative biographical overview is given in Pak's "John Calvin's Life."

its embrace of Protestantism proved a matter of geographical necessity, and this gave opportunity for Reformer Guillame Farel to persuade Calvin to stay in the city indefinitely, by appealing to Calvin's sense of commitment to God's calling.[7] So began Calvin's first efforts at advancing reform within the city as professor of theology and then pastor.

Calvin's first contributions to Geneva's reform lasted until 1538, when he and Farel faced backlash after resisting conformity with Bernese liturgical oversight and alienated political leadership in Geneva as a result. At the invitation of Reformer Martin Bucer, Strasbourg welcomed Calvin with open arms to serve as pastor of a French refugee congregation starting in September, and Calvin's years in Strasbourg proved to be a period of growth and joy under the wing of Bucer. Ministry, scholarship, and the start of a new family due to his marriage to Idellette de Bure and the adoption of her two children enriched his days. Meanwhile, Geneva's ability to advance reformation in Calvin's absence proved difficult, and by September 1541, Calvin reluctantly returned to the city to reprise his commitment to rebuilding the church and bringing order to reform underway.

The restructuring of church life began in earnest, and though his leadership faced significant opposition for more than a decade, ultimately his vision for reform found stability in 1555, when a wave of French refugees overturned the political dynamics of the city by purchasing bourgeoisie status.[8] By the time of Calvin's death in 1564, the pastoral reach of the church of Geneva had far surpassed the constraints of its modest square footage, by way of training pastors, the distribution of Geneva's publications, and notably, through the acceptance of Protestant refugees from all over Europe. The "mother church" moniker has long been used to describe Geneva's relationship to the French churches of the Reformation, but Geneva's care and involvement extended to more than just the French.[9]

During Calvin's time, Geneva's population increased by 75 percent as a result of the refugee crisis with expansion from around twelve to twenty-one thousand.[10] When English refugee and Marian Exile John Bale[11] arrived in Geneva, he marveled at the diversity of inhabitants, saying,

7. Calvin provides an account of this interaction in the preface to his Psalms Commentary (1557).

8. See Naphy, *Calvin and the Consolidation.*

9. Geneva's work as mother church continued in the eighteenth century: McNutt, *Calvin Meets Voltaire.*

10. Valeri, "Religion, Discipline, and the Economy," 127.

11. Bale initially fled England for the European continent at the end of Henry VIII's reign in 1540, with the fall of Thomas Cromwell. Shortly after his return, in 1552, he was appointed Bishop of Ossory until Mary Tudor's succession in 1553.

> Is it not wonderful that Spaniards, Italians, Scotts, Englishmen,
> Frenchmen, Germans, disagreeing in manners, speech and ap-
> parel, sheep and wolves, bulls and bears, being coupled with the
> only yoke of Christ, should live so lovingly and friendly, and
> that Monks, Laymen, and Nuns, disagreeing both in life and sect
> should dwell together, like a spiritual and Christian congrega-
> tion? Using one order, one cloister, and like ceremonies.[12]

Although his account of Geneva as an idyllic, multicultural community requires historical nuancing,[13] Bale's statement captures the wonder of find-ing refuge alongside a diversity of exiles all navigating religious convictions in the midst of personal and European-wide crises.[14] Among this gather-ing of multilingual, multiethnic exiles in Geneva, the Protestant mission found shared expression in an effort to expand the reach of vernacular Bible translations according to Renaissance humanist standards. In this regard, the refugees of Geneva were following in the footsteps of the outlaw ex-friar Martin Luther, whose first act after receiving the Imperial Ban in 1521 and being kidnapped to safety was to spend eleven weeks translating the German New Testament from the Greek. Luther's German New Testament (called the September Testament) was a monumental success from the first month of its publication in 1522 and thereafter.[15] Luther had paved the way for identifying vernacular Bible translation and publication as a central facet of the Protestant mission to restore and render accessible the pure gospel (*reines Evagelium*). Just as the Wartburg had provided time and space for Luther to advance the vernacular translation of Scripture, so too would Ge-neva to displaced Protestants.

A HARBOR FOR REFUGEE TRANSLATIONS

As Protestant refugees passed through or settled within the city,[16] Geneva also became a harbor for refugee Bible translation projects at varying stages.

12. Bale, *Pageant of Popes*. Prefatory Letter to Sulcer, Bullinger, Calvin, and Mel-anchthon, from the Oxford Text Archive, http://hdl.handle.net/20.500.12024/A02895. Updated spelling my own.

13. Geneva's citizens struggled with xenophobic sentiment due to the economic strain caused by the refugee crisis, and initial mistreatment of Calvin reflects those complexities.

14. As Spohnholz explains, "no religious group in sixteenth-century Europe was untouched by the experiences of persecution and expulsion" ("Refugees," in *John Calvin in Context*, 150).

15. Pettegree, *Brand Luther*, 185–92.

16. Innes estimates that 7,000 refugees settled in Geneva between 1535 and 1565:

Bible production was particularly advanced in the aftermath of an aggressive escalation of Protestant persecution in France during the 1550s, which led to the arrival of key refugee Bible translators and printers. These factors alongside Calvin's prolific writings would for a time transform the small city of Geneva into one of the most significant publishing centers in all of sixteenth-century Europe.[17] Importantly, France's "brain drain to Geneva" included Robert Estienne (Stephanus) and Theodore Beza,[18] whose publications of Scripture were treated as the foundational building blocks for sound vernacular translation.[19] Estienne's Greek New Testament (1550),[20] that came to be known as the *textus receptus*, and Beza's annotated Latin New Testament (1556) first published by Stephanus, were both treated as some of the finest resources used in biblical translation at the time and after.[21] The impact of their work bears out in the story of Geneva's English translation of the Bible.

The English "Geneva Bible"

The Geneva Bible took form on the heels of a season of ambiguous permissions and prohibitions during the reign of Henry VIII.[22] Past controversy involving John Wycliffe and his English Bible loomed large over the royal reception of the vernacular project.[23] At Henry's death, however, Edward VI's rule encouraged the rapid expansion of Protestant print, which revolutionized the industry and included a 1547 injunction that every church should have a Bible.[24] When Edward's reign was cut short, Mary Tudor's succession in 1553 ceased all reforming momentum, and the next English

---

Social Concern, 205.

17. Tucker, "Geneva, Its Printing Industry." Gilmont, *Jean Calvin.*

18. Monter, *Judging the French Reformation*, 114–15. Jean Crespin and Laurent de Normandie were among this group.

19. See McNutt, "From Codex Bezae."

20. Estienne had made his name by printing editions of the Bible from 1532, during the reign of King Francis I. A few years later, he was honored as King's Printer in Greek, Hebrew, and Latin. When the Chambre Ardente banned his biblical editions, he moved to Geneva in November 1550. See Armstrong, *Robert Estienne.*

21. Publishing Bibles was not a financially lucrative enterprise due to the necessity of up-front expenditure before seeing a profit. See Pettegree, "Printing and the Reformation," 159.

22. McNutt and Lauber, "That Most Precious Jewel," 1–5.

23. Pettegree, "Printing and the Reformation."

24. For an overview, see Norton, "English Bibles." Access to a complete Bible still eluded the vast majority of people due to size and cost.

Bible project was consequently conceived and birthed across borders in the arms of the Marian exiles. The boldness of the Geneva Bible is evident in its extensive reader's aids, a close reading of the original languages, and the liberal inclusion of marginalia and para-textual materials. These elements reflect its exilic disposition and lineage from the work of William Tyndale (1526 and 1534 editions) and through the contributions of Miles Coverdale. The English-speaking congregation thrived under the leadership of John Knox and was bolstered by the arrival of hundreds of exiles.[25] In 1557, though Bible printing had ceased in England, William Whittingham succeeded Knox and published a new translation of the New Testament in Geneva. The publication of the complete Geneva Bible followed thereafter in 1560 under the leadership of Whittingham and by drawing from Beza's translations and annotations.[26] Though forged in exile, the Geneva Bible was not the product of a single translator but a committee of English refugees.[27] This was a first for the English Bible, and it was made possible by Geneva's community of clergy and scholars, the availability of scholarly resources, and the willingness of a church and city to provide meaningful welfare in the midst of diaspora. Other translation projects would benefit from these dynamics as well.

The Italian Geneva Bible

The story of the Italian Bible is not as broadly known given that reforming Italians or *spirituali* were forced into exile across European borders including the English Channel, from Switzerland and Germany to England and Poland-Lithuania.[28] As a consequence of the censorship measures enacted by the Roman Catholic Church in Italy, the Italian vernacular Bible became identified with exile. Scholars Emidio Campi and Mariano Delgado explain, "the majority of the actual work of translation fell not upon the established Church, but instead on the diaspora of Italian Protestant exiles who were dispersed throughout Europe."[29] The Italian presence in Geneva was made possible by the city's geographical proximity to the Piedmont

25. Dawson, *John Knox*, 123.

26. Krans, *Beyond What Is Written*, 197. See also Norton, "English Bible," 318. Beza's final edition was published by Henri Estienne in Geneva in 1589 and dedicated to Queen Elizabeth I.

27. Norton, "English Bibles," 316.

28. See Overell's groundbreaking work, *Italian Reform*. Peter Martyr Vermigli and Bernardino Ochino fled in August 1542 to Swiss and German cities of refuge, including Geneva, before arriving in England at Thomas Cranmer's invitation.

29. Campi and Delgado, "Bibles in Italian," 358.

region of northwest Italy. Calvin, meanwhile, was fiercely protective of the Waldensians or Vaudois, who were long established in that region and considered forerunners of the Protestant Reformation.[30] The publishing of a bilingual Italian and French Bible in Geneva, which was edited by Waldensian pastor Gian Luigi Pascale, represents the profound geographical and linguistic intersection of a community forging camaraderie across borders through their Bibles.[31]

While the first Italian Bibles published in 1471 were indicative of the outworking of medieval piety at the inception of a new print culture,[32] the histories behind subsequent Italian versions illustrate the struggles faced by those navigating early modern Europe with evangelical convictions under the Roman Catholic thumb. The Bible most beloved by Italian evangelicals in exile was Antonio Brucioli's,[33] which started with a New Testament and then a complete Bible, published in Venice in 1532. Evidence of its success is noted through its republication history and the fact that Pope Paul IV listed Brucioli's translation on the Index of Prohibited Books in 1559. Stringent censorship policies were combatted by Italian evangelicals through the relocation of Italian booksellers and printers such as Giovanni Battista Pineroli to Geneva. Anonymous publications were another approach.[34] Most significantly, Geneva became the hub for the translation and publication of the anonymous Italian New Testament, *Del Nuovo Testamento di Jesu Christo* (1555),[35] which then formed the basis for Francesco Durone's publication of the complete Italian Geneva Bible (1562). During that decade, the Council of Trent's policies against vernacular Bibles further confined the Italian Bible

---

30. For background, see Cameron, *Reformation of the Heretics*. Calvin's relationship with the Italian reformers grew tense, with the exception of Peter Martyr Vermigli, over the execution of Servetus in 1553 and the anti-Trinitarian tendencies that emerged among the group in Poland: Overell, *Italian Reform*, 173.

31. *Del Nuovo Testamento di Jesu Christo nostro Signore* ([Geneva]: Per Giovan Luigi Paschale, 1555).

32. This overview is indebted to Campi and Delgado, "Bibles in Italian." See also Castaldo, "The Bible."

33. Brucioli is credited with translating the first Italian Bible from the original languages first with the New Testament (1530) and then the complete Bible (1532). Current scholarship points to his heavy reliance on updated Latin translations of Greek and Hebrew (Campi and Delgado, "Bibles in Italian," 360–61).

34. Consider the bestselling anonymous evangelical text, *Beneficio di Cristo* (1543), which was published in Venice and influenced in part by Calvin's *Institutes* (Castaldo, "The Bible," 176).

35. Campi and Delgado attribute the translation to Pilippo Rustici, who was an exile in Geneva from 1555 ("Bibles in Italian," 363).

to diaspora by prohibiting any official circulation of the Italian Bible on the peninsula from the mid-sixteenth century to the late eighteenth century.[36]

The second generation of Italian evangelicals in Geneva, meanwhile, found security enough to dispense with anonymity. Giovanni Diodati was the son of a Protestant refugee from Lucca and born in Geneva in 1576. With expertise in Hebrew, he succeeded Theodore Beza at Geneva's Academy. His *La Bibbia* was published in 1607 and then a second edition in 1641,[37] the latter of which would be printed and adopted by Italian Protestants well into the twentieth century.[38] Through the work of Diodati especially, the Italian vernacular Bible found an enduring, public voice, and this was possible because of the way that Geneva permitted Italian exiles to maintain their ethnic autonomy in the life of the church while also providing a pathway to Genevan citizenship.[39] Their leadership and legacy in Geneva continues to this day.

The Spanish Bible

The city of Geneva also contributed to the formation of the Protestant Spanish Bible. The rumblings of the Protestant Reformation did not manifest in Spain until the late 1550s. The index of prohibited books of 1559 generated a sharp divide between permitted polyglot editions for scholars (such as the Complutensian Bible printed under the authority of Cardinal Jiménez de Cisneros from 1514–1517) and vernacular Scripture for the populace. In fact, prior to 1543, Spain was the only country during the European Reformation to lack a printed translation of the vernacular Bible, until Francisco de Enzinas came along.[40]

Enzinas was educated in the Netherlands and then Wittenberg, where he was mentored and directed by Philip Melanchthon toward the work

36. Campi and Delgado write, "It is undeniable that the meticulous application of the Tridentine decrees to the biblical text and its vernacular translations meant that the Bible was consigned to the margins of Italian religious and cultural life, and fell into a long decline from which it has only recently begun to recover" ("Bibles in Italian," 371).

37. Diodati had difficulty securing permission to publish a new annotated translation of the French Bible, and this created friction between he and the Company of Pastors. See Armstrong, "Geneva and the Theology."

38. Campi and Delgado, "Bibles in Italian," 363.

39. Monter discusses the dynamics of autonomy permitted among Italian refugees: "Italians in Geneva."

40. Campi and Delgado, "Bibles in Italian," 372. Spanish humanist and Reformer Juan de Valdés translated portions of the New Testament and Psalms into Spanish paraphrase from the Greek.

of translation. On November 25, 1543, Enzinas boldly presented to Emperor Charles V his completed translation of the Spanish New Testament based on Erasmus' Greek and published in Antwerp to Emperor. Rather than a hospitable reception, Enzinas was met with prison. Upon his escape from prison, Enzinas circulated from reformer's home to reformer's home from Wittenberg with Melanchthon, to Strasbourg with Martin Bucer, Zurich with Heinrich Bullinger, and England with Thomas Cranmer. It was through the work of Juan Pérez de Pineda that the Spanish Bible project started by Enzinas was brought to Geneva. In 1556, an anonymous translation of the Spanish New Testament, *El Testamento Nuevo . . .* , was published in Geneva. In order to promote readership, the text hid the identity of the interpreter (Pérez de Pineda),[41] who was the pastor of the Spanish Reformed Church in Geneva at the time, and masked the place of publication as Venice. Dissimulation was not beyond the pale when it came to the mission of the Protestant vernacular Bible. In terms of distribution, Seville was ideal. The region had become something of a breeding ground for Protestant sympathy as Protestant books and propaganda made their way there. Pérez de Pineda's friend Juan (Juanillo) Hernández unsuccessfully smuggled the New Testaments into Seville the following year, when he was arrested by the Inquisition and burned at the stake in an *auto de fé*.[42] This event laid bare a hidden network of prominent clergy with Protestant sympathies, including friars from the Hieronymite Monastery of St. Isidore outside Seville, which was the instigating event that provoked the establishment of the 1559 *Index*.

Cassiodoro de Reina (c. 1520–1594) was a friar in the monastery and leader of the crypto-Protestants in Seville. Although he escaped safely to Geneva that year, he was still condemned by the Inquisition and burned in effigy in 1562. Reina translated on the move through Geneva and other prominent refugee cities before publishing in Basel the first complete Spanish Bible based on the original languages. Reina's Bible came to be known as the Bear's Bible or *La Biblia del Oso* (1569) in lieu of any mention of a translator or place of publication.[43] Cipriano de Valera, who had also been an exiled monk from Reina's monastery in Seville, revised the 1582 Basel edition and published in Amsterdam in 1602 to better conform with the

41. Campi and Delgado indicate that this was not a new Greek translation but a stylistic revision of Enzinas's New Testament ("Bibles in Italian," 377).

42. For further details, see Flynn, "Mimesis of Last Judgment," as well as Griffin, *The Crombergers of Seville*. With gratitude to my former MA student Juan-Fernando León, for pointing me to these resources.

43. Years later, in 1597, Reina's connection to Geneva was further solidified by his translation of Calvin's *Institutes* into Spanish.

Genevan Calvinist editions of the Bible.[44] By this act, Valera illustrates how Geneva's own contribution to the vernacular Bible through the French Geneva Bible shaped other vernacular Bibles.

THE FRENCH BIBLE FOR REFUGEES

The French Protestant Bible eventually arrived in Geneva by way of the Waldensians (the Synod of Chanforan), who had commissioned Calvin's cousin, Pierre-Robert Olivétan, to translate the French Bible based on the original languages.[45] The 1535 Olivétan Bible was printed at their expense in Neuchâtel, and this was commemorated by printer Pierre de Wingle in his ten-line acrostic poem at the end of the Olivétan Bible, wherein the translator (Petrus Robertus Olivetanus) and the Vaudois ("an evangelical people") were named as a tribute to their work and generous sacrifice.[46] In this way, the French Protestant Bible project began outside of Geneva's walls,[47] but it was quickly adopted by her Company of Pastors through the work of John Calvin as a project of their own. No other external vernacular Bible was adopted as part of the work of Geneva's ecclesiastical leadership, which is a telling indication of the way in which Geneva was first and foremost a mother to francophone Europe even while a harbor for diverse vernacular translations. Unlike the other vernacular Bibles of Geneva, then, the French Protestant Bible was not merely passing through or solely in need of time and space for translation and publication; on the contrary, the revision and publication of the French Protestant Bible was embraced as part of the primary responsibility of Geneva's Company of Pastors.[48]

Calvin contributed to the Olivétan Bible by writing three prefaces, two of which were only published in Wingle's 1535 edition and one that gained prominence beyond Olivétan's Bible. In Calvin's Latin preface, importantly, he offered a case for the legitimacy of publishing vernacular translations without royal approval, thereby countering the accepted print customs and regulations of his time and place regarding Scripture, while also opening the

44. For criticism of his project, see Campi and Delgado's summary ("The Bible in Italian," 382). Nevertheless, the Reina-Valera Bible today is based upon a 1960's revision and is the shared Bible of millions of Spanish-speaking Protestants around the world.

45. Olivétan, *La Bible*.

46. The line in the poem "Au Lecteur de la Bible" reads: "Les Vaudois, peuple évangélique, Ont mis ce thrésor en publique" (*La Bible*, n.p.).

47. Wingle was also the printer of French Humanist Jacques Lefèvre's French New Testament the preceding year: *Le nouveau testament de nostre seigneur et seul sauveur Jesus Christ*.

48. My research traces the Company's revision of the Bible until 1805.

door for refugee translations of the Bible to find dignity and acceptance.[49] This was just the beginning of his involvement. From 1543, revisions of the text itself would carry Calvin's name starting with the New Testament and then the entire Bible in 1546 and again in 1551. The second revision of the complete Bible welcomed the collaboration of Theodore Beza and Louis Budé.[50] By 1565, the year after Calvin's death, the French Geneva Bible was published in all French-speaking publications centers, including Lyons and Paris.[51] This was also the decade in which Protestantism in France expanded exponentially and religious civil war began between noble houses. In this setting, Geneva's French Bibles were not only shaped by refugees but also shaped for refugees.

The size dimensions of French Geneva Bibles warrants mention as directly reflective of a concern for the refugee plight, since material formatting was a determinative factor in the function, location, and intended audience of a Bible. The 1588 complete French Geneva Bible offers one example since it was intentionally printed in three different sizing formats (folio, quarto, octavo) of more than 10,000 copies in an effort to reach every stratum of francophone society.[52] In this regard, the 1588 was made suitable for use in the sanctuary as well as on the run.[53] As it was, Calvin's involvement in shaping the translation and publication of the French Bible aligned chronologically with France's efforts to cease the flow of print coming from Geneva across its borders.[54] Considering sizing in light of the complete Bible's mobility provides insight into how the Bible was shaped by and for its context in a time when colporteurs were illegally smuggling books into France, including Bibles, catechisms, and Psalters. Smuggling was supported in part by the *Bourse Française*, a Genevan fund for poor refugees from France, and through the book distribution networks of financier Laurent de Normandie.[55] In some cases, colporteurs lost their lives because of the books they were carrying and selling in France, and the accounts of smuggling

---

49. See Calvin's preface in the Olivétan Bible entitled, "Joannes Calvinus, Cesaribus, Regibus, Principibus, Gentibusque omnibus Christi Imperio subditis Salutem."

50. For more on Beza's contribution to biblical scholarship, see McNutt, "From Codex Bezae."

51. Chambers, *Bibliography of French Bibles*.

52. Max Engammare compares these numbers with the publication of other French Bibles to show the magnitude of the endeavor. See his "Les Bibles genevoises."

53. Customarily, sizing the Bible for mobility meant publishing the Bible in separate segments and books rather than as a complete text.

54. Books printed in Geneva were prohibited in France in April 1548 and then against with the Edict of Châteaubriand.

55. Olson, *Calvin and Social Welfare*, 50–69.

Bibles, hiding Bibles, and dying for the French Protestant Bible continued well into the eighteenth century. Smaller complete Bibles kept the cost lower, allowed mobility, and ensured that francophone Protestants would be able to engage the complete canon.[56] Therefore, it is no surprise that—comparatively speaking—Geneva tended to publish more quantities of smaller sized complete Bibles than other print markets.

The paratextual content of French Geneva Bibles is another indication of how Bibles were shaped by and for Protestant refugees. In the first place, an overabundance of confessional resources were consistently printed with or bound to French Geneva Bibles, thereby indicating a desire to equip even the remotest worshipping body of Reformed Christians in catechism, confession, prayer, and sacraments.[57] A level of uniformity and order in the midst of diaspora was made possible through this custom.

Additionally, during the escalation of religious violence and persecution against French Protestants, in 1552, a prayer specifically dedicated to the believer "held in captivity under the Antichrist" was added to "La forme des prières" section.[58] The prayer reflects a dual affirmation of God's role as both "just Judge" and "compassionate Father," who receives all who submit to him. Much of the prayer is focused on the necessity of repentance and recognizing one's sin before God so that the greatest concern for the one living in captivity is their relationship with God rather than the oppression of their context. Captivity is understood through the typological lens of Babylon and treated as God's just judgment. They are, in this way, a refugee in their own country. Earnest supplication is, therefore, offered by appealing to God's pity for deliverance from evil. The prayer is harsh in its estimation of the spiritual state of the believer with the effect of guiding the one who prays into scorning their tendency to fear "human menace rather than Your voice."[59] This is one of several indications that the prayer was meant for those literally and spiritually bound by persecution in the French context (the latter of which applies to the so-called Nicodemites, who outwardly acquiesced to Catholic ceremony while inwardly fostering evangelical convictions).[60] Above all, the prayer seeks to orient the one who prays toward dedicating their "body and soul to exalting your holy name"

56. Engammare's analysis is sound: "Les raisons principales de ces formats in-quarto et in-octavo nous semblent être le transport de ces bibles vers la France, un coût de revient plus bas, mais aussi une vocation de la Bible comme livre personnel que l'on prend avec soi" ("Les Bibles genevoises," 184).

57. I explore this aspect further in my "Word and Sacrament."

58. For an English translation, see McKee, *John Calvin*, 215–17.

59. McKee, *John Calvin*, 216.

60. On the subject, see Woo, "The House of God."

as the highest regard for their life. Free from "excessive anxiety" by God's granting, the captive is encouraged to forget themself and live according to God's Word and will. In closing, Christ alone is celebrated as their advocate and intercessor before God, thereby communicating that the only judgement that truly matters is the Lord's. The captive in France is no less a refugee than the refugee in Geneva.

Finally, French Geneva Bibles offered a record of the refugee experience through language, binding, and marginalia. In 1554, Jean Crespin, the Dutch Protestant who became a printer and author in the city of Geneva, published two of his most important works.[61] His well-known Reformed martyrology, *Le livre des martyrs*, and a reissue of his French Bible, *La Bible*.[62] Crespin would settle in Geneva by 1538 and turn from the legal profession to running a successful printing house. His Bible was one of many vernacular Bibles published by refugee printers. A copy of Crespin's 1554 French Geneva Bible is housed at Cambridge University Library, but its journey from Geneva to England began long before.

The copy is significant because it reflects the way in which a Bible printed by a refugee printer for refugee Christians could experience and reflect the life of the refugee on its own pages. In the first place, this copy is not just a French Bible, but it was also re-bound to include Sternhold-Hopkins' English metrical Psalms, which had been printed in London in 1595. The practice of binding French Bibles with the Psalms or simply publishing them with the metrical Psalms was far from unusual, but it is the bilingual dimensions of the resulting book that deserves notice. Here is evidenced the way in which francophone Protestants, grappling with diaspora, sought to maintain their native vernacular tongue of Scripture while also engaging the liturgical tongue of their refugee context. In fact, because the persecution of francophone Protestants persisted well into the eighteenth century, the ongoing publication of bilingual vernacular French Bibles is a mark of the enduring impact of geographical dislocation for francophone Protestants.[63] Spanning two worlds geographically required efficiency in two vernacular languages as well as two different "time zones."[64] Cambridge's copy of Cres-

---

61. If a printer were harboring Protestant convictions in an unfriendly country like France and without noble protection, the decision to embrace the life of the religious refugee was in some cases far preferred to the alternative of risking spiritual hypocrisy (as a Nicodemite), financial ruin, or loss of life.

62. Crespin, *La Bible*.

63. A French/Dutch Bible was published in Amsterdam (1649) and a French/German Bible was published in Berlin (1742).

64. Catholic countries had promptly embraced the 1582 Gregorian Calendar, while most Protestant powers on the continent adopted a Protestant reform of the calendar

pin's French Geneva Bible bears witness to this dynamic on the inside cover, where the owner handwrote family milestones in English, such as baptisms and weddings, while maintaining both the English and continental system of reckoning time. Clearly, one's native language, space, and time are not easily left behind even as the process of acculturation unfolded. This is one of many ways that the plight of the refugee was reflected through the vernacular Bibles themselves.

BIBLES CROSSING BORDERS

As Protestant refugees crossed borders, so did their Bibles. Mirroring the lives of their translators, they too were on the run, in transit, circumventing normative channels of approval, and crossing borders. Like their authors, editors, and owners, refugee Bibles also found ways to hide their identity and presence as well as to find their bearings in other contexts. In the sixteenth century, the arrival of refugees in Geneva contributed to its ascendancy as a premier context for biblical scholarship, print, and ecclesiastical leadership. As a harbor for refugees, Geneva also became a safe haven for vernacular Bibles translated by, shaped for, and reflective of the Protestant refugee experience. In a sense, the Bible is and has always been a book for refugees (Phil 3:20).

BIBLIOGRAPHY

Armstrong, B. M. "Geneva and the Theology and Politics of French Calvinism: The Embarrassment of the 1588 Edition of the Bible of the Pastors and Professors of Geneva." In *Calvinism in Switzerland, Germany, and Hungary*, edited by Richard C. Gamble, 195–215. Articles on Calvin and Calvinism 13. New York: Garland, 1992.

Armstrong, Elizabeth. *Robert Estienne: Royal Printer*. Cambridge: Cambridge University Press, 1954.

Bale, John. *The Pageant of Popes: Contayninge the Lyues of All the Bishops of Rome, from the Beginninge of Them to the Yeare of Grace 1555*. Translated and edited by John Sundrey. London: Thomas Marshe, 1574.

Calvin, John. Preface to *Commentary on the Book of Psalms*. Vol. 1. Translation by James Anderson. Grand Rapids: Baker, 2009.

Cameron, Euan, ed. *The New Cambridge History of the Bible from 1450 to 1750*. Cambridge: Cambridge University Press, 2016.

---

before the turn of the eighteenth century, including the city of Geneva. See McNutt, "Hesitant Steps." England continued to maintain the Julian Calendar until 1752, and it treated March 25 as the first day of a New Year, though that practice was forgotten by the later seventeenth century.

————. *The Reformation of the Heretics: The Waldenses of the Alps, 1480–1580*. Oxford: Clarendon, 1984.

Campi, Emidio, and Mariano Delgado. "Bibles in Italian and Spanish." In *The New Cambridge History of the Bible from 1450 to 1750*, edited by Euan Cameron, 358–83. Cambridge: Cambridge University Press, 2016.

Castaldo, Chris. "The Bible and the Italian Reformation." In *The People's Book: The Reformation and the Bible*, edited by Jennifer Powel McNutt and David Lauber, 171–87. Downers Grove: IVP Academic, 2017.

Chambers, Bettye Thomas. *Bibliography of French Bibles: Fifteenth- and Sixteenth-Century French Language Editions of the Scriptures*. Geneva: Librairie Droz, 1983.

Crespin, Jean. *La Bible, Qui est toute la saincte Escriture, in laquelle sont contenuz le vieil Testament, & le nouveau: translatez en François & reveuz: le vieil selon l'Hebrieu, & le nouveau selon le Grec*. Geneva: Jean Crespin, 1554.

Dawson, Jane. *John Knox*. New Haven: Yale University Press, 2015.

Engammare, Max. "Les Bibles genevoises en français au XVIe siècle: la destinée de la traduction d'Olivetan." In *La Bible en Suisse: Origines et histoire*, edited by Urs Joerg and David-Marc Hoffmann, 177–89. Bâle, Switzerland: Schwabe, 1997.

Flynn, Maureen. "Mimesis of the Last Judgment: The Spanish Auto De Fe." *Sixteenth Century Journal* 22 (1991) 281–97.

Gamble, Richard C., ed. *Calvinism in Switzerland, Germany, and Hungary*. Articles on Calvin and Calvinism 13. New York: Garland, 1992.

Gilmont, Jean-François. *Jean Calvin et le Livre Imprimé*. Geneva: Librairie Droz, 1997.

Griffin, Clive. *The Crombergers of Seville: The History of a Printing and Merchant Dynasty*. Oxford: Clarendon, 1988.

Holder, R. Ward, ed. *John Calvin in Context*. Cambridge: Cambridge University Press, 2020.

Innes, William C. *Social Concern in Calvin's Geneva*. Edited by Susan Cembalisty-Innes. Pittsburgh Theological Monographs. Eugene, OR: Pickwick, 1983.

Krans, Jan. *Beyond What Is Written: Erasmus and Beza as Conjectural Critics of the New Testament*. Leiden: Brill, 2006.

Lefèvre, Jacques. *Le nouveau testament de nostre seigneur et seul sauveur Jesus Christ*. Neuchâtel: Pierre de Wingle, 1534.

McKee, Elsie. *John Calvin: Writings on Pastoral Piety*. Classics in Western Spirituality. Mahwah, NJ: Paulist, 2001.

McNutt, Jennifer Powell. *Calvin Meets Voltaire: The Clergy of Geneva in the Age of Enlightenment, 1685–1798*. Milton Park, UK: Routledge, 2014.

————. "From Codex Bezae to *La Bible*: Theodore Beza's Biblical Scholarship and the French Geneva Bible of 1588." In *Beza at Five-Hundred: New Perspectives on an Old Reformer*, edited by Scott Manetsch and Kirk Summers, 157–76. Göttingen: Vandenhoeck and Ruprecht, 2020.

————. "Hesitant Steps: Acceptance of the Gregorian Calendar in Eighteenth-Century Geneva." *Church History* 75 (2006) 544–64.

————. "Word and Sacrament: The Gordian Knot of Reformation Worship." In *The People's Book: The Reformation and the Bible*, edited by Jennifer Powell McNutt and David Lauber, 132–51. Downers Grove: IVP Academic, 2017.

McNutt, Jennifer Powell, and David Lauber. "That Most Precious Jewel." In *The People's Book: The Reformation and the Bible*, edited by Jennifer Powell McNutt and David Lauber, 1–9. Downers Grove: IVP Academic, 2017.

McNutt, Jennifer Powell, and David Lauber, eds. *The People's Book: The Reformation and the Bible*. Downers Grove: IVP Academic, 2017.

Monter, William. "The Italians in Geneva, 1550–1600: A New Look." In *Calvinism in Switzerland, Germany, and Hungary*, edited by Richard C. Gamble, 279–303. Articles on Calvin and Calvinism 13. New York: Garland, 1992.

———. *Judging the French Reformation: Heresy Trials by Sixteenth-Century Parlements*. Cambridge: Harvard University Press, 1999.

Naphy, William G. *Calvin and the Consolidation of the Genevan Reformation*. Louisville: Westminster John Knox, 1994.

Norton, David. "English Bibles from c. 1520 to c. 1750." In *The New Cambridge History of the Bible from 1450 to 1750*, edited by Euan Cameron, 305–44. Cambridge: Cambridge University Press, 2016.

Olivétan, Pierre-Robert. *La Bible Qui est toute la Saincte escripture*. Neuchâtel, Switzerland: Pierre de Wingle, 1535.

Olson, Jeannine E. *Calvin and Social Welfare: Deacons and the Bourse française*. Selinsgrove, PA: Susquehanna University Press, 1989.

Overell, Anne. *Italian Reform and English Reformations, c. 1535–c. 1585*. Farnham, UK: Ashgate, 2008.

Pak, G. Sujin. "John Calvin's Life." In *John Calvin in Context*, edited by R. Ward Holder, 9–16. Cambridge: Cambridge University Press, 2020.

Pettegree, Andrew. *Brand Luther: How an Unheralded Monk Turned His Small Town into a Center of Publishing, Made Himself the Most Famous Man in Europe—and Started the Protestant Reformation*. New York: Penguin, 2015.

———. "Printing and the Reformation: The English Exception." In *The Beginnings of English Protestantism*, edited by Peter Marshall and Alec Ryrie, 157–79. Cambridge: Cambridge University Press, 2002.

Spohnholz, Jesse. "Refugees." In *John Calvin in Context*, edited by R. Ward Holder, 147–54. Cambridge: Cambridge University Press, 2020.

Terpstra, Nicholas. *Religious Refugees in the Early Modern World: An Alternative History of the Reformation*. Cambridge: Cambridge University Press, 2015.

Tucker, Jameson. "Geneva, Its Printing Industry, and Book Trade." In *The Brill Companion to the Reformation in Geneva*, edited by Jon Balserak, 388–408. Leiden: Brill, 2021.

Valeri, Mark. "Religion, Discipline, and the Economy of John Calvin's Geneva." *Sixteenth Century Journal* 28 (1997) 123–42.

Woo, Kenneth. "The House of God in Exile: Reassessing John Calvin's Approach to Nicodemism in *Quatre sermons* (1552)." *CHRC* 95 (2015) 222–44.

Biblical Foundations

The Image and Mission of God

Genesis as a Lens for a Biblical Discussion of Migration

M. Daniel Carroll R.

INTRODUCTION

TODAY THE NUMBER OF internally displaced persons, refugees, asylees, and immigrants[1] is in the millions (with estimates at over 270 million)[2] and growing. The enormity of this unprecedented movement is overwhelming nations across the planet, triggering adjustments to border policies, as well as generating legislation related to education, health care, security, employment, social services, and more. The causes for these demographic pressures are legion. They include social and political unrest, violence (gang-related, persecution, warfare), ecological stress, health crises (especially now with COVID-19), poverty, shrinking job opportunities, and family reunification. Not surprisingly, the study of migration now is an increasingly important academic field, producing multiple theories about its origins, factors, and

1. A helpful glossary of pertinent terms can be found at https://www.iom.int/key-migration-terms.

2. Key data is provided by the Refugees Study Center at Oxford University (https://www.rsc.ox.ac.uk), the United Nations High Commissioner of Refugees (https://unhcr.org), and the United Nations World Migration Report 2020 (https://www.un.org/sites/un2.un.org/files/wmr_2020.pdf).

effects in order to provide analytical frameworks that might point to a more viable global future.[3]

These shocking realities and their multifaceted challenges raise questions regarding the meaning of Christian identity and the role and responsibilities of the church as the twenty-first century unfolds. Unfortunately, the position espoused in some Christian circles can reflect in significant measure the negative perspectives of groups of anti-outsider sentiment and certain nationalistic narratives, with minimal input from Christian traditions and the Bible. In contrast, at the same time, a number of book-length studies have appeared that cover the entire Bible[4] as well as works on, for instance, the relevant terminology (particularly *gēr* in the Old Testament) or specific books (such as, in the Old Testament, Deuteronomy, Nehemiah, Jeremiah, and Ezekiel).[5] This chapter hopes to contribute to a more hospitable posture toward the "strangers" in our midst by exploring two themes in the book of Genesis: the image of God and the mission of the people of God.

THE IMAGE OF GOD

Citizens and media in this country routinely engage the topic of immigration through the lens of *legality*—that is, the status of the foreigner vis-à-vis established laws regulating authorized entry into the country and permissible residence, along with their requisite protocols and strictures. For many Christians, upholding current immigration legislation is a priority; this is seen as obedience to the submission to the civil authorities mandated in Rom 13:1–5. Accordingly, compliance becomes the foundational principle for treating immigration matters.[6] To these convictions, some add the right and primary obligation of a polity to define and defend the historic way of life of its citizens as over against potential changes to be wrought by outsiders from dissimilar backgrounds and cultures.[7]

These legal and cultural matters surely need serious consideration in a comprehensive treatment of immigration, but I contend that a more proper *starting point* for discussion should be immigrants' *humanity*, not their legal

---

3. E.g., Castles, de Haas, and Miller, *Age of Migration*.

4. E.g., Ruiz, *Reading from the Edges*; Hamilton, *Jesus, King*; Carroll R., *Bible and Borders*.

5. For the biblical terminology and bibliography, see Carroll R., *Bible and Borders*, 60–64; for resources on these biblical books, see the footnotes in *Bible and Borders*, 125–27. A recent publication not mentioned there is Firth, *Including the Stranger*.

6. Note especially Hoffmeier, *Immigration Crisis*.

7. For a careful articulation of this view, see Meilaender, *Toward a Theory*.

standing. Biblically, this means appreciating that every human being, including the foreigner, is created in the image of God. Acceptance of that truth can provide key foundational values for personal and community interaction and for developing public policy. For this, we begin at the beginning, in Genesis chapters one and two, the key passages that treat the image of God.[8]

Over the centuries there have been several proposals as to the meaning of the image of God. These often have been influenced by contextual philosophical trends or in accordance with specific theological traditions. Over-simplistically, these explanations can be classified broadly into three camps, within which there are variations.[9] The first are interpretations that define the image in an *essentialist* sense: the image concerns what humans possess inherently or are ontologically, dimensions that they might share with God and have in contrast to other created beings. Depending on the author, those traits can include a conscience, rationality, a will, and an immortal soul with which a person can relate to God. The image, it is said, is realized most fully in the Second Adam, Jesus Christ. This perspective is most often connected to traditional Roman Catholic dogma and certain Reformed circles.

The second set of approaches is *relational* in focus. These understand the image of God in terms of God's address to humans and their capacity through grace to know God. Some within this framework connect this relationality more specifically to the dynamics within the Trinity or to the interpersonal relationship between male and female. These interpretations, like the first option, can be heavily christological, although with a bit of a different focus. Jesus embodies the relationship with God and, because of this, is the only One truly in God's image (2 Cor 4:4; Col 1:15); he is the prototype as well as the true image to whom humans can be conformed through the work of God (Rom 8:29; 2 Cor 3:18; Eph 4:24; Col 3:10; cf. Jas 3:9).

A third perspective, the *functional* view, though not new, is the one for which most Old Testament scholars currently argue. This perspective concentrates especially on the exegesis of the Hebrew text of the early chapters of Genesis within the worldview of the ancient Near East.[10] This not to suggest that the other two sets of approaches do not have biblical support or

8. The importance of this topic surpasses what its few occurrences in the Old Testament might suggest (Gen 1:26–27; 5:1–3; 9:6). In many ways, the meaning of the image is unpacked in the rest of Genesis and the Old Testament (Davis, *Scripture, Culture, and Agriculture*, 55–56; Briggs, "Humans in the Image of God").

9. For a helpful survey, see Demarest, *Integrative Theology*, 2:123–33; more extensively, Peterson, *Imago Dei*.

10. For much of what follows, see conveniently Middleton, *Liberating Image*; Walton, *Genesis 1*; Walton, *Old Testament Theology*, 84–99.

do not provide key insights. Interestingly, recent studies that work with the conviction that this topic must be informed dogmatically and canonically incorporate this third view, albeit in a subordinate role to what is deemed a fuller theological understanding.[11] On the other hand, some Old Testament scholars integrate the relational aspect into their functional persuasion.[12]

In the biblical account,[13] humans—male and female—appear as the culmination of God's creative work. The sovereign King puts in order and fills the chaotic void (1:3–25) and then brings humanity into being (1:26–30). With this final step, all is "very good" (1:31; the seventh occurrence of the term "good"). In 1:26–28 the term *image* (*ṣelem*) appears three times and *likeness* (*dəmût*) once.[14] For our purposes, it is important to underline that the image of God in these verses clearly is associated with exercising authority over all the other creatures and subduing the earth. In other words, the image is correlated with royal prerogatives and dignity.[15]

This orientation regarding humanity stands in sharp contrast to other ancient creation stories. In those accounts, humans were created to be the gods' servants. Humanity's role in the cosmic order was to provide them food and drink (through sacrifices and other rituals) and housing (by building and maintaining their temples). These activities were necessary for humans to secure protection and provision from the deities and to maintain the cosmic order.[16] In Genesis, however, humans are the pinnacle of God's creation, and it is *they* who receive provision from God (1:29; cf. 2:8–9, 16)! A second surprise is that *every* human being is made in God's image.[17] In

11. Note, e.g., Treier, *Introducing Theological Interpretation*; Peterson, *Imago Dei*; Levering, *Engaging Doctrine*; cf. Briggs, "Humans in the Image of God."

12. E.g., McConville, *Being Human*, 11–45; cf. Fretheim, *God and World*. Rogerson takes this in a different direction, with relationality connected to becoming more humane toward others as an expression of God's grace and purposes in the world (*Theology of the Old Testament*, 171–95).

13. Our exposition is based on the final, or canonical, form of the biblical text and does not engage debates on composition. This, we believe, is the primary text for doing theology and missiology. For a thoughtful discussion that reflects this essay's position, see Moberly, *Theology of Book*, 1–20. Of course, not all agree (e.g., Schmid, *Historical Theology*).

14. For technical studies of *ṣelem* and *dəmût*, see the commentaries and entries in the standard lexicons; cf. Middleton, *Liberating Image*, 45–48.

15. Crouch argues that the ancient background suggests instead the parent-child relationship as the principal source domain ("Genesis 1:26–27 as a Statement").

16. Walton, *Old Testament Theology*, 56–65; and Walton, "Theological Implications of Covenant."

17. While this essay, with most scholars, understands the image of God to apply to each human person, John H. Walton argues that the concept refers to humanity corporately (*Old Testament Theology*, 86–88).

ancient Egypt and Mesopotamia, royal ideologies sustained that only the king (and sometimes the priest) was made in the image of the deity (and in Egypt the pharaoh himself was divine).[Genesis announces the democratization of the divine image, whereby all individuals have this status. There is no hierarchy of superiority among persons and social relationships (including male and female).]

Noticeably, humanity's sovereignty is directed at the nonhuman world (cf. Ps 8). The two verbs expressing this dominion are "rule" (*rādâ*; 1:26, 28) and "subdue" (*kābaš*; 1:28). The first is used of kings in various passages (e.g., Ps 72:8; 110:2; Ezek 34:4); the second can refer to subjection by force (e.g., 2 Sam 8:11; Josh 18:1). In this context, their meaning must be determined by the actions and attitudes of the one delegating this authority, God.[18] In Genesis 1–2, his sovereignty is peaceful, wisely organizing, life-giving, and blessing-bestowing—ideals that were to be determinative for Israel's rulers (e.g., Ps 72:1–8; cf. Isa 11:1–9). These were the attributes to be made manifest in humanity's role upon creation: "As to the image of God, they are to mirror God to the world, to be as God would be to the nonhuman, to be an extension of God's own creative activity in the continuing development of the world."[19] God appoints humanity to continue the work of organizing and directing the world toward its proper ends.[20] There is no place, to use Pope Francis's phrase, for "tyrannical anthropomorphism."[21]

Another connection to ancient kingship was the practice of kings setting up images of themselves in regions where they could not be physically present. These statues could serve as memorials to these monarchs, but they also symbolized authority and jurisdiction over those lands. Sometimes such images were placed in temples to represent the king before the cult statues of the gods, communicating his constant gratitude for and dependence on their good graces. In the case of Genesis 1, the divine King has formed humans in his image to represent him on the earth as his vice-regents, as it were—both a privilege and a responsibility.

18. Brown, *Ethos of the Cosmos*, 42–52; Wright, *Old Testament*, 118–26; Fretheim, *God and World*, 49–53; cf. Davis, *Scripture, Culture, and Agriculture*, 53–64. These authors correctly argue that these verbs do not validate the violation of creation, an accusation made sometimes in ecology discussions. Cf. Lapsley, "Ethics and Creational Dignity." Key theological questions would be, would "rule" and "subdue" have had negative connotations before the sin and expulsion from Eden in Genesis 3? How did sin distort these mandates?

19. Fretheim, *God and World*, 55.

20. The temptation of 3:5, to aspire to be like God, is the ultimate reversal and betrayal of God's original intent for humanity and brings all sorts of perversions to the mandate to rule as God's representatives.

21. Pope Francis, *Praise Be to You*, 52; cf. parr. 65–69, 89–92.

Genesis 1–2 offers additional insight into humanity's function in creation. Features in these chapters reveal that the earth, and the garden of Eden in particular, are conceived as a cosmic sanctuary in which God desires to dwell (cf. Isa 66:1–2). Here we find echoes of vocabulary and concepts related to the tabernacle and the Jerusalem temple.[22] Among the many pertinent details are the two verbs "work" (*'ābad*) and "keep" (*šāmar*) that comprise the commission of Genesis 2:15. While these verbs are broad in their significance, both can refer to worship responsibilities. "Work" can be translated as "serve," and it is used in connection with worship of God generally (e.g., Exod 9:1, 13) or the service of the Levites (e.g., Num 4:23–24, 26). Likewise, "keep," although often associated with obeying the Torah (e.g., Exod 13:10; 20:6), can refer to guarding the tabernacle (Num 1:53; 3:7–8). Both terms appear together in reference to the Levites (Num 3:7–8; 8:26; 18:5–6; cf. 1 Chr 23:32; Ezek 44:14). Said another way, the work assigned to humanity is conceived at some level as service to God within the earthly temple that is the garden of Eden. Humans are designed to be priests of the creator God.

Additionally, elements in the narrative of Genesis 2 are reminiscent of the Mesopotamian *mīs pî* ("mouth washing") and *pīt pî* ("mouth opening") rituals, in which images of the deities were consecrated and readied to be placed in temples.[23] Through various ceremonies, these objects transitioned from being products of human hands to become the handiwork of the gods. The image would be vivified ritually and declared to be able to speak, see, and hear. Now, as a powerful representative of the deity, the image would be moved into the temple. This notion of vivification resonates with the imparting of God's breadth to humanity in 2:7. What God had shaped out of the dust of the ground is installed in the earthly temple as his living image.

The three sets of interpretations of the meaning of the image of God emphasize human worth and dignity. The particular contribution of the functional approach is that this truth about human beings, individually and corporately, is grounded distinctively in their unique royal and priestly status and roles.[24] Immigrants, of course, have the same value as everyone else. Theologically, their country of origin, culture, socioeconomic class, educational level, and legal standing are irrelevant before God. At the same time, a functional understanding of the image moves beyond the shared conviction that all humans have infinite worth to the insight that humans

22. E.g., Gordon J. Wenham, "Sanctuary Symbolism in the Garden of Eden Story," in *Proceedings of the Ninth World Congress*, 19–25; Middleton, *Liberating Image*, 81–88; Walton, *Genesis 1*, 100–119, 178–92; Brown, *Ethos of the Cosmos*, 82–89.

23. Middleton, *Liberating Image*, 127–29; McDowell, *Image of God*.

24. Carroll R., *Bible and Borders*, 13–17; cf. Middleton, *Liberating Image*, 204–12.

also possess boundless potential because of the divine design for all to be rulers. The biblical text instructs all humanity, as God's royal and priestly representatives, to rule and subdue the earth, to partner in the ongoing work of God. Accordingly, each person, again including the immigrant, is gifted with aptitude and capabilities. These can be harnessed to fulfill their divinely given role of stewarding creation and serving as God's proxies.

These competencies would not only operate for the immigrants' own benefit; they also can be channeled to impact the national good in positive ways. This perspective could alter common narratives for both the host nation and immigrants. In terms of the former, the stigmatization of immigrants as a burden and even as a possible menace can be reshaped toward a fresh conceptualization of immigrants as prospective and energetic contributors to society. Historical and current data bear out this fact in multiple fields, such as agriculture, construction, the creation of small businesses, education, health care, and more. In addition, within Christian circles, thousands of immigrant churches (and the many thousands of foreign believers in host culture congregations), and the ever-growing variety of ministries are having a major influence.

Consequently, this functional perspective can affect the purposes and tone of immigration legislation. Instead of working with a largely punitive, discriminatory, and exclusionary focus, greater attention can be paid to putting laws into place that might facilitate immigrant integration into society and more open participation in national life. Finally, for immigrants, this functional approach underscores that they are more than victims of unfortunate circumstances (of whatever kind), though that often is the case. They, too, have God-given abilities to develop and of which to be proud. They can have agency as persons created in the image of God in the new world in which they are embedded; they can grow into a deeper sense of their authentic standing before God and others in the world and move more confidently toward a better future in the various spheres in which they live.

MIGRATION AND MISSION

The second part of this chapter moves beyond the first two chapters of Genesis that focus on the identity and function of humankind in general to the topic of mission in the rest of the book, particularly as it relates to migrants and migration. In a sense, 1:28 sets the stage with the injunction to "fill the earth." This, of course, requires ongoing movement out of and away from the garden of Eden. Human history could be described then as the history of migration.[25] It truly characterizes human existence since the beginning. Perhaps one could even say that migration is in humanity's DNA. It certainly is central to Genesis. The missiologist Andrew Walls has gone so far as to say, "The first book of the Bible might also as readily have been called 'Migrations' as Genesis."[26]

In the Genesis narrative, this movement does not commence as it should have, in obedience to the divine directive. Rather, the inverse is true. Adam and Eve are expelled from Eden and prohibited from returning (3:23–24). After murdering Abel, Cain is sent to wander as part of God's judgment (4:12–14). The generations that stem from Noah's three sons—Shem, Ham and Japheth—are listed in part according to their diverse geographic locations (10:5, 20, 31), "from these the nations spread out over the earth after the flood" (10:32; NIV 2011). Chapter 11, the account of the Tower of Babel, reveals that this dispersion of peoples in chapter 10 finds its source in the judgment of God on a humanity that refused to heed God's design to fill the earth (11:4, 8–9). In other words, one could say that the nations of the earth are born at Babel.[27] In each case, humanity's movement is related to judgment on sin. Indeed, the narrative of Genesis 1–11 portrays the entire world as full of violence and death (4:8, 14–15, 23–24; chapter 5; 6:11, 13; cf. 2:17) and with an overwhelming propensity toward evil (6:5–7, 12; 8:21; 11:6).

The migrations of the people of God in Genesis begin after the Babel story with the tôlədōt ("generations") of Terah (11:27). Terah leads his family (Abram and his wife Sarai and nephew Lot) out of "Ur of the Chaldees" (11:31)[28] to Haran in northwestern Mesopotamia. Years later it is from there that Abram, the father of the faith, sets out for a land he does not know, Canaan (12:4–5). So commence the peregrinations of the patriarchs. Abraham (his name change occurs in Genesis 17), Isaac, Jacob, and Jacob's sons apparently were pastoral semi-nomads, who lived in tents and whose livelihood was taking care of herds of sheep across seasonal pasturelands.[29]

25. This is true generally but also in terms of world religions. E.g., Hanciles demonstrates that the history of the global church until 1500 is intimately connected to migration (*Migration and the Making of Global Christianity*). This would be true in all periods.

26. Walls, "Mission as Migration," 19. Walls goes on to trace the centrality of migration throughout church history.

27. In other words, the order in Genesis 9–11 is theological and literary, not chronological (i.e., the global spread of the peoples in chapter 10 begins with the dispersion of chapter 11). This also is an act of grace to forestall the potential for evil when humanity gathers together in defiance against God (11:6).

28. The location of Ur is disputed. Most link it to the old Sumerian capital of that name along the lower Euphrates, but some argue for a site in northern Mesopotamia (e.g., Beitzel, *Moody Bible Atlas*, 98–100).

29. For ancient nomadism, see Younger, *Political History*, 63–80.

Those patterns on occasion were complicated by famine, which generated their relocation to different areas of Palestine and even to as far away as Egypt (12:10; 26:1; 42:5; 43:1; 47:4, 13). When Abraham seeks to acquire a plot of land to bury his wife, he aptly describes himself to the Hittites as a "sojourner and foreigner" (*gēr vǝtôšǎb*) among them (23:4). At the end of Genesis, the reader once more is reminded of the patriarchs' occupation. When Joseph prepares his father and brothers for their initial meeting with the Pharaoh, he instructs them to say that they are shepherds (46:32—47:6). Finally, in the subsequent ritual calendar of Israel, the people are told to declare at the Feast of First Fruits, "A wandering Aramean was my father" (Deut 26:5),[30] indicating that the Israelites conceived of their early history as migratory. The exception, of course, is Joseph, but he too is a victim of what today we might call forced migration or human trafficking, as this young shepherd is sold to a caravan of traders (37:25–28).[31] Eventually, his entire extended family ends up in Egypt as immigrants. Fittingly, recent studies approach the patriarchal narratives as experiences parallel to the travails of migration today, which, like then, is generated by sociopolitical, economic, and ecological reasons.[32]

In the Genesis narrative the patriarchal migrations are connected to the launching of God's mission. That is, the protagonists of this divine work are Abram the migrant and his descendants.[33] This mission can be summed up as their being chosen as the medium for communicating God's blessing to the peoples of the world, all of whom are made in the image of God (Gen 12:1–3).[34] Wright says it well:

> God's answer to the international blight of sin was a new community of international blessing, a nation that would be a pattern and model of redemption, as well as the vehicle by which

30. For the translation of *'ōbēd* as "wandering" or "perishing," see Younger, *Political History*, 99–104. For the latter, note Alter, *Hebrew Bible*, 704.

31. To this notion of forced migration could be added Jacob's flight to the area of Haran and his time with the family of Laban (Gen 27–31).

32. Ruiz, *Reading from the Edges*, 57–70; Ruiz, "José in Egypt"; Hamilton, *Jesus, King*, 14–29; Strine, "Study of Involuntary"; Strine, "Your Name Shall No Longer Be Jacob, but Refugee"; Carroll R., *Bible and Borders*, 19–23, 27–28.

33. For some of what follows, see Van Engen, "Biblical Perspectives on Role"; Carroll R., "Biblical Perspectives on Migration"; and Gallagher, "Abraham on the Move."

34. For divine blessing and mission in Genesis, see especially Carroll R., "Blessing the Nations"; Wright, *Mission of God*, 191–221; Alexander, *From Paradise*, 146–60. These sources also discuss the options of translating the niphal verbal form (*nibrǝkû*) in 12:3b. As in most English versions, the choice here is for the passive ("will be blessed") and not the reflexive ("will bless themselves"). For yet another understanding, see Moberly, *Theology of Book*, 141–61.

the blessing of redemption would eventually embrace the rest of humanity.[35]

The blessing theme first appears in the opening creation account (1:22, 28), where it is linked to fertility (it is juxtaposed to "be fruitful and multiply"). The notion of God's blessing as material bounty is enhanced in Genesis 2 in the description of an idyllic garden that God creates for the first human couple. The rest of the book presents many instances of God's good hand in the bearing of children, the increase in flocks, and finding water. The fact that God blesses and sets apart the seventh day as holy (2:1–3) establishes that divine blessing also has a spiritual dimension (the Sabbath is explicitly grounded in creation in Exodus 20:8–11). The earliest exemplars of faith in this unfolding story are Seth (Gen 4:26) and Enoch (Gen 5:22–24). The greatest of all was to be Noah (Gen 6:8, 9), whose name (Nōaḥ) is a word play on the verbal root nwḥ ("to rest"); Genesis 5:29 suggests that he will reverse the effects of the "curse" of 3:16–19. When the flood waters recede and creation has a new beginning (note the echo of Genesis 1:26–28 in 9:1–3, 7), Noah's building of an altar and his offering acceptable sacrifices, and the divine promise never again to bring a similar judgment (Gen 8:20–22), as well as the covenant sealed with the rainbow (Gen 9:8–17), bode well for the future.

Yet the Noah narrative closes with him drunk, passed out in his tent (Gen 9:20–24). The hope of the world, as it were, fails spectacularly. The disappointment escalates to involve all of humanity in Genesis 11. There humanity declares its intention to build a city, in conscious contravention of God's directive to fill the earth (1:28; 9:1), and to construct a tower that would reach to the heavens (11:4)—perhaps to have access to where God is (or provide a gateway for God to come to humans), since their expulsion from the divine presence made direct interaction impossible (3:24). The ambitious desire for renown ("a name") and autonomy leads to the dispersion of humanity, the very thing that they had wanted to avoid.

It is at this point that Abram is called by God to migrate: to leave his native land, his kin (that is, his cultural and familial setting), and his father's house (hence, any claim to his inheritance).[36] Abram obeys at the ripe old age of seventy-five (12:4), and migrates with his family and servants to a new place, Canaan. He does so trusting in a promise of the blessings of land and progeny from God's hand (12:1–2a). Abram also is promised a "great name" as he fulfills his God-given task of being the conduit of blessing to all the mišpǝḥōt ("peoples," NIV2011; "families," NRSV, ESV, CEB) of the

---

35. Wright, Old Testament Ethics, 49.

36. It might have entailed leaving as well the family's traditional religion (Josh 24:2).

earth. Three textual observations are particularly important. The first is the promise of a "great name." Abram's renown will be bestowed as he obeys God's mandate; quite a contrast to the self-focused reach for fame by the rest of humanity (11:4)! Second, the term "peoples" in 12:3 is the same as that used in the summary statements of the genealogies of the descendants of Noah's three sons who covered the known earth (10:5, 20, 31, 32). This lexical connection intimates that the very "peoples" that were born at the rebellion and the dispersion at Babel (11:8–9) are the very "peoples" that will be blessed through the migrant Abram and his family![37] The third point flows from the sequence in 12:1–3. Abram and his descendants receive God's blessings (12:1–2a) in order to be agents of that blessing to others (12:2b–3). Experience of the grace of God precedes mission. Said another way, the people of God were created for mission.

Reflective of that initial part of the sequence of 12:1–3, the patriarchs do enjoy the blessings of children (21:1–3; 25:1–11; 29:31—30:24; 35:22–29; 46:8–27; 47:27). They accumulate flocks, servants, and wealth (13:2; 24:35; 26:12–14; 30:43; 39:5), and they find water when others cannot (26:17–22). Joseph will rise to unexpected power in Egypt (39:2–6, 21–22; 41:41–45), and the shepherd Jacob is received by Pharaoh when he and his clan enter Egypt (45:16–20; 47:1–12). The blessing of the patriarchs has its spiritual component, too. They build altars and call on God (12:7–8; 13:4, 18; 21:33; 26:25; 28:18; 35:7), and they obtain divine help on several occasions.

The second part of the sequence, mission to others as the conduit of divine material and spiritual blessing, also is evident. Abram rescues Lot from capture (chapter 14); Jacob serves Laban for many years, yielding the multiplication of his father-in-law's flocks (29:20, 27–30; 30:29–30). As second to Pharaoh, Joseph helps organize Egypt to prepare for seven years of famine (41:14–44, 53–57). Blessing comes, too, through interceding for others: Abram for Sodom (18:22–33; 19:29) and Abimelech (20:7, 17–18). The patriarchs testify verbally as well before others of their God: he has provided wealth (30:30; 31:5–13; 33:10–11; cf. 24:35), protection and guidance (31:42; 50:20; cf. 24:40–49, 56), children (33:5), and the interpretation of dreams (40:8; 41:12–16, 25–33, 50–52). The impact of these words and of the reality of God's hand upon those with whom Abraham and the others come into contact is impressive. Abimelech (21:22–24; 26:26–29), Laban (24:31, 50; 30:27; 31:29, 50, 53), and even Pharaoh (41:39) acknowledge the God of Abraham. Significantly, Abraham responds to the blessing of Melchizedek by naming the "God Most High" lauded by that king-priest as

---

37. In the narrative note that God does not choose a nation as the medium for mission. All the nations originate at Babel and are born in rebellion. Instead, God sets aside a man and will create a new people with a different history.

Yahweh in his own blessing (14:19–20, 22). Here, Genesis 12:3 finds its most obvious fulfillment: the patriarch blesses the one who blesses him.

The portrayal of the patriarchs, however, is not all positive. They violate their moral ideals and betray their sacred calling to be a blessing to other peoples. For example, several times the males ask their wives to pose as sisters (chapters 12, 20, 26). This astonishing action is illumined by comparisons to the desperate choices immigrants often make in dramatic situations where they fear physical harm, but the moral disquiet remains.[38] Jacob lies to acquire his father Isaac's blessing (chapter 27), and the brothers of Dinah slaughter the Shechemites (chapter 34; facilitated by the incapacitation of the men because of circumcision, the sign of the covenant!). Joseph did help Egypt avoid starvation, but in exchange he expropriated much of the land for Pharaoh, thereby, ironically, playing a part in creating the monstrous state that would oppress the people of God in the book of Exodus (47:13–26).

Genesis presents the pilgrimage of faith of these migrants as an integral component of its very *realistic* mission story. The patriarchs—flesh and blood individuals—continually are put in situations in which they are given the opportunity to choose the way of trust in God or to succumb to compromise. The high points of that trajectory come in chapters 15 and 22. In the former, Abram has doubts about the divine promise of a son and of many descendants (15:1–3). After being shown the vast array of the stars in the sky to which the number of his offspring will be compared, Abram believes and is commended by God (15:4–6). The climax of faith in the book occurs in chapter 22. Abraham's willingness to sacrifice the son of promise, his only son, is proof that he truly fears God (22:12). The words of the angel of the Lord, accompanied by the divine oath, repeat the promise of 12:2–3 and underscore his brave obedience (22:16–18; cf. 18:17–19). To be sure, there are other exemplary moments, such as Joseph's gracious response to his brothers in 50:20–21, in which he declares his confidence in God's sovereign ways—but none rise to the heights of Abraham's selfless act on Moriah.

Many aspects of this cursory exposition of the inauguration of the mission of God and its development across the book of Genesis may be familiar to readers. What may be new, however, is its correlation with migration. From Abram forward, the protagonists of this mission are migrants. They do mission in the diaspora, scattered among other peoples and interacting with other cultures and polities. These mobile individuals, families, and clans participate in an array of activities of all kinds in various situations and

---

38. Ruiz, *Reading from the Edges*, 64–68; Carroll R., *Bible and Borders*, 19–21; and Hamilton, *Jesus, King*, 16–27.

contexts as they live out the calling to be the means by which God blesses all the peoples of the earth. Their engagement is both materially tangible and spiritually confessional, with successes and breakdowns, that under the sovereign hand of God advance the divine mission of blessing in the world.

As with the discussion of the image of God, there are several lessons to be drawn from the biblical text for host culture Christians and immigrant believers alike. To start with, this material underscores again that immigrants can be key players in the work of God. Yet, how many sermons have been preached and books written about the persons and events of Genesis 12–50 without any awareness at all of the migration dimensions of these accounts and of their migrant characters! Some compare the Christian life to a journey of discipleship that might require abandoning deep roots, an exile of sorts;[39] this is all well and good and true, but migrants live these realities in tangible ways . . . as did the patriarchs so very long ago—not in some sort of metaphorical way. And, the patriarchs set the stage for the rest of the biblical story and the history of the people of God across millennia!

At the same time, these texts can encourage immigrant audiences to take up, as best they can within their limitations, the mantle of being a blessing to other peoples, even as the patriarchs did so many years ago. Not only the *recipients* of Christian mission, they can become *participants* and *catalysts* of mission. The many immigrant churches and ministries around the country embody this call, something of which the many denominations and Roman Catholic Church in this country are increasingly aware and are trying to support. In addition, the recent and growing field of diaspora missiology, in a more formal way, is examining the life and ministry of diaspora peoples worldwide and is committed to mobilizing them for kingdom work within their new context (both to their own people groups and the host culture) and in global mission.[40] All of this activity and projects must be laced with the complex and honest realism about host culture and immigrant challenges and failures. Mission *to*, *among*, and *by* each do not occur in an idealistic vacuum, but is part of their pilgrimage of faithfulness.

CONCLUSION

The purpose of this essay has been to look at two important interconnected themes in the book of Genesis, the image of God and the mission of the people of God, and demonstrate their relevance for contemporary debates

39. Brueggemann, *Genesis*, 117–22.

40. See Im and Yong, eds., *Global Diasporas and Mission*; and Tira and Yamamori, eds., *Scattered and Gathered*.

about immigration and immigrants. A brief foray into some lessons on immigration follows each biblical discussion. Those attempts to sketch connections between the biblical text and immigration and immigrants suggest fresh perspectives for both host culture and immigrant readers—hopefully, as conversation starters and as a stimulus for self-reflection and constructive action. The biblical material can impact each audience in distinct ways, so that hopefully each could appropriate new insights and then share these with the other group for the benefit of all, both within and beyond church walls.[41]

For readers of the host culture, this exposition may provide a different lens for looking at migration and immigrants and yield an appreciation of them as a gift from God. For immigrant readers, these themes can be an encouragement as they highlight their value and potential contributions as divine image-bearers and their significance for God's work in the world.

BIBLIOGRAPHY

Alexander, T. Desmond. *From Paradise to the Promised Land: An Introduction to the Pentateuch*. 3rd ed. Grand Rapids: Baker Academic, 2012.

Alter, Robert. *The Hebrew Bible: A Translation with Commentary*. Vol. 1, *The Five Books of Moses*. New York: Norton, 2019.

Azaransky, Sarah, ed. *Religion and Politics in America's Borderlands*. Lanham, MD: Lexington, 2013.

Beitzel, Barry J. *The New Moody Bible Atlas of the Bible*. Chicago: Moody, 2009.

Briggs, Richard S. "Humans in the Image of God and Other Things That Genesis Does Not Make Clear." *Journal of Theological Interpretation* 4 (2010) 111–26.

Brown, William P. *The Ethos of the Cosmos: The Genesis of Moral Imagination in the Bible*. Grand Rapids: Eerdmans, 1999.

Brueggemann, Walter. *Genesis*. Interpretation. Atlanta: John Knox, 1982.

Carroll R., M. Daniel. *The Bible and Borders: Hearing God's Word on Immigration*. Grand Rapids: Brazos, 2020.

———. "Biblical Perspectives on Migration and Mission: Contributions from the Old Testament." *Mission Studies* 30 (2013) 9–26.

———. "Blessing the Nations: Toward a Biblical Theology of Mission from Genesis." *Bulletin for Biblical Research* 10 (2000) 17–34.

———. "How to Shape Christian Perspectives on Immigration? Strategies for Communicating Biblical Teaching." In *Religion and Politics in America's Borderlands*, edited by Sarah Azaransky, 57–77. Lanham, MD: Lexington, 2013.

———. "Latino/Latina Biblical Interpretation." In *Scripture and Its Interpretation: An Ecumenical, Global Introduction to the Bible*, edited by Michael J. Gorman, 311–23. Grand Rapids: Baker Academic, 2017.

Castles, Stephen, et al. *The Age of Migration: International Population Movements in the Modern World*. 5th ed. New York: Guilford, 2014.

41. E.g., for Latino/a audiences, see Carroll R., "How to Shape Christian Perspectives"; Carroll R., "Latino/Latina Biblical Interpretation."

Crouch, C. L. "Genesis 1:26–27 as a Statement of Humanity's Divine Parentage." *JTS* 61 (2010) 1–15.

Davis, Ellen F. *Scripture, Culture, and Agriculture: An Agrarian Reading of the Bible.* New York: Cambridge University Press, 2009.

Demarest, Bruce. *Integrative Theology.* Grand Rapids: Zondervan, 1990.

Firth, David G. *Including the Stranger: Foreigners in the Former Prophets.* NSBT 50. London: Apollos; Downers Grove: IVP Academic, 2019.

Fretheim, Terence E. *God and World in the Old Testament: A Relational Theology of Creation.* Nashville: Abingdon, 2005.

Gallagher, Sarita D. "Abraham on the Move: The Outpouring of God's Blessing through a Migrant." In *God's People on the Move: Biblical and Global Perspectives on Migration and Mission,* edited by Van Thanh Nguyen and John M. Prior, 3–17. Eugene, OR: Pickwick, 2014.

Gorman, Michael J., ed. *Scripture and Its Interpretation: An Ecumenical, Global Introduction to the Bible.* Grand Rapids: Baker Academic, 2017.

Hamilton, Mark W. *Jesus, King of Strangers: What the Bible Really Says about Immigration.* Grand Rapids: Eerdmans, 2019.

Hanciles, Jehu J. *Migration and the Making of Global Christianity.* Grand Rapids: Eerdmans, 2020.

Hoffmeier, James K. *The Immigration Crisis: Immigrants, Aliens, and the Bible.* Wheaton, IL: Crossway, 2009.

Im, Chandler, and Amos Yong, eds. *Global Diasporas and Mission.* Regnum Edinburgh Centenary Series 23. Oxford: Regnum, 2014.

Jonker, Louis C., ed. *Congress Volume Stellenbosch 2016.* VTSup 177. Leiden: Brill, 2017.

Lapsley, Jacqueline E. "Ethics and Creational Dignity in the Old Testament." In *Congress Volume Stellenbosch 2016,* edited by Louis C. Jonker, 93–114. VTSup 177. Leiden: Brill, 2017.

Levering, Matthew. *Engaging the Doctrine of Creation: Cosmos, Creatures, and the Wise and Good Creator.* Grand Rapids: Baker Academic, 2017.

McConville, J. Gordon. *Being Human in God's World: An Old Testament Theology of Humanity.* Grand Rapids: Baker, 2017.

McDowell, Catherine L. *The Image of God in the Garden of Eden: The Creation of Humankind in Genesis 2:5—3:24 in Light of* mīs pî pīt pî *and* wpt-r *Rituals of Mesopotamia and Ancient Egypt,* Siphrut 15. Winona Lake, IN: Eisenbrauns, 2015.

Meilaender, Peter C. *Toward a Theory of Immigration.* New York: Palgrave, 2001.

Middleton, J. Richard. *The Liberating Image: The Imago Dei in Genesis 1.* Grand Rapids: Brazos, 2005.

Miglio, Adam, et al., eds. *For Us, but Not To Us: Essays on Creation, Covenant, and Context in Honor of John H. Walton.* Eugene, OR: Pickwick, 2020.

Moberly, R. W. L. *The Theology of the Book of Genesis.* Old Testament Theology. Cambridge: Cambridge University Press, 2009.

Nguyen, Van Thanh, and John M. Prior, eds. *God's People on the Move: Biblical and Global Perspectives on Migration and Mission.* Eugene, OR: Pickwick, 2014.

Peterson, Ryan S. *The* Imago Dei *as Human Identity.* JTISup 14. Winona Lake, IN: Eisenbrauns, 2016.

Pope Francis. *Praise Be to You, Laudato Si': On Care for Our Common Home.* San Francisco: Ignatius, 2015.

Proceedings of the Ninth World Congress of Jewish Studies, Jerusalem, August 4–12, 1985; Division A: The Period of the Bible. Jerusalem: World Union of Jewish Studies, 1986.

Rogerson, J. W. *A Theology of the Old Testament: Cultural Memory, Communication and Being Human.* London: SPCK, 2009.

Ruiz, Jean-Pierre. "José in Egypt: Reading Genesis 37–50 with People on the Move." *Perspectivas* 22 (2020) 1–10.

———. *Reading from the Edges: The Bible and People on the Move.* Maryknoll: Orbis, 2011.

Schmid, Konrad. *A Historical Theology of the Hebrew Bible.* Grand Rapids: Eerdmans, 2018.

Strine, C. A. "The Study of Involuntary Migration as a Hermeneutical Guide for Reading the Jacob Narrative." *Biblical Interpretation* 26 (2018) 485–98.

———. "Your Name Shall No Longer Be Jacob, but Refugee: Insights into Gen. 25:19—33:20 from Involuntary Migration Studies." In *Scripture in Social Discourse: Social Scientific Perspectives on Early Jewish and Christian Writings,* edited by C. A. Strine et al., 51–69. London: Bloomsbury T. & T. Clark, 2018.

Strine, C. A., et al., eds. *Scripture in Social Discourse: Social Scientific Perspectives on Early Jewish and Christian Writings.* London: Bloomsbury T. & T. Clark, 2018.

Tira, Sadiri Joy, and Tetsunao Yamomori, eds. *Scattered and Gathered: A Global Compendium of Diaspora Missiology.* Rev. ed. Carlisle: Langham Global Library, 2020.

Van Engen, Charles. "Biblical Perspectives on the Role of Immigrants in God's Mission." *ERT* 34 (2010) 29–43.

Treier, Daniel J. *Introducing Theological Interpretation of Scripture: Recovering a Christian Practice.* Grand Rapids: Baker Academic, 2008.

Walls, Andrew F. "Mission as Migration: The Diaspora Factor in Christian History." In *Global Diasporas and Mission,* edited by Chandler Im and Amos Yong, 19–37. Regnum Edinburgh Centenary Series 23. Oxford: Regnum, 2014.

Walton, John H. *Genesis 1 as Ancient Cosmology.* Winona Lake, IN: Eisenbrauns, 2011.

———. *Old Testament Theology for Christians: From Ancient Context to Enduring Belief.* Downers Grove: IVP Academic, 2017.

———. "The Theological Implications of Covenant as Vassal Treaty in Israel." In *For Us, but Not to Us: Essays on Creation, Covenant, and Context in Honor of John H. Walton,* edited by Adam Miglio et al., 174–95. Eugene, OR: Pickwick, 2020.

Wenham, Gordon J. "Sanctuary Symbolism in the Garden of Eden Story." In *Proceedings of the Ninth World Congress of Jewish Studies, Jerusalem, August 4–12, 1985; Division A: The Period of the Bible,* 19–25. Jerusalem: World Union of Jewish Studies, 1986.

Wright, Christopher J. H. *The Mission of God: Unlocking the Bible's Grand Narrative.* Downers Grove: IVP Academic, 2006.

———. *Old Testament Ethics for the People of God.* Downers Grove: InterVarsity, 2004.

Younger, K. Lawson, Jr. *A Political History of the Arameans: From Their Origins to End of Their Polities,* Archaeology and Biblical Studies 13. Atlanta: SBL, 2016.

Migration and the Prophetic Imagination

C. L. Crouch

INTRODUCTION

THE HEBREW SCRIPTURES ARE the story of migrants. Adam and Eve are evicted by their landlord (Gen 3). Cain wanders the earth in search of asylum (Gen 4).[1] Noah and his family flee climate change (Gen 6–9). The ancestral narratives (Gen 12–50) begin with God's instruction to Abram to "leave your country and your father's house" (Gen 12:1), setting the stage for four generations of migrations due to famine (Gen 12; 26; 42–23), civil conflict (Gen 27), and human trafficking (Gen 37).[2] The Hebrews leave economic exploitation and attempted genocide in Egypt (Exodus) and spend decades as stateless persons (Exodus–Numbers). After settling in the Cisjordan, cultural inflexibility presents difficulties for life alongside the host population (Deuteronomy–Judges). David migrates repeatedly to evade threats to his life (1 Sam 19–24; 27; 2 Sam 15–19); his ancestresses Ruth and Naomi were both migrants (Ruth).[3] Political instability and military invasions trigger refugee flight and forced displacement from the northern kingdom of Israel (2 Kgs 17), followed by similar migrations from the southern kingdom of

1. González Holguin, *Cain, Abel, and Politics.*
2. Strine, *Get Thee Out*; Southwood and Strine, eds., "Involuntary Migration and Joseph Narrative."
3. Strine, "Fear and Loathing in the Levant"; Flanders, "'Without Ruth.'"

53

Judah (2 Kgs 23–25). Some of the descendants of the population deported to Babylonia eventually return to the homeland (Ezra–Nehemiah).[4] Much of the latest literature in the Hebrew Scriptures directly addresses the challenges of life in diaspora (Esther, Daniel, Gen 37–50).

The prophetic books are especially attentive to the concerns of migrants. Amos is a Judahite from Tekoa who migrates to the environs of Samaria in pursuit of prophetic work, where he warns his host population of their own looming deportation (Amos 4–7). Hosea, though not himself a migrant (as far as we know), also warns the people that they will be expelled from their homeland as a result of political and cultural issues (Hos 8–11). Ezekiel speaks from the experience of those deported from Jerusalem to rural Babylonia in the sixth century BCE, lamenting the loss of the homeland and attempting to explain why such a catastrophe has occurred. Jeremiah responds to this and to subsequent waves of forced migration to Babylonia, as well as to the internal displacements that characterized the experience of those remaining in the homeland. Second Isaiah (Isa 40–55) seeks to persuade those who have grown up in a foreign land to migrate back to their parents' and grandparents' traditional homeland, even though they have never seen it themselves.

The Hebrew Scriptures preserve the story of God's migrant people: a story written by migrants, for migrants, and about migration.[5] The pervasiveness of migration in the Hebrew Scriptures not only affirms the ongoing significance of migration for Christian life and practice, but brings to the fore the power of migratory experiences as catalysts of personally and communally transformative theology. To recognize the recurring role of migration in the story of God's people is to admit not only that the Old Testament is indispensable to a Christian theology of migration in the twenty-first century, but to recognize that experiences of migration have stood at the heart of the theological project for more than three millennia.

The Hebrew Scriptures' extended attention to stories of and issues arising from migration means that they preserve a variety of voices on the subject. This polyphonic chorus acknowledges many different forms of migration, as well as a wide range of possible theological responses to it. A contemporary theology of migration must likewise recognize the diversity of modern migratory experiences, together with the legitimacy of a wide range of individual and collective responses to these experiences. The range of perspectives offered by the prophets, in particular, model theological innovation, adaptation, and flexibility in rapidly and radically changing

4. Southwood, *Ethnicity and Mixed Marriage Crisis*.

5. Strine, "Migration, Dual Identity, and Integration," 106.

circumstances. The following attends especially to Jeremiah and Ezekiel, the two prophetic books that respond to the destruction of Jerusalem and the end of the Judahite kingdom in the sixth century BCE. These events triggered multiple instances of displacement, to which these books respond in complex ways.

JEREMIAH

The book of Jeremiah preserves a multilayered collection of prophetic material, produced in response to the changing social, political, and theological circumstances that accompanied decades of repeated displacements. The fluidity of the Jeremiah traditions—this "book" is preserved in two different versions, both with canonical status in the Christian churches—gives the impression that this literature represents theological work in progress.[6] Each version captures the tradition at a different moment and, together, they convey the extent to which rapidly shifting circumstances required an ongoing commitment to theological creativity.

Though it is not often observed, Jeremiah is one of the most robust scriptural witnesses to displacement, depicting the repeated migrations of the population of Judah in the run-up to and in the aftermath of the Babylonian assault on Jerusalem in 586 BCE.[7] The final decades of Judah's independent existence were dominated by a series of ill-advised political decisions, in which the small kingdom's loyalty vacillated between the major empires of Babylonia and Egypt. Most of the book already presupposes the deportation of the kingdom's senior leadership to Babylonia in 597 BCE, attending instead to the politically, socially, and geographically tumultuous decade that followed. Despite the consequences that the Babylonians inflicted in 597 BCE for Judah's refusal to pay taxes and submit to imperial authority—including the deportation of its king, Jehoiachin, and other senior leaders—those who remained in the kingdom continued to look for a route to greater independence. After deporting Jehoiachin, the Babylonians put one of Josiah's sons, Zedekiah, on the throne, hoping that his indebtedness would make him pliably subservient. This turned out to be a misplaced hope; although the narratives about Zedekiah in the Masoretic

6. On the two books of Jeremiah, see Crouch, *Introduction to the Study*, 31–37. This essay follows the numeration of the Masoretic tradition that lies behind most modern translations. For an accessible English translation of the Greek tradition, see Pietersma and Wright, eds., *New English Translation*.

7. But see Davidson, "Imperial End"; Strine, "Embracing Asylum Seekers"; Crouch, *Israel and Judah*.

Text of Jeremiah depict him as weak-willed, they also intimate that he was willing to entertain the possibility of alliances with Egypt and with the other smaller kingdoms of the Levant (Jer 27:3; 37:6–7).[8] These ventures were deemed by the Babylonians to constitute rebellion against the empire, prompting a second invasion into the kingdom of Judah and an eighteen-month siege of the capital city of Jerusalem (2 Kgs 24:20—25:4 // Jer 52:3–7; also Jer 32–35; 37–39).

As the Babylonians began their approach to Jerusalem, many of the kingdom's rural residents concluded that to remain in their hometowns and villages posed a greater risk to their lives than any risk that flight could pose to their livelihoods, and elected to seek refuge in the fortified capital of Jerusalem.[9] The Rechabites of whom Jeremiah makes an example in Jeremiah 35 are internally displaced migrants of this kind, as are perhaps the Judahites who witnessed Jeremiah's acquisition of a field in Jeremiah 34.[10] This type of migration, in search of security from political violence, is a common cause of refugee movements even today.[11]

With the Babylonians camped on Jerusalem's doorstep, however, and ultimately bursting through its gates, the capital ceased to be the hoped-for refuge (Jer 8:14–15). Again, people fled in search of safety, some dying in the attempt (Jer 6:1; 39:4–9; 52:7).[12] Some of these people escaped across the Jordan River, into neighboring Ammon, Moab, and Edom (Jer 40:10–11). The dominance of the Transjordanian territories in the named destinations of displaced Judahites probably reflects the fact that "refugees cannot simply

---

8. In *Last King(s) of Judah*, Birdsong argues that this is expressed more strongly in the MT than the LXX.

9. On factors influencing decisions to migrate, see Chatty, *Displacement and Dispossession*, 16–17. Sarah K. Lischer cites work by Will Moore and Stephen Shellman that "one will leave one's home when the probability of being a victim of persecution becomes sufficiently high that the expected utility of leaving exceeds the expected utility of staying" ("Conflict and Crisis," 324; the cited work was later published as Moore and Shellman, "Whither Will They Go?").

10. On the Rechabites as involuntary migrants, see Strine, "Embracing Asylum Seekers." Steed V. Davidson examines the presentation of this otherwise unknown group as "drawn into the center and absorbed by the center," in "'Exoticizing the Other,'" 198.

11. Lischer, "Conflict and Crisis," 319.

12. Mortality rates among those displaced in or from Judah in the early sixth century BCE are unknown. Estimates of death rates during Middle Eastern involuntary migrations in the eighteenth and nineteenth centuries CE, cited by Chatty, range from 20 to 50 percent (*Displacement and Dispossession*, 94, 96, 102). Chatty also notes the consistency with which narratives of migration across a wide range of population groups describe "traumatic physical hardship, accompanied by disease, starvation, and death" (295). The deaths of Zedekiah's sons narrated explicitly in Jer 39:6 are probably only the elite tip of a very large iceberg.

appear in another country and take over 'empty' space; they can only live in areas where they are able successfully to negotiate access with the local residents."[13] In practice, "such negotiations require a good understanding of the language, the structure of the local society, and usually some pre-existing relationship"; these conditions are "most likely to be found when refugees flee across the border into the neighboring country."[14] For those fleeing Judah, the language and cultural barriers to survival were lower across the Jordan than they might have been elsewhere. If the account of Jeremiah 27 is an accurate reflection of the era's political machinations, these countries' earlier interest in supporting Judah against the Babylonians may also have suggested them as potentially welcoming allies for those displaced by the empire. Those fleeing Jerusalem as it fell were probably also joining people who had fled across the Jordan directly from their homes, rather than going first to Jerusalem. Once the immediate military crisis had abated, a number of those who had fled chose to return to Judah (Jer 40:11; 43:5). Insofar as there is less interest in return migration among self-settled involuntary migrants, others may have decided to stay in the Transjordan.[15]

In 586 BCE, after Jerusalem's final defeat and the deportation of its remaining leaders (Jer 39:7–9; 52:11–23, 27–30 // 2 Kgs 25:7–17, 21), the government was relocated by the Babylonians to Mizpah, about seven miles north of Jerusalem. This is where those who had fled into the Transjordan are said to have gone upon their return (Jer 40:11–12). Given Mizpah's previously minor status in the kingdom, most of these "return" migrants probably originated elsewhere. The influx may well have overwhelmed the town; urban centers often "suffer serious consequences because of displacement," as incoming populations "overload social services, water supplies, and sanitation facilities and thereby hasten the deterioration of the urban infrastructure, already weakened by conflict."[16] Arrival at Mizpah may have represented a symbolic return home, but in practice this return was unlikely to have been accompanied by an easy transition back to the way things used to be.[17]

These already-repeat migrants were soon on the move again, anyway. After some unspecified amount of time, an assassination plot against

13. Bakewell, "Encampment and Self-Settlement," 133; cf. Cohen and Deng, *Masses in Flight*, 29.

14. Bakewell, "Encampment and Self-Settlement," 133; cf. Harrell-Bond, *Imposing Aid*, 7.

15. Malkki, *Purity and Exile*, 182–83, 190–92; Colson, "Forced Migration," 7–10; Chatty, *Displacement and Dispossession*, 297.

16. Cohen and Deng, *Masses in Flight*, 25; cf. 42.

17. For a summary of the challenges of return migration, see Southwood, *Ethnicity and Mixed Marriage Crisis*.

Gedaliah—the native but non-royal Judahite appointed as local governor over the newly formed province—and ensuing civil war put the people on the road to Egypt (Jer 41–44). Gedaliah is killed by some distant member of the royal family, and the surviving leadership fears Babylonian reprisals for an act likely to be perceived as insurrection (Jer 41:1, 17–18). They seek safety in Egypt, pressing the remaining population into accompanying them. This includes Jeremiah and Baruch, despite Jeremiah's vociferous opposition.[18] The text suggests that these migrants do not intend to remain in Egypt; rather, they desire to return to Judah as soon as it is safe to do so, just as others had returned from the Transjordan (Jer 44:14; cf. Jer 40:11–12). This sort of temporary flight, or envisioned temporary flight, is especially common in civil wars, as people flee an area of fighting in the expectation of rapid return. The prophet denies that such a return will be possible, but the narrative acknowledges that at least a few of those who seek temporary refuge in Egypt will be able to return to the homeland (Jer 44:14, 28). In the meantime, the unrelenting instability raises serious questions of faith among the displaced, who wonder whether—or which—God is able to save them (Jer 42–44). In modern terms, some of the migrants depicted in the book of Jeremiah are internally displaced-involuntary migrants, while others are externally-displaced involuntary migrants or refugees.[19]

The migrants depicted in the book of Jeremiah also vary in the degree of agency they have over the decision to migrate. Almost all appear to migrate involuntarily—meaning under some degree of duress—although the nature of the pressure to move varies in kind and intensity.[20] At one extreme, Zedekiah and certain other individuals migrate to Babylonia because they are forced out of Judah by Nebuchadnezzar and his army (Jer 39:7, 9). Jeremiah and Baruch also appear to be taken to Egypt against their will (Jer

18. Reimer, "There—but Not Back Again." Schiffauer's discussion of the function of morality and moralizing in the aftermath of violence-induced migration may illuminate the intensity of Jeremiah's rhetoric, insofar as remaining in the homeland to fight is commonly valorized over flight ("Migration and the Structure," 72).

19. Cohen and Deng define internally displaced persons as those "who have been forced or obliged to flee or to leave their homes or places of habitual residence, in particular, as a result of, or in order to avoid the effects of, armed conflict, situations of generalized violence, violations of human rights or natural or human-made disasters, *and who have not crossed an internationally recognized state border*"; this is slightly modified from a 1992 definition employed by the United Nations (Cohen and Deng, *Masses in Flight*, 18, italics added). The distinction between these and externally displaced persons, as highlighted, concerns state authority and national responsibility; it seeks to address the assumption of international movement assumed by most definitions of the term *refugee*. For discussion, see Cohen and Deng, *Masses in Flight*, 16–18.

20. On the difficulty of establishing adequate terminology vis-à-vis "voluntary" and "involuntary" migration see Chatty, *Displacement and Dispossession*, 16–17.

43:5–6). Harder to quantify, if no less real, were the consequences of the Babylonian presence in the region—first as an invading army, terrorizing the countryside with destruction and death, then as an occupying power, possessed of absolute authority to kill or deport anyone remaining. The final siege of Jerusalem also produced severe famine in the city and possibly beyond it, as the invading army disrupted agricultural activities and supply lines (Jer 52:6). Many of those faced with these realities weighed the odds and concluded that flight was their best, or only, chance of survival. The diversity of destinations named by the text—Egypt, Ammon, Moab, Edom, and the catch-all reference to "all the other lands" (Jer 40:11)—suggests that the displaced may have had some degree of choice in the places to which they fled, as well as offering a hint of the diverse lengths to which people were prepared to go to escape the danger at home.

The narrative that the book of Jeremiah tells of Judah and Jerusalem's destruction thus acknowledges many different kinds of migration, incorporating all of them into the story of the people of God. The tradition depicts even the prophet as an involuntary migrant, forced to abandon the beloved homeland in which he is desperate to remain (Jer 40:4–6; 43:6). Nevertheless, Jeremiah's experience of migration is not the only one acknowledged by the book; there are many others. The book recognizes that no two experiences of migration are the same; the causes of displacement, the destination of the displaced, the desire or lack thereof to return, and the impact of this displacement on faith are all deeply personal, even as they form part of a wider social and historical picture. Especially significant is the way the book's portrayal of these experiences honors the fact that displacement, even in cases where migrants have some limited autonomy over departure and destination, is often deeply traumatic. The book's strange, disordered contents have sometimes been perceived as a stumbling block that must be overcome in order to discern the divine word; more recent readings have recognized that its unusual form reflects the disruption and disorientation inflicted by displacement and its trigger events, including war, political violence, and famine.[21] The acuity of this distress is so extreme that God weeps (Jer 8:18—9:1). Acknowledgment of traumatic suffering as fully within the life of the people of God is a crucial part of the divine word that Jeremiah conveys, even as this suffering raises questions about the nature of the God who allows it.

21. O'Connor, *Jeremiah*.

EZEKIEL

The trauma of involuntary migration provokes a deep and dangerous dive into the nature of God in the book of Ezekiel, too. Unlike Jeremiah, Ezekiel responds to a specific instance of involuntary migration, namely, the deportation in 597 BCE of the kingdom's senior leadership to Babylonia. This was triggered, in political terms, by the Judahites' decision to shift their loyalties away from the Babylonians and to the Egyptians, whose imperial ambitions in the southern Levant appeared to be in the ascendant as the seventh century came to a close. Unfortunately, the Judahite leadership's loyalties were misplaced; the Egyptians, as in centuries past, would prove to be unreliable allies when the Babylonian king came to reassert his dominance. Already weakened by attacks from its nearer neighbors (2 Kgs 24:2), the kingdom capitulated quickly—encouraged, perhaps, by the fact that its king, Jehoiakim, had died shortly after rebelling. His young son Jehoiachin ruled for only three months before surrendering to Nebuchadnezzar (2 Kgs 24:8–24). The royal family and some other members of the most senior leadership were deported to and held captive in Babylon, but most of the deportees were resettled on rural agricultural estates in rural Babylonia. The book of Ezekiel witnesses to the experience of one of these; there may also have been others in the area.

Ezekiel's community was located somewhere along a waterway referred to as the Chebar River, or perhaps the Chebar Canal (Ezek 1:1, 3; 3:15, 23; 10:15, 20, 22). Once the settlement is referred to as Tel Abib (Ezek 3:15). Its exact location is unknown, although it was probably in the environs of Nippur; a number of later cuneiform documents refer to individuals with Yahwistic names living in a place called āl-Yaḫudu ("Judah-town"), which seems to have been in this area.[22] Many of these documents are loan contracts, attesting to the eventual economic success of some of the deportees' later descendants. The original deportees were mostly settled on royal agricultural estates, where they were obliged to adopt a completely different kind of existence than what they had known as members of Jerusalem's royal, priestly, and administrative families (2 Kgs 24:12, 14–16). Although this reconstituted community may have sometimes been obliged to supply workers for imperial building projects, they were not slaves; the arrangement was more like a feudal system, in which the deportees were responsible to Babylonian administrators for the taxable proceeds of the property on which they had been settled. The quotidian conditions at Tel Abib are difficult to determine, but the lack of references to interactions between the

---

22. The texts published thus far appear in Pearce and Wunsch, *Documents of Judean Exiles*; Wunsch, with Pearce, *Judeans by the Waters of Babylon*, is eagerly awaited.

community and either Babylonian or other outsiders suggests that it was fairly isolated, away from major urban centers, and that the community was made up mostly or exclusively of other Judahites.

With these circumstances in mind, Ezekiel's theology bears strikingly similarities to the reactions of other involuntary migrants resettled in similarly isolated contexts. The nearest modern analogy for Ezekiel's circumstances is the refugee camp, where migrants are settled in close proximity to other members of their originating community, with few opportunities for engagement with members of the host community. This kind of isolation tends to provoke a particular anxiety about the community's physical and cultural boundaries, as well as a strong sense of the importance of the past. These interests are linked by the community's present circumstances, which constitute such a dramatic departure from previous experience that they require intentional explanation. This is most frequently sought in past events, with a special focus on transgressions within the community that led to the catastrophe. These transgressions are often identified as failures to maintain the community's cultural boundaries: the disaster is interpreted as the consequence of assimilation and "willful mixing" with outsiders.[23] This phenomenon has been extensively documented, and Ezekiel's accounts of Israel's history of transgression (Ezek 16; 20; 23) bears striking similarities to these more recent accounts, explaining that the people have been deported to Babylonia in punishment for their persistent worship of foreign gods.[24] In Ezekiel's case this explanation has a specific theological purpose, as well: what happened was not the random consequence of chance, nor the result of other powers' successes, but the result of crimes committed by the Israelite community, to which a just and almighty God has responded with appropriate severity.[25]

Ezekiel's depiction of a God whose commitment to justice leads to catastrophic punishment is one that many Western Christians find difficult to engage, having been raised on a spiritual diet that emphasizes God's love to the exclusion of almost all other divine attributes. Scripture reveals both a more complex deity and one that recognizes the spiritual and psychological needs of involuntary migrants. Surviving the defeat of Jerusalem

23. Malkki, *Purity and Exile*, 216.

24. Malkki, *Purity and Exile*. Chatty argues that historicizing occurs also among migrants not isolated in mono-ethnic migrant camps, but acknowledges that it is more intense in camp settings (*Displacement and Dispossession*, 297).

25. The ability of stories about the past to transform to serve explanatory purposes was observed most influentially by Halbwachs, in *On Collective Memory*, but is now widely discussed. We are here less interested in the historicity of Ezekiel's narrative than we are in its function.

and deportation to Babylonia required making sense of what had happened—re-telling the story of Israel in a way that could take account of and include these catastrophic changes.[26] Indeed, this "ability to tell a coherent story of our life" appears to be one of the most essential elements of socially and psychologically stable identity.[27] Traumatic events like displacement threaten people's ability to narrate: they disrupt the structure and sequence of daily life, undermine the perceived causality of events, and challenge beliefs about divine justice. Displacement, in particular, creates a radical break between past and present—one that is physical, social, and psychological. Communally-shared stories are one of the things that support the (re-)construction of the social networks and theological systems that have been broken down by dislocation.[28] Ezekiel's attention to Israel's history of sin, though unremittingly negative, is a way of re-establishing the coherence of the world and the God that rules over it. As such, it is critical for the individual and group survival of Ezekiel's involuntary migrant community.

Moreover, identifying the Israelites' own behavior as the cause of the catastrophe powerfully reasserts their moral autonomy, even as such intense negativity appears to outsiders to be a dangerous form of self-blame. By denying that they have been passive victims of foreign domination, Ezekiel's narrative shifts the responsibility for what has happened onto the people—and thereby empowers them as moral agents going forward. As Daniel Smith-Christopher has observed, "*Our own* mistakes offer hopeful possibilities in ways that outside imperial conquest does not."[29] Though disastrous, the past points the way toward a better future.

26. On these events as traumatic, see Poser, *Das Ezechielbuch als Trauma-Literatur*, 121–248.

27. King, *Memory, Narrative, Identity*, 23. Individual and collective memory do not work identically, but King suggests that in key respects they mirror each other, especially in the context of nationalist movements and in the context of traumatic events that have taken on a central role in the group's identity (5). The narrativization of the individual as a cipher for the community has been ably explored with reference to Jeremiah; see O'Connor, *Jeremiah* and "Terror All Around." On the significance of narrative in processing trauma, see Alexander, *Trauma*; Caruth, *Unclaimed Experience*; Herman, *Trauma and Recovery*; Leys, *Trauma*; and Eyerman et al., eds., *Narrating Trauma*.

28. Feldman, "Home as a Refrain"; Peteet, "Transforming Trust."

29. Smith-Christopher, "Reading Jeremiah as Frantz Fanon," 116–17 (italics original); cf. Poser, "No Words," 36–38. In a similar vein, Joo has suggested that one of Ezekiel's key preoccupations is the narration of a history in which the migrant experience is fully reflected. Reading Ezekiel contrapuntally with Rushdie's *The Satanic Verses*, she suggests that both are characterized by an "off-centering" perspective designed to undermine officially-circulating versions of history—"an alternative story to the authoritative history . . . embodying the experiences of the migrant" ("Off-Centering," 64). In Ezekiel's case, this is aimed at denying the theological and historical reality presented

THEOLOGY

Perhaps the greatest theological challenge posed by the books of Jeremiah and Ezekiel arises from the fact that they are theological works composed largely in the midst of the events they describe. As such, they constitute emergency theology: urgent attempts to respond to a cascading series of crises, more or less as they are happening. Neither of these books are the kind of pristine, precisely arranged work that might have been composed in the uninterrupted quiet of a private study, though both have fueled profound work of this kind by later theologians. Both Jeremiah and Ezekiel are depicted as literally down in the dirt as a consequence of their efforts to convey the word of God: Jeremiah in a filthy pit serving as a makeshift prison (Jer 38:6–13), Ezekiel prostrate on the ground for weeks on end (Ezek 4:4–7). Both are also portrayed as deeply ensconced in and representative of the story of the people as a whole, including the people's experiences of involuntary migration—Jeremiah is taken to Egypt, Ezekiel to Babylonia.

Given such circumstances, it should come as little surprise that the canonical forms of both books preserve a kind of theological messiness. In Jeremiah's case this is especially and overtly so, with a chaotic structure and inconsistent style that makes it very difficult to read as a book at all. In its disorderliness, the book offers scriptural acknowledgment of the disorientation and confusion common to experiences of involuntary migration and other forms of trauma.[30] Ezekiel, at the other end of the spectrum, appears orderly to a fault, scrambling to regain solid footing in a world turned upside-down—but the theology it conveys was perceived by the rabbis to be so potent, so radical, that the faithful were advised not read it until well into adulthood, and never alone.[31] Both of these prophets draw on deep reservoirs of older theological tradition, but are driven by their circumstances into the creation of something new. Radical circumstances call for radical theology.

Because both of these books underwent subsequent revision—in Jeremiah's case, probably quite significant revision—the fact that this roughness survives is worth pause. One might have expected the scribes who passed on these prophetic voices to smooth out their oddities, tone down their rhetoric, and bring them more closely in line with older orthodoxy. Instead, the prophetic traditions have been canonized in ways that recognize the exasperating elusiveness of speech about God in circumstances

---

by the Babylonian conquerors.

30. O'Connor, *Jeremiah*.

31. Simon, "Ezekiel's Geometric Vision."

where everything known and familiar has been yanked out from under one's feet. They recognize that attempts to articulate a theology appropriate to such circumstances may produce work that is imprecise, ambiguous, or even imperfect—and that, in the midst of crisis, such efforts are acts of true faith.[32] The contribution of the involuntary migrant theologies of Jeremiah and Ezekiel to theology—not only to theology specifically concerned with migration, but to all kinds of theology—provides a model for theological and community conversations today. Like those whose voices are heard in Scripture, contemporary migrants' insights into the nature of God are a gift to the whole church.

BIBLIOGRAPHY

Alexander, Jeffrey C. *Trauma: A Social Theory*. Cambridge: Polity, 2012.

Bachmann-Medick, Doris, and Jens Kugele. *Migration: Changing Concepts, Critical Approaches*. Concepts for the Study of Culture 7. Berlin: de Gruyter, 2018.

Bakewell, Oliver. "Encampment and Self-Settlement." In *The Oxford Handbook of Refugee and Forced Migration Studies*, edited by Elena Fiddian-Qasmiyeh et al., 127–38. Oxford: Oxford University Press, 2014.

Becker, Eve-Marie, et al., eds. *Trauma and Traumatization in Individual and Collective Dimensions: Insights from Biblical Studies and Beyond*. Göttingen: Vandenhoeck & Ruprecht, 2014.

Birdsong, Shelley L. *The Last King(s) of Judah: Zedekiah and Sedekias in the Hebrew and Old Greek Versions of Jeremiah 37(44):1—40(47):6*. FAT 2/89. Tübingen: Mohr Siebeck, 2017.

Boase, Elizabeth, and Christopher G. Frechette, eds. *Bible through the Lens of Trauma*. Semeia Studies 86. Atlanta: Society of Biblical Literature, 2016.

Caruth, Cathy. *Unclaimed Experience: Trauma, Narrative, and History*. Baltimore: Johns Hopkins University Press, 1996.

Chatty, Dawn. *Displacement and Dispossession in the Modern Middle East*. Cambridge: Cambridge University Press, 2010.

Cohen, Robert, and Francis M. Deng. *Masses in Flight: The Global Crisis of Internal Displacement*. Washington, DC: Brookings Institution, 1998.

Colson, Elizabeth. "Forced Migration and the Anthropological Response." *Journal of Refugee Studies* 16 (2003) 1–18.

Crouch, C. L. *An Introduction to the Study of Jeremiah*. T. & T. Clark Approaches to Biblical Studies. London: Bloomsbury, 2017.

———. *Israel and Judah: Migration, Trauma and Empire in the Sixth Century BCE*. SOTSMS. Cambridge: Cambridge University Press, 2021.

Daniel, E. Valentine, and John C. Knudsen, eds. *Mistrusting Refugees*. Berkeley: University of California Press, 1995.

Davidson, Steed V. "'Exoticizing the Other': The Curious Case of the Rechabites in Jeremiah 35." In *Prophecy and Power: Jeremiah in Feminist and Postcolonial*

---

32. See also O'Connor, "How Trauma Studies," 216.

Perspective, edited by Christl M. Maier and Carolyn J. Sharp, 189–207. LHBOTS 577. London: Bloomsbury, 2013.

———. "The Imperial End: How Empire Overtakes Refugees in Jeremiah." *Political Theology* 19 (2018) 460–77.

Diamond, A. R. Pete, and Louis Stulman, eds. *Jeremiah (Dis)Placed: New Directions in Writing/Reading Jeremiah*. LHBOTS 529. London: T. & T. Clark, 2011.

Eyerman, Ron, et al., eds. *Narrating Trauma: On the Impact of Collective Suffering*. London: Paradigm, 2011.

Feldman, Ilana. "Home as a Refrain: Remembering and Living Displacement in Gaza." *History & Memory* 18 (2006) 10–47.

Fiddian-Qasmiyeh, Elena, et al., eds. *The Oxford Handbook of Refugee and Forced Migration Studies*. Oxford: Oxford University Press, 2014.

Flanders, Denise. "'Without Ruth': The Transformative and Liberating Blessing of the Immigrant." Paper presented at The Bible on the Move: Toward a Biblical Theology of Migration, Pasadena, California, January 17, 2020.

Girma, Mohammed, and Cristian Romocea, eds. *Christian Citizenship in the Middle East: Divided Allegiance or Dual Belonging*. London: Jessica Kingsley, 2017.

González Holguin, Julián A. *Cain, Abel, and the Politics of God: An Agambenian Reading of Genesis 4:1–16*. London: Taylor & Francis, 2017.

Halbwachs, Maurice. *On Collective Memory*. Edited, translated, and introduction by Lewis A. Coser. Heritage of Sociology. London: University of Chicago Press, 1992.

Harrell-Bond, Barbara E. *Imposing Aid: Emergency Assistance to Refugees*. Oxford: Oxford University Press, 1986.

Herman, Judith L. *Trauma and Recovery: The Aftermath of Violence—from Domestic Abuse to Political Terror*. New York: Basic, 1992.

Joo, Samantha. "'Off-Centering' in *The Satanic Verses* and the Book of Ezekiel: Postcolonial Response to Alienation." *JSOT* 39 (2014) 55–78.

King, Nicola. *Memory, Narrative, Identity: Remembering the Self*. Tendencies. Edinburgh: Edinburgh University Press, 2000.

Leys, Ruth. *Trauma: A Genealogy*. Chicago: University of Chicago Press, 2000.

Lischer, Sarah Kenyon. "Conflict and Crisis Induced Displacement." In *The Oxford Handbook of Refugee and Forced Migration Studies*, edited by Elena Fiddian-Qasmiyeh, et al., 317–29. Oxford: Oxford University Press, 2014.

Maier, Christl M., and Carolyn J. Sharp, eds. *Prophecy and Power: Jeremiah in Feminist and Postcolonial Perspective*. LHBOTS 577. London: Bloomsbury, 2013.

Malkki, Liisa H. *Purity and Exile: Violence, Memory, and National Cosmology among Hutu Refugees in Tanzania*. London: University of Chicago Press, 1995.

Moore, Will H., and Stephen M. Shellman. "Whither Will They Go? A Global Study of Refugees' Destinations, 1965–1995." *International Studies Quarterly* 51 (2007) 811–34.

O'Connor, Kathleen. "How Trauma Studies Can Contribute to Old Testament Studies." In *Trauma and Traumatization in Individual and Collective Dimensions: Insights from Biblical Studies and Beyond*, edited by Eve-Marie Becker et al., 210–22. Göttingen: Vandenhoeck and Ruprecht, 2014.

———. *Jeremiah: Pain and Promise*. Minneapolis: Fortress, 2011.

———. "Terror All Around: Confusion as Meaning Making." In *Jeremiah (Dis)Placed: New Directions in Writing/Reading Jeremiah*, edited by A. R. Pete Diamond and Louis Stulman, 67–79. LHBOTS 529. London: T. & T. Clark, 2011.

Pearce, Laurie E., and Cornelia Wunsch. *Documents of Judean Exiles and West Semites in Babylonia in the Collection of David Sofer.* CUSAS 28. Bethesda, MD: CDL, 2014.

Peteet, J. M. "Transforming Trust: Dispossession and Empowerment among Palestinian Refugees." In *Mistrusting Refugees*, edited by E. Valentine Daniel and John C. Knudsen, 168–86. Berkeley: University of California Press, 1995.

Pietersma, Albert, and Benjamin G. Wright III, eds. *A New English Translation of the Septuagint and the Other Greek Translations Traditionally Included under That Title.* Oxford: Oxford University Press, 2007.

Poser, Ruth. *Das Ezechielbuch als Trauma-Literatur.* VTSup 154. Leiden: Brill, 2012.

———. "No Words: Ezekiel as Trauma Literature and a Response to the Exile." In *Bible through the Lens of Trauma*, edited by Elizabeth Boase and Christopher G. Frechette, 27–48. Semeia Studies 86. Atlanta: Society of Biblical Literature, 2016.

Reimer, David J. "There—but Not Back Again: Forced Migration and the End of Jeremiah." *Hebrew Bible and Ancient Israel* 7 (2018) 359–75.

Schiffauer, W. "Migration and the Structure of the Imaginary." In *Migration: Changing Concepts, Critical Approaches*, edited by D. Bachmann-Medick and J. Kugele, 63–80. Concepts for the Study of Culture 7. Berlin: De Gruyter, 2018.

Simon, Bennett. "Ezekiel's Geometric Vision of the Restored Temple: From the Rod of His Wrath to the Reed of His Measuring." *Harvard Theological Review* 102 (2009) 411–38.

Smith-Christopher, D. L. "Reading Jeremiah as Frantz Fanon." In *Jeremiah (Dis)Placed: New Directions in Writing/Reading Jeremiah*, edited by A. R. Pete Diamond and Louis Stulman, 115–24. LHBOTS 529. London: T. & T. Clark, 2011.

Southwood, Katherine E. *Ethnicity and the Mixed Marriage Crisis in Ezra 9–10: An Anthropological Approach.* Oxford Theological Monographs. Oxford: Oxford University Press, 2012.

Southwood, Katherine E., and C. A. Strine, eds. "Involuntary Migration and the Joseph Narrative: Interdisciplinary Perspectives." *Hebrew Studies* 60 (2019) 39–106.

Strine, C. A. "Embracing Asylum Seekers and Refugees: Jeremiah 29 as Foundation for a Christian Theology of Migration and Integration." *Political Theology* 19 (2018) 478–96.

———. "Is 'Exile' Enough? Jeremiah, Ezekiel, and the Need for a Taxonomy of Involuntary Migration." *Hebrew Bible and Ancient Israel* 7 (2018) 289–315.

———. "Fear and Loathing in the Levant: King David as Asylum Seeker and Refugee." Paper presented at The Bible on the Move: Toward a Biblical Theology of Migration, Pasadena, California, January 17, 2020.

———. *Get Thee Out of Thy Country: Involuntary Migration and the Development of the Ancestral Narrative (Gen 12–50).* ANEM. Atlanta: SBL, 2021.

———. "Migration, Dual Identity, and Integration: A Christian's Approach to Embracing Others across Enduring Lines of Difference." In *Christian Citizenship in the Middle East: Divided Allegiance or Dual Belonging*, edited by Mohammed Girma and Cristian Romocea, 103–20. London: Jessica Kingsley, 2017.

Wunsch, Cornelia. *Judeans by the Waters of Babylon: New Historical Evidence in Cuneiform Sources from Rural Babylonia.* With Laurie E. Pearce. Babylonische Archive 6. Dresden: ISLET, forthcoming.

The Migrant Messiah and the Boundary Crossing

Messianic Community in Luke-Acts

Joshua W. Jipp

DOES LUKE'S NARRATION OF the story of Jesus (in the Gospel of Luke) and his foundation story of the rise of the messianic community—what we refer to as the church (in the Acts of the Apostles)—address our most pressing contemporary social and ethical concerns?[1] To answer this question, at least two challenges must be addressed: one concerning the antiquity of our texts (i.e., "historical distance") and the other having to do with their genre as narratives. For example, Luke narrates prison escapes and speaks of Jesus engaging in liberation for the captives, but of course he knows nothing of the 2.3 million persons incarcerated in our country. Luke is well acquainted with how ethnic and cultural stereotypes harm and stigmatize minority peoples (e.g., think Samaritans, eunuchs, barbarians), but of course he does not directly address our country's history of race-based slavery, Jim Crow, or contemporary manifestations of white nationalism. With respect to this volume's theme, Luke knows that the history of Israel is one of migration, that the God of Israel is a God who demands hospitality for the vulnerable, that Jesus was an itinerant wanderer dependent upon hospitality from others, and that the early church too was a migrant people pursuing mission on the move and creating all kinds of unusual and surprising friendships for the sake of the gospel. And yet Luke, of course, says nothing about public

---

1. There are a variety of helpful ways of reading Luke and Acts. On my decision to read them as Luke-Acts, see Jipp, *Reading Acts*, 1–13.

policy, legislative proposals, or questions related to borders and modern nation-states.

To clarify then: The first challenge in drawing upon Luke-Acts for contemporary social and ethical matters is that it is an ancient text that does not know of and, therefore, is not able to speak with the degree of directness to our situation that we might desire. The second hermeneutical challenge is that of genre: Luke and Acts are narratives. They tell stories about Jesus and the church. Any contemporary use of these narratives, therefore, cannot be simply an extraction of universal rules or laws; neither will it be a simplistic replication or imitation of the characters in the stories.

I will suggest that these two potential objections are easily overcome. I highlight them, however, precisely because they have been used as a means of avoiding the robust, prophetic, and unsettling contemporary call to practice the moral and social vision of Luke-Acts (and other Christian Scriptures) as it pertains to discerning how the church responds to the contemporary challenge of migration (among other many other matters). Let me say it this way: the correspondences between our contemporary situation and that of the ancient world of the Bible will always be inexact.[2] Searching for laws, policies, and patterns to replicate cannot be the way forward, then, for moving from Scripture to the contemporary world, from biblical narrative to ethics. Instead, those of us wanting to practice theology do better to "learn again how to live in the world Scripture produces."[3] Given that Luke-Acts witnesses to a God once engaged *and still engaged* with the world he created, to a reign of an enthroned messianic king who is present in our world through the Holy Spirit, our reading of Luke-Acts is inherently self-involving as it invites us to believe, confess, and act in ways that are congruent with its literary and theological imagination.[4] The world that is imagined by Luke-Acts claims to give definition to all of reality, the situation of all of humanity, and the purpose of God's messianic people. The world of Luke-Acts, then, is not merely story; it is a totalizing vision which claims to constitute the world of its readers.[5] In what follows, then, I intend to read Luke-Acts attentive to how its scriptural vision can call us to faithful practice in our world. I read Luke-Acts, in the words of Eric Barreto, "searching for a theological imagination that can encourage prophetic action, compassionate

2. This is rightly noted by Heimburger, *God and the Illegal Alien*, 5–10.

3. Johnson, "Imagining the World Scripture Imagines," 165.

4. I have articulated this approach in much more detail in Jipp, "Beginnings of a Theology."

5. See throughout the similar theological reflections in the important work of Rowe, *World Upside Down*. My way of stating this is also obviously indebted to the likes of Hans Frei.

care, and a communal identity open to God's transformative activity among and with us."[6] How then do we develop such a theological imagination that will enable us to respond with compassion, hospitality, and humility as the people of God? I examine three important literary and theological threads of Luke-Acts that, I hope, will help us do exactly that.

Thesis #1: God's saving presence is embodied in the vulnerable stranger-guest Jesus. In other words, Jesus is the king and savior of strangers precisely because he himself is the stranger-guest par excellence. Jesus' identity as vulnerable and poor stranger corresponds precisely to the identity of his followers.[7]

The early chapters of Luke make it emphatically clear that Jesus is the singular agent of God's saving visitation of his people. Luke's birth narrative has three epiphanies where angelic messengers come *from heaven* to earth and announce a coming figure from heaven (Luke 1:5–25; 1:26–38; 2:8–20). Zechariah's hymn twice praises God for making good on his promise to visit his people. Zechariah declares, "Blessed is the Lord the God of Israel for he has *visited* his people and brought redemption for them" (1:68); and "from the compassionate mercy of our God, the dawn from on high *will visit us*" (1:78).[8] The language of divine "visitation" connotes a downward spatial movement of God from heaven to earth.

Stories of divine visitors—God or the gods—descending to earth to make a test of peoples and societies are pervasive in antiquity. The plot is fairly simple. God, or the gods, descend wearing the guise of impoverished travelers. The reason for their descent and disguise is that they have come to test the piety of the peoples and lands they visit. Quite obviously, the appropriate response to the disguised deity will be one of hospitality and, conversely, inhospitality to the seemingly vulnerable strangers will reveal the impiety of the people. And, of course, the peoples' response will have significant consequences: blessings and rewards vs. curses and punishment. The stories are quite obviously moralizing as they function as literary symbolizations of piety versus impiety.[9]

In the Gospel of Luke, Jesus, of course, is the singular agent of God's visitation whose identity as the Son of God is hidden—even disguised—from

---

6. Barreto, "A Gospel on the Move," 176.

7. Foundational here is Moessner, *Lord of the Banquet*.

8. Here and throughout, the translation is the author's.

9. See also Weaver, *Plots of Epiphany*.

the people he visits.[10] Luke presents Jesus as an itinerant wanderer, with little connection to family ties, with no home, and even birthed away from home during a journey, and spending the night in the open air (Luke 2:1–7).[11] Luke Johnson notes this Lukan dynamic well: "[Jesus] does not have a fixed abode. He does not occupy a cult center. Instead, Luke shows him constantly on the move."[12] In the words of René Padilla: "[Jesus'] entire ministry is marked by a constant identification with the destitute—an identification that won him the title 'Friend of tax collectors and sinners.'"[13] While this theme pervades the entirety of Luke, it is highlighted most powerfully in Luke's travel narrative. Luke repeatedly describes Jesus as an itinerant journeyer, a wandering stranger (e.g., 9:51–62; 10:38; 13:22, 33; 14:25; 18:31, 35, 36; 19:1, 11, 28). Jesus' journey begins with an opening vignette indicating that Jesus' journey will be marked by inhospitality and vulnerability. When his disciples go on ahead to find places for him to lodge in Samaritan villages, Luke narrates: "they did not receive him" (9:53a). Thus, in the very next scene, when a would-be disciple declares his desire to travel with Jesus on his journey: "I will follow you wherever you go" (9:57b), Jesus' response ("the Son of Man has nowhere to lay his head"; 9:58b) is a direct reference to the Samaritan village's refusal to show hospitality to him and his disciples, a situation that will characterize his journey as a whole. In other words, the rejection of Jesus and his mission is quite literally evident in Jesus' current homeless state. Ensuing inhospitality scenarios will take place between Jesus and Israel's religious leaders, who consistently break hospitality protocols as they use meals as opportunities to criticize and insult the journeying guest (11:37–44; 14:1–6; cf. 7:36–50).

The theme of inhospitality to Jesus during his journey gradually builds and leads to the sad climax, occurring at the end of the journey narrative, where Jesus weeps for God's people who have "not recognized the time of its [divine] visitation" (19:41–44). While this scene foreshadows Jesus' ultimate rejection in Jerusalem, not all is bleak, however. Jesus will experience hospitality, kindness, and welcome—e.g., from women (Mary and Martha in 10:38–42), sinners (5:27–32; 7:36–50), the poor and ritually unclean (9:11–17), and tax-collectors (5:27–32; 19:1–10). The inhospitality Jesus receives as a journeying guest is, of course, deeply related to the company he keeps

10. E.g., Jesus' identity is disclosed to infants but is hidden from the wise and powerful (10:21–24). A blind beggar "sees" (18:41–43), while his identity as the suffering Son of Man is "concealed" from his disciples (18:34).

11. Cadbury, "Lexical Notes on Luke-Acts. III," 317–19.

12. Johnson, *Prophetic Jesus, Prophetic Church*, 100–101.

13. René Padilla, "Mensaje bíblico y revolución," *Certeza* 10 (1970) 197; quoted from Escobar, *In Search of Christ*, 169.

in his own hospitality encounters. As is well known, one of the major marks of Jesus' table-practices is his indiscriminate and non-calculating offer of hospitality to all people. Jesus is tangibly extending God's welcome to those who, in the eyes of others, are unrighteous, have a low status, and are viewed as unworthy of friendship with God. Jesus is rejected, because he eats with the "wrong people," thereby incorporating them into God's family.[14]

Why do some extend hospitality to Jesus, seemingly recognizing him and his message as God's saving visitation of his people, whereas others treat him with inhospitality? It seems to me that Jesus' identity as stranger/guest functions as something of an embodied parable of his teaching. Jesus is the stranger *par excellence* precisely because he is the king and savior of strangers. In his poverty, homelessness, vulnerability, and dependence upon others, Jesus reveals—to those who are able to see—that God himself is in the deepest solidarity with the poor, the sojourner, the vulnerable refugee, and the journeying immigrant. Just as Jesus portrays himself in the parable of the sheep and the goats in Matthew 25 as "the hungry, thirsty, naked, homeless migrant" and as a "king who comes to the unsuspecting disciples as a beggar," so also Luke makes the deepest connection between Jesus' identity as stranger-guest and the recipients of God's saving visitation:[15] Jesus himself declares, "The Spirit of the Lord is upon me, for he has anointed me to proclaim good news to the poor; he has sent me to preach release to the captives, sight to the blind, to bring release to the oppressed, to proclaim the year of the Lord's favor" (4:18–19); "Blessed are the poor for yours is the kingdom of God" (6:20); and, "When you give a feast, invite the poor, the maimed, the lame, and the blind" (14:13). Again, Jesus is the king of strangers, the poor, and the humble precisely because he takes to himself the identity of the poor, vulnerable stranger guest.

Thesis #2: The church continues the ministry of Jesus and enacts God's mission precisely through crossing borders, settling in new lands, and engaging in deeply surprising, even unsettling, friendships.

Luke's Gospel repeatedly makes it clear that God's salvation is universal in scope. It is "for all people" (e.g., Luke 2:10, 32; 3:4–6; 24:44–49). As such, God's salvation—like the journeying Jesus—is constantly on the move in the book of Acts. One of the fabulous aspects of this book consists in the reader's entering into new lands and encountering all kinds of peoples. As

14. See my *Saved by Faith*, 22–24; Barreto, "A Gospel on the Move," 182.

15. This language comes from Hamilton, *Jesus, King of Strangers*, 129.

Barreto rightly notes: "The gospel cannot stay in one place, for it is God's uncontainable grace that propels witnesses to every corner of the world."[16]

Throughout the book of Acts, God's mission is propelled forward by means of God's Spirit. Peter's initial Pentecost Sermon declares what attentive readers of Luke's Gospel already know: the Spirit is the Spirit of the resurrected and enthroned-in-heaven Messiah Jesus. Peter declares that with God's exaltation of Jesus to his right hand, this resurrected Jesus has now poured out the Spirit upon those dwelling in Jerusalem (Acts 2:33; cf. Luke 24:47–48; Acts 1:4–5). In other words, the risen Jesus is responsible for the incredible event at Pentecost, whereby the pilgrim Jews in Jerusalem are able to hear the proclamation of God's mighty acts in their native languages.

If the Spirit poured out upon God's people at Pentecost flows from the very person of Jesus, now enthroned in heaven, we should expect that this Spirit will enable God's people to embody the mission, character, and very marks of Jesus. In fact, we find God's Spirit throughout Acts enabling God's people to share in his mission in surprising ways, in ways that require movement and through engaging in unusual friendships. This theme is foreshadowed in Acts 2:1–13, when the Spirit's powerful presence is manifested in the ability to speak in unlearned languages. The emphasis on speech is obvious as tongues like fiery flames descend upon the community, enabling them to speak in different languages "just as the Spirit gave them the ability to proclaim" (2:4). The Diaspora Jews are perplexed as they are enabled to hear these Galilean Jews speaking in their own dialects (2:8). Luke's listing of the virtual table of nations from Genesis 10, the emphasis upon language and hearing, and the note that the content was "the mighty deeds of God" (2:11) indicates that the function of the Spirit is to enable God's people to engage in cross-cultural testimony. It seems likely that Luke has alluded to both the Table of Nations (Gen 10) and the Tower of Babel (Gen 11) to show that the multiplication of languages will serve God's purposes to reach all peoples.

Just as the journeying Jesus extended God's salvation and hospitality to surprising people in the Gospel of Luke, so the Spirit of the risen Jesus is constantly pressing and pushing God's people to share God's blessing through crossing borders and unusual friendships. Before we look at some of these border crossings, note how Stephen's speech, strategically placed right before the gospel's movement beyond the borders of Jerusalem in Acts 8, prepares us to share Luke's conviction that God's presence is not bound to one geographical locale. Throughout his speech, Stephen argues that God's glory and presence knows no geographical restriction. In fact,

16. Barreto, "A Gospel on the Move," 182.

Stephen portrays Israel and its patriarchs as a migrant people, a people who are on the move and who encounter both God's presence outside the land of Israel as well as the challenges and vulnerabilities common to migrants and refugees. Willie Jennings says it well: "God took hold of Abraham and made him new by turning him into a sojourner and making in him something new, creating a people who were sojourners."[17] Thus, God's glory appears to Abraham in Mesopotamia (Acts 7:2); God is with Joseph in Egypt (7:9); Moses is raised in Egypt where he receives an Egyptian education (7:22–23); God visits Moses in the burning bush at Sinai and refers to the place as "holy land" (7:30–33); God is present with the wilderness generation in a moveable tent (7:44–45). God's people, however, also experience the vulnerabilities of a migrant people: leaving behind of family and friends (7:1–5), imprisonment (7:9–10), movement due to famine (7:11–12), the violent rage of tyrants (7:19), and the abuse and exploitation that stems from Pharaoh's fear (7:19–29). Stephen rightly understands that numerous portions of the biblical tradition, specifically the Torah, have inscribed a migrant identity into Israel such that the experience of being an immigrant—both the vulnerabilities and the possibilities for experiencing God's presence—is built into the very fabric of Israel's identity (see also Lev 25:23; Deut 26:1–11; 1 Chr 29:15; Ps. 39:13).[18]

The death of Stephen results in a great persecution against the church in Jerusalem such that the believers are forced to leave Jerusalem and are "scattered" throughout the regions of Judea and Samaria (8:1–4). Thus begins the move of the gospel to new lands and peoples. Without analyzing the historical intricacies and literary texture of Luke's storytelling here, we simply note the following surprising border crossings:

a. *Samaritans*: The persecution of the believers in Jerusalem leads to some travelling into Samaria, where the gospel message of Christ is proclaimed (8:4–5). Luke's repeated references to "Samaria" (Acts 8:1, 5, 14, 15, 25), along with the concluding narratival summary in Acts 9:31 ("So then all the church in the entirety of Judea, and Galilee, and Samaria had peace"), draws attention to Luke's concern to show the surprising friendship and the eradication of the long-seated hostility between Jews and Samaritans.[19]

b. *Ethiopian Eunuch*: The surprises continue as Philip now meets up with an Ethiopian eunuch. That this is a divinely ordained encounter is

17. Jennings, *Acts*, 70–71.

18. See further Knauth, "Alien, Foreign Resident." I have written more on this in *Divine Visitations and Hospitality*, 151–56.

19. I have learned much here from Pao, *Acts and Isaianic New Exodus*, 127–29.

clear from the fact that God sends an angel to tell Philip to "go south to the road that goes down from Jerusalem to Gaza" (8:26) and concludes with the Spirit snatching Philip away (8:39). Jennings again: Philip "witnesses a God whose love expands over every road and transgresses every bordered identity. The Spirit is Lord of the road."[20] Why is an Ethiopian eunuch portrayed as an ideal or model convert? A few things stand out. First, while there are a variety of descriptors for ancient Ethiopians and some positive, one more frequently finds references to them as symbols of vice and sexual desire. Second, Luke repeatedly refers to the man as a "eunuch" (8:24, 34, 36, 38, 39). Eunuchs often served as royal officials, just as this man does, in part so that there would be no worries of sexual liaisons with the nobility. Despite this, eunuchs were frequently stereotyped as salacious and sexually ambiguous monstrosities.[21] The Law speaks of eunuchs as excluded from the "assembly of the Lord" and from worshipping God in the temple (e.g., Deut 23:1; Lev. 21:16–23). The eunuch is, in short, a symbol of an outcast, one who conjures up exotic cultural, gender, and ethnic stereotypes.[22] Luke activates none of these potentially negative stereotypes. Instead, the man recognizes the God of Israel as the true God; he is reading the prophet Isaiah; he responds with belief and enthusiasm to Philip's teaching of the gospel; and he presses Philip for baptism. Luke's point is clear: Nothing like physical disability, or exotic ethnicity, or geographical distance can exclude one from encountering the powerful presence of Christ who meets this man through Philip.

c. *Pagans*: The proclamation of the gospel has now expanded beyond the borders of Jerusalem through new witnesses, in surprising ways, and to unexpected peoples. God has used the Greek-speaking Hellenists Stephen and Philip to bring the gospel to the Samaritans and outcasts. Luke's narration of the movement of the gospel into new territories "stokes confidence about venues the gospel has yet to find. Even the places that the book's original readers might consider new, unfamiliar, distant, or curious await the gospel."[23] We should not be shocked if God continues to use surprising people to bring the gospel to new

20. Jennings, *Acts*, 82.

21. Jennings, *Acts*, 83: "His difference is marked by his origin in Ethiopia, the outer limits of the known world, and is even signified by his blackness. His difference is also marked by his sexuality, neither unambiguously male nor female."

22. See especially Wilson, *Unmanly Men*, 113–49; also Pao, *Acts and Isaianic New Exodus*, 140–42.

23. Skinner, *Intrusive God, Disruptive Gospel*, 65.

places and widen the expansiveness of those included in the people of God. This prepares us for the biggest shock: the narration of the foundation event whereby gentiles are included within the people of God. Luke uses a lot of words, even repeating the Peter-Cornelius encounter three times, to indicate its central importance. Here I only point to the experiential process whereby Peter is led to recognize the surprising act of God in his encounter with the Roman centurion Cornelius.[24] The story begins with two accounts of the human experience of divine activity: Cornelius's vision of the angel of God who commands him to call for Peter, and Peter's simultaneous vision while he is praying. Peter is deeply unsettled as the voice from heaven commands him to eat both clean *and* unclean food. Peter is perplexed by the vision (10:17, 19). Peter obeys the voice of the Spirit, who tells him to go without discrimination to the home of Cornelius (10:23). The rest of the story narrates Peter's progressive growth in his ability to interpret God's activity within these events. Finally, within Cornelius's home, Peter declares that, even though it is not permissible for a Jew to associate with a Gentile, "God has shown me that I should not call any person defiled and unclean" (10:28b). Through reflection on the visions, through the shared hospitality, Peter goes even further and claims: "Truly I now perceive that God shows no partiality" (10:34). Further, when the Spirit comes upon Cornelius and the other gentiles and inspires ecstatic declaration of God's deeds (10:44–46), Peter rightly declares that they belong to the people of God, since they have received the Spirit of God "just as even we had" (10:47). Peter's affirmation of God's surprising activity is the result of a process of *experience and encounter* of divine work: visions from heaven, hospitality with strangers, and the work of the Spirit. Luke's narration of God's inclusion of the Gentiles marks a new point in the narrative of Acts. If Greek-speaking Jews (Stephen and Philip), Samaritans, Ethiopian eunuchs, and now pagans are part of God's people, then there are no limitations in terms of peoples or geographical locales to which God's gospel can move. Jesus is, in fact, as Peter had declared "Lord of all" (10:36).

d. The crossing of boundaries, the unusual friendships, and the diverse cast of characters and lands continues throughout Acts: the ethnic diversity in the church in Antioch (13:1), Lydia the Philippian God-fearer (16:11–15), the Philippian jailer (16:25–34), Athenian intellectuals (17:16–34), barbarian islanders on Malta (28:1–10)—all of

24. I am indebted to Johnson, *Scripture and Discernment*; Gaventa, *From Darkness to Light*.

this helps us grasp that, according to the witness of Acts, the church is a multiethnic people engaged in mission, crossing borders, embracing ethnic and cultural differences as gifts from God, and attentive to God's ongoing work to establish new and surprising friendships.[25] The Spirit is the Spirit of cross-cultural testimony who enables people to cross geographical borders and transgress cultural stigmas.

Thesis #3: Luke's ethnic reasoning subverts the popular belief that ethnic and cultural differences are problems to be overcome. Rather, Luke disrupts notions of the other as a source of fear, pollution, or inferiority. He does this through the subversion of ethnic and cultural stereotypes and through working within rather than demonizing the cultural and religious logics of non-Jewish peoples.

To support my third thesis, I want to examine two aspects of Luke's ethnic reasoning. By "ethnic reasoning" I refer to Luke's use of "culturally available understandings of human difference, which we can analyze in terms of our modern concepts of 'ethnicity', 'race', and 'religion' . . ."[26] First, I suggest that Luke consistently overturns and subverts common stereotypes, so much so that one can suggest this is an intentional Lukan strategy whereby ethnic, gender, and cultural difference is seen as a gift of God rather than a problem. Second, I look at how Luke appropriates diverse religious and cultural scripts and stories to proclaim the gospel.

One of the defining features of God's hospitality in Jesus for his people is that this welcome does not correspond to some prior existing social worth of the individual. God's welcome is for male and female, Jew and Gentile, Pharisees and sinners, rich and poor, apostles and outcasts. By frequently raising a negative cultural stereotype only then to reject or subvert it, Luke shows that God's friendship is for all people and not predicated upon social and cultural norms. A few examples suffice. I have written at length about how Paul's shipwreck on Malta plays on the stereotypes of the supposedly exotic islanders as uncivilized barbarians. Only here does Luke use the language "barbarian" (Acts 28:2, 4), and it seems this is almost certainly his intention to raise the stereotype of the barbarian, the non-Greek, as one who is prone to prey on shipwrecked strangers and who lacks the civilized

25. See Barreto, "A Gospel on the Move," 185: "Counter to this racialized way of thinking, Acts can help us imagine that our differences are gifts from God, not problems to overcome or obstacles on the way to becoming God's church."

26. Buell, *Why This New Race*, 2.

custom of hospitality.[27] The reader is prepared, then, for an impending *in-hospitality* scenario as Paul and his fellow prisoners wreck on the island. But Luke raises this stereotype only to reject it as a poor means of making sense of the Maltese. Luke pairs "barbarian" together with *"philanthropia"* ("philanthropy") and this is intentionally jarring for the reader. The Maltese execute hospitality protocols as well as any of the other characters through-out Luke-Acts. They make a fire to warm the prisoners (28:1–2); Paul receives a friendly and hospitable welcome in Publius's home (28:7–9); and the Maltese provide Paul with what he needs for his journey as they grant honors to him (28:9–10).

Luke does something similar, of course, with the parable of the Good Samaritan in Luke 10. One aspect of Jesus' genius is seen in his forcing the lawyer and reader, to use the insights of John Dominic Crossan, "to put together two impossible and contradictory words for the same person: 'Samaritan' (10:33) and 'neighbor' (10:36) . . . The story demands that the hearer respond by saying the contradictory, the impossible, the unspeakable."[28] The story packs the punch that it does precisely because the reader struggles to say: "The *Samaritan* was the neighbor to the man," and maybe even harder, "The *Samaritan* obeyed and fulfilled the commands of the Law of Moses."

We have already noted that Luke's transformation of stereotypes occurs in Luke's portrait of the Ethiopian eunuch, a man considered a sexual deviant by most ancient standards. The Torah forbid castrated men from full participation in the temple (see Lev. 21:16–23; Deut. 23:1). The prophet Isaiah in fact draws upon the eunuch as a representative for the kinds of outcasts who will be welcomed into God's people when God fulfills his promises (Isa 56:3–8). Eunuchs were frequently portrayed as soft, feminine, and sexually deviant as they did not conform to the masculine stereotypes of virility and strength.[29] Despite Luke's fronting of the man's identity as "eunuch" (Luke 8:27, 34, 38, 39), he activates none of the stereotypes about eunuchs. Rather, the man is humble and inquisitive as he reads Isaiah and seeks interpretive help from Philip. He welcomes Philip's interpretation and pursues baptism and goes back home rejoicing—a model Lukan character to be sure.

Roman centurions, women, people representing other ethnic stereo-types (e.g., Pontus, Acts 18) and those with physical disabilities could be examined in detail to see that the previous three examples are not acciden-tal but instead point to a fundamental feature of Luke-Acts: the worthless-ness of stigmatizing stereotypes for making sense of human existence. The

27. See Jipp, "Hospitable Barbarians."
28. Crossan, *In Parables*, 64.
29. See further Jipp, *Saved by Faith*, 33.

recipients of divine welcome in Luke-Acts are some of society's most stig-matized (and often vulnerable) peoples: sinners, tax-collectors, eunuchs, Sa-maritans, the poor and the hungry, the physically disabled, and barbarians. Jesus is remarkably unconcerned with a fear of the stranger, being polluted by a sinner, or conforming to societal standards and cultural norms.[30] Amos Yong has suggested that this theme indicates that those on the margins of society are included within God's people as they are, so that they can stand "as a testimony to the power of God to save all of us 'normal' folk from our discriminatory attitudes, inhospitable actions, and exclusionary social and political forms of life."[31]

Second, Luke further disrupts the notion of the other as a source of fear, pollution, and inferiority through appropriating the religious and cultural logics of non-Jewish peoples. Since Christianity does not sacralize any par-ticular language or culture, every new culture is, thereby, destigmatized as well as relativized.[32] Lamin Sanneh has emphasized the significance of the fact that the earliest Christians did not spread the gospel message through diffusion or cultural adoption, but rather through translation, which "rests on the persuasive nature of the idioms adopted in religious practice."[33] The contents of the Christian proclamation were "received and framed in the terms of its host culture; by feeding off the diverse cultural streams it en-countered, the religion became multicultural. The local idiom became the chosen vessel."[34] When we turn to the book of Acts and its engagement with Greco-Roman religions and cultures, it presents a similar missionary dynamic that becomes a defining feature of Christian identity throughout its history. Acts makes abundant use of Greco-Roman religious discourses in order to show that the early Christian movement embodies supremely the superior elements of Greco-Roman religiosity and philosophy.[35] Acts portrays its characters and movement as working within the cultural and religious logic of a variety of aspects of Greco-Roman religiosity as a means of simultaneously criticizing and disrupting pagan beliefs, allegiances, and ways of life, *and* using said Greco-Roman cultural scripts to portray Christianity as *the* superior Greco-Roman religion. Christianity—or at least Christian discourse—emerges out of intense conflict with Greco-Roman

30. On Luke-Acts' subversion of popular physiognomic norms, see Parsons, *Body and Character.*

31. Yong, *Bible, Disability, and the Church,* 69.

32. Flett, *Apostolicity,* 276–77.

33. Sanneh, *Translating the Message,* 33–34.

34. Sanneh, *Disciples of All Nations,* 26.

35. I have written in more detail on this and reproduced a short section from "Did Paul Translate."

religiosity. But, its employment of Greco-Roman religious scripts, themes, and philosophy results in deep cultural convergences between Christianity and pagan religion as the former emerges out of the latter. The Acts of the Apostles provides significant testimony to this dynamic, as it both adapts to and criticizes aspects of the culture within which it takes root.

For example, we see Luke adapting scripts, themes, and traditions from ancient Mediterranean culture as means of communicating the gospel. In addition to the well-known example of Paul's appropriation of Stoic philosophy in his proclamation in Athens (Acts 17:16–34), I think of the following as indicating Luke's adaptation of the gospel to Greco-Roman cultural patterns and traditions: Luke's literary prefaces and their similarities to Hellenistic historiography (Luke 1:1–4; Acts 1:1–2), the portrait of Jesus as participating in four symposia (Luke 5:27–30; 7:36–50; 11:37–54; 14:1–24), the transformation of the traditions of Jesus' crucifixion into that of noble death (Luke 23; cf. Acts 4:29; 5:29), the shaping of Jesus' resurrection appearance in the literary guise of a theoxeny (Luke 24:13–35; cf. Acts 28:1–10), the use of philosophical friendship language to exalt the Jerusalem church's common life (Acts 2:41–47; 4:32–35), God's validation of the Christian movement as exemplified in the apostles' prison escapes (Acts 5:19–20; 12:1–17; 16:25–34), and the depiction of the Christian movement's power and success as validated through victorious turf wars against its competitors (8:14–25; 13:5–12; 19:11–20; 28:3–6). Throughout Acts, Luke portrays the Christian witnesses both disrupting the cultural and religious allegiances of his Greco-Roman audience, even as he works within, rather than mocking or demonizing, their cultural and religious logics.

CONCLUSION: CONTEMPORARY REFLECTIONS ON FOLLOWING OUR MIGRANT MESSIAH

So where does our analysis of Luke-Acts leave us as we attempt to give a faithful Christian response to the complex challenges and questions surrounding immigration? It is true that the Bible does not contain specific prescriptions for public policy, but it most certainly does provide us with a contemporary moral vision or theological imagination that can enable us to discern what faithful discipleship looks like in our world.[36] Let me offer three exhortations that move from the world of Luke-Acts to our contemporary world.

First, Luke-Acts calls us to a consistent rejection of xenophobia based upon irrational stereotypes. More than forty years ago Henri Nouwen said something that seems to me to be sadly even more true today: "our society

36. I set forth some thoughts on what this might look like in *Saved by Faith*, 142–46.

seems to be increasingly full of fearful, defensive, aggressive people anx-iously clinging to their property and inclined to look at their surrounding world with suspicion, always expecting an enemy to suddenly appear, in-trude and do harm."[37] Following Jesus our stranger-king necessitates a criti-cal awareness and rejection of the irrational fears of our age, fears which, if left unchecked, cause us at best to turn away from our neighbors and, at worst, to participate in various forms of dehumanization, exclusion, and violence directed toward those whom we fear.[38]

The compelling force at work in anti-immigrant rhetoric is almost invariably *fear*, fear that the other will contaminate.[39] This fear often cen-ters upon three common threads: fear that the immigrant will corrupt our nation's cultural identity (related to language, religion, laws, and sense of shared history); fear that the immigrant will threaten national security (related to terrorism, violent crime, drug trafficking); and fear that the im-migrant will harm the economy and national institutions (related to taxes, welfare, health care).[40] Fear that the other will pollute the purity of our na-tion, then, often produces all kinds of irrational ethnic stereotyping and scapegoating.[41] The stereotyping can take many forms: Us vs. Them, Hard-working vs. Lazy, Civilized vs. Barbaric, Moral vs. the Wicked, even Alien vs. Citizen (the coining of the term "alien" was for the purpose of labeling one as an enemy and threat to a nation).[42] The cultivation of a theological imagination from Luke-Acts will have none of this in the church. We have seen that dehumanizing stereotypes and exclusionary practices are entirely antithetical to the gospel Jesus and his disciples preach.[43]

Second, and deeply related, if Jesus is the King of Strangers, the travel-ling and itinerant stranger-guest, and his identity is revealed among those

---

37. Nouwen, *Reaching Out*, 66.

38. So also von Balthasar, *The Christian and Anxiety*.

39. Also at work is the fear of scarcity, namely, fear that immigrants and refugees will take our jobs and harm the economy. Consumer societies can distract and blind us from the needs (physical and relational) of those who are lonely, hungry, and socially alienated from society. We are unable to share our resources, possessions, and live with others because we are constantly afraid that we will not "have enough" to satisfy our own desires and needs.

40. Snyder, "Fright: The Dynamics of Fear within Established Populations," in Sny-der, *Asylum-Seeking*, 85–126. See also Koser, *International Migration*, 61.

41. On stereotyping and scapegoating, see Snyder, "Fright," 102–4.

42. See further Volf, *Exclusion and Embrace*, 57–64. On the history of the term *alien*, see Heimburger, *God and the Illegal Alien*, 25–44, 65–94.

43. Personal friendships are the best way to learn about experience of migrants and refugees. In addition, I recommend reading two recent novels: Zadie Smith's *White Teeth* and Mohsin Hamid's *Exit West*.

who hospitably welcome him on the road, then the church should expect God's presence to be found and his mission extended through "strangers," disciples "on the move," and itinerants who are disconnected from family and homeland.[44] If we take seriously Jesus' words such as "Blessed are the poor for yours is the kingdom of God" (6:20), and if Jesus embodied God's salvation as an itinerant guest dependent upon the provisions of others, then perhaps we should expect to find God working in places and people that surprise us. If the church today imagines itself as continuing the same story and mission of Jesus, then many of our churches need to reject their obsession with the so-called normal, with strict boundaries, over the consistent witness that the church is comprised of unusual friendships, that it is a group of disciples crossing borders, transgressing boundaries and norms, to extend and receive the presence of Christ as embodied in one another.

Third, we should expect that the gospel mission can and will be facilitated through faithful disciples who speak in so-called "other tongues and languages." The Spirit of God in Acts is the Spirit of cross-cultural testimony. The Spirit enables God's people to hear God's mighty deeds not in one language only but with all the diversity and multiplicity of different languages, stories, cultural scripts, and worldviews. As Oscar Garcia-Johnson notes: "The Pentecost narrative points to the mandate and power for the church . . . to become everlastingly a flourishing intercultural community, the embodiment of the new humanity of Jesus Christ . . ."[45] Rather than eradicating difference or forcing those different from us to assimilate, Luke-Acts testifies to a form of life where different tongues, ethnicities, and cultures are not merely tolerated but are lovingly embraced as the means whereby the church continues to hear afresh the word and work of God.[46] Those comfortably part of majority culture thereby are called not only to extend hospitality but to act as a guest willing to learn from and hear the gospel in the rituals, practices, stories, and experiences of his/her neighbor, embodying a posture and mentality whereby they are not only the hosts and givers but guest and recipients of the gospel.[47]

---

44. For some reflections upon the contemporary practice of Luke's vision of itinerancy, see Johnson, *Prophetic Jesus, Prophetic Church*, 126–28.

45. Garcia-Johnson, *Spirit Outside the Gate*, 258.

46. See Jennings, *Acts*, 87–89.

47. See also Yong, *Hospitality and the Other*, 125, 132.

BIBLIOGRAPHY

Alexander, T. Desmond, and David W. Baker, eds. *Dictionary of the Old Testament: Pentateuch.* Downers Grove: IVP Academic, 2003.

Barreto, Eric D. "A Gospel on the Move: Practice, Proclamation, and Place in Luke-Acts." *Interpretation* 72 (2018) 175–87.

Buell, Denise Kimber. *Why This New Race: Ethnic Reasoning in Early Christianity.* Gender, Theory, and Religion. New York: Columbia University Press, 2005.

Cadbury, Henry J. "Lexical Notes on Luke-Acts. III, Luke's Interest in Lodging," *JBL* 45 (1926) 305–22.

Crossan, John Dominic. *In Parables: The Challenge of the Historical Jesus.* New York: Harper and Row, 1975.

Escobar, Samuel. *In Search of Christ in Latin America: From Colonial Image to Liberating Savior.* Downers Grove: InterVarsity, 2019.

Flett, John G. *Apostolicity: The Ecumenical Question in World Christian Perspective.* Missiological Engagements. Downers Grove: InterVarsity, 2006.

Garcia-Johnson, Oscar. *Spirit Outside the Gate: Decolonial Pneumatologies of the American Global South.* Downers Grove: IVP Academic, 2019.

Gaventa, Beverly Roberts. *From Darkness to Light: Aspects of Conversion in the New Testament.* Minneapolis: Fortress 1986.

Hamid, Moshin. *Exit West.* New York: Riverhead, 2018.

Hamilton, Mark W. *Jesus, King of Strangers: What the Bible Really Says about Immigration.* Grand Rapids: Eerdmans, 2019.

Heimburger, Robert W. *God and the Illegal Alien: United States Immigration Law and a Theology of Politics.* Cambridge: Cambridge University Press, 2018.

Jennings, Willie James. *Acts.* Belief. Louisville: Westminster John Knox, 2017.

Jipp, Joshua W. "The Beginnings of a Theology of Luke-Acts: Divine Activity and Human Response." *Journal of Theological Interpretation* 8 (2014) 24–43.

———. "Did Paul Translate the Gospel in Acts 17:22–31? A Critical Engagement with C. Kavin Rowe's *One True Life.*" *Perspectives in Religious Studies* 45 (2018) 361–76.

———. *Divine Visitations and Hospitality to Strangers in Luke-Acts: An Interpretation of the Malta Episode in Acts 28:1–10.* NovTSup 153. Leiden: Brill, 2013.

———. "Hospitable Barbarians: Luke's Ethnic Reasoning in Acts 28:1–10." *JTS* 68 (2017) 23–45.

———. *Reading Acts.* Eugene, OR: Cascade, 2018.

———. *Saved by Faith and Hospitality.* Grand Rapids: Eerdmans, 2017.

Johnson, Timothy Luke. "Imagining the World Scripture Imagines." *Modern Theology* 14 (1998) 165–80.

———. *Prophetic Jesus, Prophetic Church: The Challenge of Luke-Acts to Contemporary Christians.* Grand Rapids: Eerdmans, 2011.

———. *Scripture and Discernment: Decision-Making in the Church.* Nashville: Abingdon, 1996.

Knauth, R. J. D. "Alien, Foreign Resident." In *Dictionary of the Old Testament: Pentateuch,* edited by T. Desmond Alexander and David W. Baker, 27–33. Downers Grove: IVP Academic, 2003.

Koser, Khalid. *International Migration: A Very Short Introduction.* Very Short Introductions. Oxford: Oxford University Press, 2016.

Moessner, David P. *Lord of the Banquet: The Literary and Theological Significance of the Lukan Travel Narrative*. Minneapolis: Fortress, 1989.

Nouwen, Henri J. M. *Reaching Out: The Three Movements of the Spiritual Life*. New York: Doubleday, 1986.

Pao, David W. *Acts and the Isaianic New Exodus*. WUNT 2/130. Tübingen: Mohr Siebeck, 2000.

Parsons, Mikeal C. *Body and Character in Luke-Acts: The Subversion of Physiognomy in Early Christianity*. Grand Rapids: Baker Academic, 2006.

Rowe, C. Kavin. *World Upside Down: Reading Acts in the Graeco-Roman Age*. Oxford: Oxford University Press, 2009.

Sanneh, Lamin. *Disciples of All Nations: Pillars of World Christianity*. Oxford Studies in World Christianity. Oxford: Oxford University Press, 2008.

———. *Translating the Message: The Missionary Impact on Culture*. Rev. ed. Maryknoll: Orbis, 2009.

Skinner, Matthew L. *Intrusive God, Disruptive Gospel: Encountering the Divine in the Book of Acts*. Grand Rapids: Brazos, 2015.

Smith, Zadie. *White Teeth*. New York: Vintage, 2001.

Snyder, Susannah. *Asylum-Seeking: Migration and Church*. Explorations in Pastoral and Empirical Theology. London: Ashgate, 2012.

Volf, Miroslav. *Exclusion and Embrace: A Theological Exploration of Identity, Otherness, and Reconciliation*. Nashville: Abingdon, 1996.

Von Balthasar, Hans Urs. *The Christian and Anxiety*. San Francisco: Ignatius, 2000.

Weaver, John B. *Plots of Epiphany: Prison-Escape in Acts of the Apostles*. BZNW 131. Berlin: de Gruyter, 2004.

Wilson, Brittany. *Unmanly Men: Refigurations of Masculinity in Luke-Acts*. Oxford: Oxford University Press, 2015.

Yong, Amos. *The Bible, Disability, and the Church: A New Vision of the People of God*. Grand Rapids: Eerdmans, 2011.

———. *Hospitality and the Other: Pentecost, Christian Practices, and the Neighbor*. Maryknoll: Orbis, 2008.

James and 1 Peter through the Eyes of a Migrant

Nelson Morales

AT THE BEGINNING OF the decade of 2010, due to the so-called Arab spring, thousands of people were displaced from their homes. Currently, as a consequence of that uprising, the Syrian conflict still generates massive displacements. Political and financial problems in Latin America also provoked displacement from unstable and poor countries to other places, with the migrants looking for work and better opportunities in life. The COVID-19 pandemic has aggravated the situation of those millions of migrants. What has been the role of the church in the midst of this crisis? What should be our response? Without a doubt, before answering those questions, we need to evaluate our concept of diaspora. We need to think theologically about migration. This article explores the concept of diaspora and reflects theologically about migration from the perspective of the letters of James and 1 Peter. With this foundation, we are better equipped to answer the aforementioned questions. I write this chapter from the view of a migrant, who has lived outside his native country for more than twenty-seven years.

IDEAS ON DIASPORA THAT GUIDE THIS CHAPTER

Both James and Peter send their letters to people in the *diaspora* (Jas 1:1; 1 Pet 1:1). The noun *diaspora/dispersion* appears three times in the New Testament. Besides James and Peter, John uses the word with the historical sense of Jewish communities outside of Palestine. John 7:35 presents a conversation between Jewish leaders, where they ask one another if Jesus intends to go to the diaspora, namely that of the Jews among the Greeks. James and Peter, instead, use the concept not literally, but metaphorically. For James, his addressees are the twelve tribes in the diaspora. For Peter, they are exiles of the dispersion in Asia Minor. Besides this noun, Peter also uses the words *paroikos/paroikia* (foreigner/sojourn) and *parepidēmos* (exiles) to describe his addressees and their situation.

In the same vein, following Shively T. J. Smith's proposal, one idea developed in this chapter is that diaspora and its related words serve as a literary trope used by James and Peter to frame their letters to believers.[1] It is apparent throughout the present analysis that what Smith notes in 1 Peter regarding diaspora is true in both letters. She states that "diaspora is not the creation and action of God against the people. Rather, diaspora life is the product of people's faithful response to God's action through Christ as they embrace their newfound identity and kinship, now called 'Christian.'"[2]

In order to compare the way both James and Peter use the notion of diaspora, this chapter follows the recommendations of Kim Butler. She studies the contemporary concept of diaspora and presents a proposal that permits the comparison of different social groups living in this situation. In her important work "Defining Diaspora, Refining a Discourse," she presents a synthesis of the basis for an analysis of a diaspora. Her insights help us to set the methodological approach followed here. Butler highlights four features of any diaspora. First, "after dispersal, there must be a minimum of two destinations." Second, "there must be some relationship to an actual or imagined homeland." Third, "there must be self-awareness of the group's identity." Fourth, "diasporas are multi-generational: they combine the individual migration experience with the collective history of group dispersal and regenesis of communities abroad."[3] In our case, these features can be observed in Christianity beginning in Acts 8. With these characteristics, Butler develops the basis for the comparative study of any diaspora.

She presents five dimensions of diaspora analysis which helps us to compare the topic in James and in 1 Peter:[4]

1. Reasons for and conditions of the dispersal
2. Relationship with the homeland
3. Relationship with hostlands

1. Smith, *Strangers to Family*, 12.
2. Smith, *Strangers to Family*, 21.
3. Butler, "Defining Diaspora," 192.
4. Butler, "Defining Diaspora," 195.

4. Interrelationships within the communities of the diaspora

5. Comparative studies of different diasporas

The first four dimensions help us to analyze each epistle. With this analysis, it is possible to compare the diaspora groups or perspectives found in these epistles, the fifth dimension.

Another point of comparison between the concept in James and in 1 Peter is the temporality of the diaspora. The duration of diaspora is limited. It is for a little while, if necessary, Peter says (1 Pet 1:5). The end of exile is an important theological metanarrative which runs throughout the New Testament and, in particular, these epistles. Thus, it is better to separately analyze how each author presents the idea in his letter and then compare its impact to the concept of diaspora.

A READING OF JAMES

This letter shows a rich flavor of everyday life pastoral concerns. I assume James, the brother of Jesus, to be its author.[5] Regardless of how one identifies James, the author of the epistle, the first verse presents him as the intended author: James, a servant of God and of the Lord Jesus Christ (Jas 1:1). The letter deals with different situations that James wants his addressees to correct. He builds his ethics upon the Old Testament and Jesus' teachings. Furthermore, his main focus is to strengthen the community of believers by pointing out and correcting those attitudes and actions that threaten the cohesion of the people of God.

Reasons for and Conditions of the Dispersal

James begins his letter by calling his addressees "the twelve tribes in the diaspora" (1:1). There is no explicit reference in the letter for the reason of the dispersion nor a specific place where they are located. Some authors understand the phrase "the twelve tribes in the diaspora" to refer to Jewish Christian communities living among Jewish diaspora groups, in places such as Antioch of Syria or Asia Minor,[6] or Jewish Christian communities that were dispersed outside Palestine because of persecution,[7] or in a more

5. There is an ongoing debate about the authorship of this letter. A good discussion on different approaches is found in Allison, *Commentary on Epistle of James*, 3–31. For a good defense of James's authorship, see Blomberg and Kamell, *James*, 32–34.

6. Davids, *Epistle of James*, 64; Martin, *James*, 9.

7. Moo, *Letter of James*, 50.

metaphorical sense, the true Israel, namely all the Christians, Jewish or Gentile,[8] or even, a mixed audience of Christian and non-Christian Jewish communities scattered throughout the world.[9] In any case, the implied readers are represented as the whole Israel scattered in the world.

Although it is not clear where the audience lives, from the letter one may infer some conditions of the dispersal. The community is facing trials of different kinds (1:2–4). Some of them live in poverty or extreme poverty (1:9; 2:1–6, 15). Some of them are laborers who experience oppression (5:4). Also, there are some widows and orphans among them or nearby, living in affliction (1:27). Rich people have dragged some of the addressees into courts (2:6; 5:6), without any possibility of resistance from them. But not all is negative. The life of the community seems to revolve around the synagogue (2:1–4, 14–16). Some of the addressees are business people who do commerce abroad (4:13).

Relationship with the Homeland

There is no explicit mention of the homeland in the letter. If James, the brother of Jesus, is the author, then the letter probably is from Jerusalem, where James was pastor/elder of the church. In that case, the word *diaspora* would have a more standard meaning. In the letter, however, there is a contrast between above and the earth (3:15). Thus, in one sense, their homeland is above, from where every good gift comes (1:17). It is the place from where wisdom comes (3:15, 17). It is the dwelling of God the Father (1:17, 27), the Lord of hosts (5:4).

Relationship with the Hostland

There are a few references to the hostland. The hostland is represented negatively as *kosmos*, the world. Believers, the twelve tribes, are scattered around that world. In the letter, *kosmos* represents the sinful standards and worldview that surround the community. When speaking about true religion, James exhorts his audience to keep themselves unstained from the world (1:27), or as the NLT puts it, "refusing to let the world corrupt" them.

There are some tensions within the community because of the standards of that world. Precisely for that reason, James points out the severe problem of discrimination against the poor committed by his addressees

8. Richardson, *James*, 54–55.
9. Allison, *Commentary on Epistle of James*, 131–32.

(2:2–4). One of the causes of that attitude is that the poor are wrongly evaluated by the standards of the world. They are poor in the world, but in God's eyes, they are rich in faith and heirs of his kingdom (2:5). Furthermore, friendship with the world's standards, insists James, is enmity against God; it is unfaithfulness to God (4:4).

In the same vein, James criticizes the rich. Almost every time that James uses the word *plousios* (*rich*), he describes them negatively (1:10–11; 2:6–7; 5:1–6). The rich represent several manifestations of those sinful standards of the world. For example, they drag believers into courts (2:6) and also blaspheme the good name of Jesus that was invoked over them (2:7). As landlords, they exploit their laborers and live a luxurious life with the money obtained (5:2–5). They also condemn the righteous person without any possibility of resistance (5:6). The intolerance of those situations puts at risk the cohesion of the diaspora community. When believers side with those standards and practices they contradict God's perspective and become judges with evil thoughts (2:4).

Interrelationship within the Diasporic Group

When living in a foreign land, one looks for a sense of belonging. For that reason, a diasporic community becomes the source of emotional, spiritual, and physical strength for each one of its members. Accordingly, it is important to note that the health and quality of the relationships in the community is the main focus of James's concern. His advice and exhortations confront and guide his addressees on the importance of the diasporic community. Almost every chapter of the letter contributes to building strong relationships within the community.

The letter begins with an emphasis on the community. The first exhortation is addressed to the group (1:2–4). The expression *adelphoi mou*, "my brothers and sisters" (1:2), highlights this sense of community (1:2, 16, 19; 2:1, 5, 14; 3:1, 10, 12; 5:12, 19). Also, there is a grammatical contrast between the second person plural in 1:2–4 and the third person singular in the next textual unit, 1:5–8. Thus, as a community, they should face trials with the correct attitude. Even though James does not specify what kind of trials he has in mind, throughout the letter he engages the different hard circumstances which his addressees experience. In the midst of those trials, they should consider it as great joy the opportunity of perfecting their faith and developing perseverance (1:2–4).

James deals with several problems that deteriorate the solidity of the diaspora community. One of the first situations that threatens the community is the improper handling of anger (1:19–21). Uncontrolled anger does not produce the type of justice that God desires for his people scattered around the world. Another important danger is the uncontrolled use of the tongue (1:26). Both aspects are presented in chapter 1, but developed later in the letter. James 3:1–12 intertwines both themes. The wisdom from above is the solution for those problems (3:13–18). Anger is not the only sin that undermines the stability of the community. James also denounces other sins, such as bitter jealousy (3:14), ambition (3:14), quarrels and fights due to envy and covetousness (4:1–3), speaking evil against one another (4:11), judging one another (4:12), and grumbling against one another (5:9). Again, wisdom from above is the solution to combat directly those sins which erode the basis of a strong diaspora community.

Not all people who live in a diasporic situation face the same degree of hardship. The poor tend to be more vulnerable to abuse. Furthermore, they are more exposed to illness or lacking clothing and food, as the COVID-19 pandemic made evident. Additionally, they also tend to lack social and political connections. James reflects on each of these aspects. He reminds his readers that true worship of God should include visiting widows and orphans in their afflictions (1:27). In that vein, he draws attention that instead of being an example of caring for the poor, the community has focused on their own beneficial connections with the rich (2:1–6). James criticizes the community for the way they are acting toward the poor among them and the patronage they are looking for. For James, discrimination is as heinous as adultery or murder (2:10–11). The solution is to show true love (2:8) and mercy to the poor (2:13). Only by having this nondiscriminatory attitude toward the poor do they fulfill the royal law and strengthen the diaspora community (2:8).

Likewise, their lack of concern for the well-being of the poor among them is a demonstration of incongruence of faith (2:14–16). In an inclusio, James frames that incongruence with the rhetorical question "what good is it?" (2:14, 16). Even though the poverty and need of some members of the community are patent, instead of helping the poor, some close their eyes and respond to the need with clichés such as "go in peace, be warmed and filled" (2:16). Probably, some of those poor believers are the laborers who are experiencing severe deprivation because of oppression (5:4). They cry to God looking for justice (5:4). Thus, the community should provide refuge and help. Otherwise, what good is it?

In this context, it is noteworthy that James presents Rahab as an example of true faith (2:24). He chooses a poor woman, a prostitute who lives in the walls of Jericho, as an example of someone who shows a congruent faith. She evidenced her faith by receiving messengers, even at risk of her life. She as a foreigner in Israel becomes an example of hospitality.

The End of Exile

Usually, one of the main hopes of a migrant is to go back to his/her homeland. That person will save enough money to build a new life to go back home, when peace returns to the homeland, or at least at the end of his/her life. Christians also long for the end of diaspora, the end of this earthly exile. The key event that will put an end to that diaspora and exile is the Lord's coming. James exhorts his audience to be patient until that time (5:7, 10). They should act like the farmer, with a militant patience, with the correct perspective of the temporary situation they face (5:7–11). For the same reason, they should be attentive to bring back those who are wandering from the truth (5:19–20). The Lord is at the gate, almost arrived and ready to put an end to the exile (5:9). This imminence of the Lord's coming gives hope to the community and helps them to persevere while living in exile.

Vindication and punishment are distinctives of the end of the exile (1:9–11; 5:1–6). Both are expressions of the compassion and mercy of God (5:11). This double manifestation of the end of the exile gives hope to the diasporic community as it faces trials. This hope also brings support to the daily life in the diaspora. It permits the humble brother to boast in the exaltation he will receive (1:9). It is what strengthens the poor to wait for their inheritance (2:5) and believers to act with justice and mercy under the law of liberty (2:12–14). At the same time, the warning of imminent punishment of the unjust gives hope to those who suffer and should motivate those who are acting sinfully against the members of their own community to change their attitude and conduct (1:10–11; 2:1–5; 5:1–6).

A READING OF 1 PETER

This letter also reflects a deep pastoral concern. In fact, the author presents himself as a fellow elder (1 Pet 5:1). I assume the Apostle Peter is its author (1:1).[10] The letter shows that hostility and persecution of some sort is progressively increasing not only in Asia Minor, but also in other regions of the Roman empire. Peter deals with this issue throughout the letter by highlighting the diasporic nature of the people of God. As Shively Smith

---

10. See a detailed and strong argument to support Petrine authorship in Jobes, *1 Peter*, 5–19.

convincingly demonstrates, Peter strengthens and exhorts the community around their duality as *parepidēmoi kai paroikoi en tē diaspora*, "sojourners and exiles in the diaspora," and *oikos tou theou*, "the household of God."[11]

Reasons for and Conditions of the Dispersal

The addressees are geographically located in Asia Minor: Pontus, Galatia, Cappadocia, Asia, and Bithynia (1:1). Even though they live in their own towns, among their own fellow citizens, Peter calls them "exiles of the diaspora." Not only are they living in the diaspora, Peter also locates himself and his community in exile in Babylon (5:13). Furthermore, there are communities of believers throughout the world experiencing similar situations (5:9). It is clear at this point that Peter is metaphorically using the concept of diaspora. However, his depiction of diaspora differs from the common negative connotation of God's punishment associated with that word group in the Septuagint (cf. Eph 2:19; in the LXX, Deut 28:25; 30:4; 2 Esd 11:9; Ps 146:2; Jdt 5:19; Isa 49:6; Jer 15:7; 41:17; Dan 12:2; 2 Macc 1:27; Pss Sol 8:34).

As mentioned above, in 1 Peter, diaspora is a desired status. To follow Jesus implies to enter into diaspora (2:9–11). People become strangers and sojourners in their own towns by believing in Christ. They became Christians when they heard the message of the gospel (1:3–12). It is through Christ that they become believers in God the Father (1:18–21). Through the sacrifice of Christ, they were redeemed/ransomed/liberated from their former way of life inherited from their forefathers (1:18). In other words, their diaspora is not genetic but spiritual.[12] This new status as an exile has introduced them into a new family, new siblings through the preaching of the word of the gospel (1:22–25), new responsibilities toward God and their new family (2:1–8), and a new relationship with their former life (4:1–6). They now are a new nation, the people of God (2:9–10), the household of God (4:17).

This condition of diaspora brings some temporal suffering. As discussed below, their relationship with the hostland entails a degree of distress. However, Peter says, even though these trials are necessary, they are temporary (1:6–7; 5:10). There is no mention of overt political or religious persecution, but different concrete expressions of hostility.[13] For example, some people

11. Smith, *Strangers to Family*, 1–86.

12. Scot McKnight argues for a literal understanding of diaspora, even though he recognizes that the spiritual understanding of the concept is the scholarly consensus. McKnight, *1 Peter*, 51–52.

13. The expression "fiery ordeal" in 1 Pet 4:12 does not necessarily reflect physical

slander believers as evildoers (2:12). In fact, some people are surprised that believers do not run with them in the same excess of dissipation (4:4). Some unbelieving masters mistreat their Christian slaves (2:18). Some Christian wives may suffer violence by their non-believing husbands (3:1–2).

Relationship with the Homeland

There are some connections between believers and their homeland. Peter describes that home as heaven (1:4, 12; 3:22). Heaven is the place where God's throne is, where Jesus is at his right hand (3:5), and from where the Holy Spirit was sent (1:12). From there, Jesus will be revealed and will bring grace (1:13; 3:7), salvation (1:9), and honor (5:4, 6). Peter reminds his readers that they have an inheritance in heaven (1:4–5). The purpose of their calling is to inherit blessing (3:9). Moreover, both men and women are co-heirs of that grace (3:7).

Relationship with the Hostland

Those in the hostland are labeled in different ways. They are named in generic terms, such as the world (2:11; 5:9) and *éthnē* ("gentiles"; 2:12), but also with more derogatory terms such as foolish people (2:15), disobedient to the word (2:8; 3:1), even darkness (2:9). Furthermore, the hostland is the place where the adversary, the devil, the roaring lion is present (5:8–9).

Peter explicitly mentions the sociopolitical world of the diaspora. The political system is called *anthrōpine ktisis*, a human authority system (2:13). Kings and governors of that world should be righteous in their function and be obeyed by the people (2:13–15). Socially speaking, there is also a system of slavery in which some believers live as slaves. Some of their masters are gentle but others are harsh (2:18).

The relationship with the hostland is a mixed one. There is some form of political protection for those who do right/good (2:13). For that reason, they should respect the political structure of the place where they live (i.e., the king and governors, 2:13–17) and do what is culturally good (2:14–16; 3:1–2, 16–17). However, hostility is stronger than that protection. There is hostility toward them from some people of the land, but believers should respond with Jesus as the model of suffering (2:18–25; 3:18–22). Gentiles speak against believers as evildoers. For that reason, Christians should live

persecution. It is more probably an expression of testing, or, as Jobes says, "trials faced by Christians that test the mettle of their faith." See a good evaluation of the term in Jobes, *1 Peter*, 8–10.

honorably, so that the gentiles might glorify God in the day of visitation due to their correct conduct (2:12). Also, gentiles are surprised by their new conduct and bully them (4:1–6). Believers should not be surprised by that persecution (4:12–16). Servants are a particular case of suffering (2:18–25), but all the believers are exposed to the same trials (3:13–17). Again, Jesus is their model (2:21–25; 3:18; 4:1). When they suffer unjustly, they share the sufferings of Christ (4:12).

While this overt hostility exists, believers have a clear mission of proclaiming the gospel. Furthermore, with their actions in the daily life, they should demonstrate the implications of the gospel in the midst of an adverse world. Believers were rescued from their former life, so that now they can proclaim God's excellences (2:9–10). Their conduct and message should impact others in such a way that people will glorify God in the day of visitation (2:12); even unbelieving husbands will be won by the behavior of their believing wives (3:1). For that reason, believers should be prepared to give an account for their hope before those who ask them (3:15) and live according to the standards of the gospel (3:8–14).

Interrelationship within the Diasporic Group

This diaspora community is described locally and abroad. Peter focuses his exhortations on believers in the diaspora on these two fronts. Locally, love is central to build community in the diaspora. Believers should love each other deeply and earnestly (1:22–25; 3:8; 4:8). Also, Peter urges them to have unity of mind and other attitudes and practices that will strengthen the diaspora community (3:8–9). They should use their gifts to spiritually serve one another (4:10–11). Communities should not repay evil or revile, neither inside nor outside the community (3:10–12). Elders should promote unity in the community by shepherding them as a flock (5:2), not lording over them but being examples to them (5:3). Likewise, congregations should live in a peaceable and humble relationship in submission to their elders (5:5–6). Men should care for their wives (3:7).

Peter also gives instructions to the community in relation to the other Christian communities abroad. He points out that they should be conscious that other diaspora communities also experience suffering (5:9). As the Apostle John reminds us in his third epistle, hospitality is an important characteristic for the successful travel of believers between communities (3 John 7–11). For that reason, it is noteworthy that not only does James mention this quality by recalling Rahab's hospitality (Jas 2:25), but Peter does so in a more emphatic way. In the context of the end of exile (4:7), he reminds the community to show hospitality without complaint or grumbling (4:9). As Paul Achtemeier highlights, hospitality in this context "was a necessary way to express love . . . and to show support for one's fellow Christians who also lived as exiles and aliens in a culture from which they could expect no support."[14] It is not a paternalistic help to a displaced member of another community; it is an open door of dignity to a fellow citizen of the kingdom, no matter from where he or she comes.

The End of Exile

In James this theme is important, but in Peter it is central. Believers live by hope, waiting for their inheritance reserved in heaven. Even though it is ready (1:4), this inheritance will be manifest in the last time (1:5), when Jesus comes (1:7, 13). With this hope, they should face trials with the correct perspective (1:4–9) and live the holiness God demands (1:13–16) during the time of exile/*paroikia* (1:17). The imminence of the end of all things is a motivator for correct attitudes, actions, and service within the community (4:7–11). Moreover, the time has come for judgment; the present suffering of believers is evidence of the imminent punishment of those who do not obey the gospel of God (4:17–19). These trials are temporary. They should remember every day of their exile that after a little while, the God of all grace will perfect, confirm, strengthen, and establish them (5:10).

CONTRASTS AND EMPHASES

There are many similarities but also clear differences between the way both authors use the metaphor of diaspora. These differences and similarities will permit us to reflect on the issue of migration today. The way James and Peter conceive of diaspora fits well in the way Shively Smith conceptualizes it. Both apostles describe the diaspora community as living in multiple places. James and Peter depict the homeland metaphorically. Both of them emphasize throughout their letters the importance of the group's identity. Finally, diaspora is a multigenerational experience in both communities.

Reasons of and Conditions for Dispersal

In both letters the causes of the exile are not explicit. Peter, however, clearly conceives of all Christians as living in exile. Both authors depict the

14. Achtemeier, *1 Peter*, 297.

conditions of exile. In the Letter of James, the external or political situations are less explicit, almost absent. The rural and agricultural environment where the addressees seem to live presents the main challenges to the community. In fact, poverty is the focus. The diasporic community should develop a network of protection for the weak, in particular for those laborers, widows, and orphans among them.

In contrast, in the Epistle of Peter, there is an important connection with the external world. For the Lord's sake, the political system should be respected. In that way, when acting rightly in society, believers in the diaspora will silence the ignorance of foolish people (2:15). This conduct also implies a good relationship with those outside the community. The most extreme situations are those of Christian slaves and of some women. The social structure of slavery presented an important source of trials for Christian slaves. Additionally, there are tensions in some mixed marriages. In both cases, the good conduct of believers can contribute to a better situation or even to the conversion of unbelievers.

Relationship with the Homeland

Both letters metaphorically describe the homeland. Even though Peter is more explicit in his imagery than James, both refer to God's presence as their home. Heaven is the homeland. It is the place from where wisdom and blessings come. Their inheritance remains secure in heaven, awaiting Jesus' imminent manifestation.

Relationship with the Hostland

James seems more negative toward the hostland. He describes the world, its standards, and in particular the rich in negative terms. For his part, Peter presents a more positive approach to that world. Although he recognizes that there is persecution, there still is an opportunity of proclamation. In the midst of that hostility, believers should make permanent efforts for living rightly, not giving opportunity for defamation. As Smith properly notes, "First Peter does not gloss over the realities of a social location characterized by subjectivity, servility, subordination, and invisibility, nor does it endorse that existence as ordained by God. It is a reality that must be maneuvered and managed, not subscribed to."[15]

---

15. Smith, *Strangers to Family*, 62.

Interrelationship within the Diasporic Group

Although both authors are concerned with sound relationships within the group, James is more focused on the importance of the strength of those relationships. The protection and care of the vulnerable should be high in the range of priorities of the diaspora community. It is the unequivocal signal of a congruent faith. It is, furthermore, one of the concrete ways to express the command of love. Additionally, wisdom should characterize all their relationships. This wisdom should overflow all their discourses and the emotions they express to one another. Peter, on the other hand, highlights the importance of the spiritual care of the community. Love, service, and pastoral care should characterize the diaspora community.

The End of Exile

The end of exile is an important theme in both letters. The authors build their ethical discourse on the eschatological hope of the end of exile. This hope rests on two axes: imminence/temporality and vindication/punishment. Temporality is one of the key factors in James's and Peter's diaspora mentality. The exile does not last forever. The Lord's return or his manifestation will put an end to the exile. The imminence of this event gives the diaspora communities support for facing trials and hostility in the world. Additionally, it stimulates correct relationships and mutual service within the community and the proclamation of the gospel. The other side of the coin is vindication and punishment. The Lord brings with him the inheritance that believers will receive. The humble brother will receive his exaltation. At the same time, the unjust will receive the punishment due to their disobedience to the word, the gospel of God. The wicked rich will be humiliated due to their abuse of the just, the poor, and laborers.

SOME REFLECTIONS ON MIGRATION

This diaspora mentality present in James and Peter is a good framework for our discussion of migration today. This same mentality has remained through the centuries. The early church testifies to this perspective. The Reformers experienced displacement and forced migration many times. *The Pilgrim's Progress* written by John Bunyan (1678) also testifies to this perspective. Even the Second Vatican Council describes the church, as a "pilgrim in a strange land."[16]

Connections between the Church and World Today

James and Peter present different types of exile, and different attitudes concerning the world. Each one has an important contribution to make to a theology of migration that should include this diversity. It is necessary to remember that we live in a fallen world. James reminds us that the standards of that world many times fight against the standards of the kingdom. Thus, we should be attentive and not accommodate ourselves to those standards but confront them. Sadly, in many places it is more and more common to see mistreatment of migrants as normal, even as an expected attitude. A huge number of migrants move from their places without many resources. They are vulnerable and at risk. Thus, the church should not accept those worldly attitudes, but be a community that cares for those in need because it is also a community in diaspora.

Additionally, in James's letter, the rich use the legal system in their favor against the community of believers. Instead, the church today should side with those who suffer and support laws that protect them. As Carroll R. suggests, "A biblical theology of immigration, therefore, must have an orientation toward immigrants as people made in the image of God and should provide moral (indeed, theological) guidance to legislation."[17] Diaspora is temporary, thus rather than having a complacent attitude toward the world and resignation before those injustices, the community should have a militant patience to face them with deep hope in the imminent manifestation of the Lord. In that way, the church demonstrates that it is a friend of God and not of the world.

Peter reminds us that there is a duality in the way we relate to the world. Even though we are foreigners and exiles in this world, we have some responsibilities toward the place in which we live. The diaspora community should submit itself to the political system where it is present and do what is right in that place, but never at the cost of its loyalty to God and his kingdom. This disposition could imply suffering for the sake of Christ. Sadly, many of us today avoid suffering at all cost. At the same time, Peter reminds us that we have the opportunity to proclaim the gospel in this world, something

16. Vatican Council, *Lumen Gentium*, §7. Groody makes the same connection between migration and the Vatican Council II, when he points out that migration is in the spiritual genes of believers. See Groody, "Homeward Bound," 299.

17. Carroll R., "Towards an Hispanic Biblical Theology of Migration," 113.

that also implies the proper treatment of the stranger. As Jesus says: "And when did we see you a stranger and welcome you, or naked and clothe you? . . . And the King will answer them, 'Truly, I say to you, as you did it to one of the least of these my brothers, you did it to me'" (Matt 25:38, 40 ESV).

Connections with Migration Issues and Attitudes

Having a diaspora perspective permits the church to be sensitive to migration problems around the world. James and Peter show us what it implies to have that attitude in all the spheres and dynamics of a community. In his reflections on these texts, Carroll R. points out: "Immigrants understand this metaphor in their very being. For the native born, the metaphor may be an abstract concept, but for the foreigner, it is lived experience. In a sense, it might be said that the Christian church of the host country may need immigrants in their midst to be reminded of what it means to be strange, of what being a follower of Jesus entails."[18] Having a diaspora mentality permits us to focus on the church's mission of reconciliation, as Daniel Groody says, the mission "which gives primacy to the human and relational costs associated with migration rather than remaining centered on political and economic costs."[19] Peter and particularly James demonstrate that the diaspora community should be strengthened through sound relationships, pastoral care, and brotherly love.

Challenges for the Mission of the Global Church around the World

Peter reminds us that the whole church lives in the diaspora.[20] Diaspora communities around the globe spread the gospel of salvation. Beside the proclamation of this message, the church of Christ should be conscious of the suffering of others, not just of those of its own group. This consciousness demands that we draw near to and care for the migrant. As Groody says, "In its care for all, especially those most in need, the church not only goes beyond borders but unites itself with those on the other side of them, giving expression to its interconnectedness as the body of Christ."[21]

18. Carroll R. "Towards an Hispanic Theology of Migration," 117.

19. Groody, "Homeward Bound," 300.

20. Carroll R. also notes the implications of this reality of strangeness in this world for all Christians. See Carroll R., *Bible and Borders*, 99–101.

21. Groody, "Homeward Bound," 309.

CONCLUSIONS

James and Peter invite us to think with a diaspora mentality. We are sojourners and exiles living in diaspora. Jesus' return will put an end to this exile. Meanwhile, we have to strengthen the diaspora community and proclaim the gospel. This perspective permits us to face the issues of migration with a theological perspective. What has been the role of the church in the midst of the phenomenon of migration in the last decade? What would be our response? Sadly, the response of the church has been mixed. Some local churches in different continents have developed programs to support migrants. As a result, new opportunities to express mercy and love have appeared.[22] However, other Christian groups have assumed an antagonistic attitude and actions against migrants. James and Peter teach us that we, as the people of God, live in diaspora until the coming of our Lord. With this in mind, we should reflect the love of our Lord as sojourners and exiles in diaspora.

BIBLIOGRAPHY

Achtemeier, Paul J. *1 Peter: A Commentary on First Peter*. Hermeneia. Minneapolis: Fortress, 1996.

Allison, Dale C., Jr. *A Critical and Exegetical Commentary on the Epistle of James*. International Critical Commentary. New York: Bloomsbury, 2013.

Blomberg, Craig L., and Mariam J. Kamell. *James*. Zondervan Exegetical Commentary on the New Testament 16. Grand Rapids: Zondervan, 2008.

Butler, Kim D. "Defining Diaspora, Refining a Discourse." *Diaspora* 10 (2001) 189–219.

Carroll R., M. Daniel. *The Bible and Borders: Hearing God's Word on Immigration*. Grand Rapids: Brazos, 2020.

———. "Towards an Hispanic Biblical Theology of Migration." In *Immigrant Neighbors among Us: Immigration across Theological Traditions*, edited by M. Daniel Carroll R. and Leopoldo A. Sánchez M., 109–21. Eugene, OR: Pickwick, 2015.

Carroll R., M. Daniel, and Leopoldo A. Sánchez M., eds. *Immigrant Neighbors among Us: Immigration across Theological Traditions*. Eugene, OR: Pickwick, 2015.

Davids, Peter H. *The Epistle of James: A Commentary on the Greek Text*. New International Greek Testament Commentary. Grand Rapids: Eerdmans, 1982.

Groody, Daniel G. "Homeward Bound: A Theology of Migration for Fullness of Life, Justice and Peace." *Ecumenical Review* 64 (2012) 299–313.

22. For example, some churches in Chile have created programs to help unemployed immigrants to survive the quarantines due to the COVID-19 pandemic. Some churches in Greece have created programs to support immigrants that flee from Syrian war. However, some churches have promoted attitudes and legislation to limit the number of strangers into their countries, or they are silent in the face of unjust immigration laws.

Jobes, Karen H. *1 Peter*. Baker Exegetical Commentary on the New Testament. Grand Rapids: Baker Academic, 2005.

Martin, Ralph P. *James*. WBC 48. Waco, TX: Word, 1988.

McKnight, Scot. *1 Peter*. NIV Application Commentary. Grand Rapids: Zondervan, 1996.

Moo, Douglas J. *The Letter of James*. Pillar New Testament Commentary. Grand Rapids: Eerdmans, 2000.

Richardson, Kurt A. *James*. New American Commentary 36. Nashville: Broadman & Holman, 2001.

Smith, Shively T. J. *Strangers to Family: Diaspora and 1 Peter's Invention of God's Household*. Waco, TX: Baylor University Press, 2016.

Vatican Council. *Lumen Gentium*. In *Vatican Council II: Constitutions, Decrees, Declarations*. Vatican City: Libreria Editrice Vaticana, 2011.

Theological Reflections

Home Land, Foreign Land, Our Land

A Christian Theology of Place in Migration

Peter C. Phan

THIS CHAPTER INTENDS TO examine the role and significance of land in migration and the lives of migrants from the perspective of the Jewish-Christian faith. The three expressions in its title, "home land," "foreign land," and "our land," are meant to be taken both literally and figuratively.[1] Literally, "land" designates an area of ground, including its water and air, which today is often, albeit not always, identified with a country, and more narrowly, a nation-state with well-demarcated borders. Metaphorically, "land" is a metonymy for all the things that constitute the basic elements of human existence, including but not limited to, material and non-material artifacts, economics, politics, culture, society, and religion. Furthermore, "home," "foreign," and "our," as qualifiers of "land," represent roughly the three stages which, normally though not necessarily, most migrants go through, namely, their departure from their "home land" (the country of origin) their arrival to and life in a "foreign land" (the country of destination), and the transformation of the land of the receiving country into "our land," "our" referring to the migrants and the natives together.

This "our land" emerges from the collaborative work of both the migrants and the natives into some new and common land. These three stages

1. In standard English, "home land" is written as one word ("homeland"). Here, I intentionally depart from this orthography and separate it into two words, not simply to match the other two expressions, "foreign land" and "our land," but also to give strong emphasis on the reality of land in migration and in the lives of migrants rather than "home."

do not always occur in every migration, nor, should they occur, do they form a linear and sequential progression from emigration to permanent residence to citizenship, with one stage left behind and leading to the next. Rather, more often than not, they are overlapping existential conditions in which migrants move back and forth and in which home land, foreign land, and our land acquire new connotations as migrants experience their displacement and settlement in different individual, familial, and collective contexts.

Multiple academic disciplines have delineated this process of migration and the migrants' subsequent acculturation to the predominant culture of the country of destination. These disciplines include chiefly history, geography, anthropology, sociology, politics, and law. While acknowledging the necessity of a multidisciplinary approach in the study of migration and presupposing here the findings of these social-scientific sciences on migration, this chapter studies the role of land, understood both literally and metaphorically, in migration and the migrants' lives from the religious perspective, more specifically that of the Jewish-Christian faith. It delves into the sacred Scriptures of Judaism and Christianity as well as the Christian tradition to formulate a theology of land. The chapter is structured in three parts corresponding to the three stages of migration: home land, foreign land, and our land.

A preliminary observation on migration and what is meant by "migrant" in this chapter is in order. By any standard, migration is currently a phenomenon of global and immense proportions, such that our time has been rightly dubbed "The Age of Migration."[2] According to the annual *Global Trends* report of the United Nations Refugee Agency, United Nations High Commissioner for Refugee (UNHCR), released on June 19, 2018, a day before World Refugee Day, worldwide forced displacement as a result of war, violent conflicts, persecutions, and human rights violations reached a new high in 2017 for the fifth year in a row, with 68.5 million *refugees* or forcibly displaced persons by the end of 2017.[3] It is to be noted that the UNHCR uses the term *refugee* to designate people who have been forced to change residence across national borders (international migrants),

2. This is the title of the best one-volume study of international migration: Castles et al., *Age of Migration*. On migration, the historical, sociological, anthropological, and political studies, in addition to specialized journals and websites, are numberless. The following general works are worth consulting: King, *People on the Move*; Collier, *Exodus*; Portes and DeWind, *Rethinking Migration*; Bretell and Hollifield, eds., *Migration Theory*; Gutiérrez and Hondagneu-Sotelo, eds., *Nation and Migration*; Faist et al., *Transnational Migration*; Carens, *Ethics of Immigration*; O'Reilly, *International Migration and Social Theory*; and Quayson and Daswani, eds., *Companion to Diaspora*.

3. See www.unhcr.org/en-us/. . ./unhcr-projected-global-resettlement-needs-2018.html.

permanently or for a long time, usually at least a year, due to "well-founded fear of being persecuted for reasons of race, religion, nationality, membership of a particular social group or political opinion."[4] The UNHCR does not use the generic term *migrant* to designate people of forced migration. While this restricted use of the term *refugee* to designate people of forced migration is rooted in international legal instruments, there is no reason for limiting the consideration of migration and migrants to refugees. Refugees, of course, are not the only migrants; every refugee is a migrant, but not every migrant is a refugee.

Migration is an enormously complex and varied phenomenon. Besides the distinction between forced migrants (refugees) and voluntary migrants, other dichotomies include: temporary vs. permanent, legal vs. illegal (or undocumented), skilled vs. unskilled, and, most importantly, international vs. internal—the number of the latter (Internally Displaced Persons) being vastly larger than that of international migrants. In this chapter, I use "migrant" to designate not only refugees, forcibly displaced communities, and stateless persons who have been forced to flee from their countries by war and violence, political and religious persecution, but also those forced to migrate due to poverty, lack of economic opportunities, climate change, and environmental degradation in search of a better life for themselves and their families.

THE HOME LAND: THE PLACE OF EMIGRATION

The inevitable question that migrants, especially if they are not white or speak with a foreign accent, are often asked by the natives of their host country upon their first encounter is: "Where do come from?" In official applications for permanent residence and citizenship, applicants are required to state not only their country of origin but also specifically their "place of birth," usually city or province. Migrants are thus defined by their country of origin/origination or their home land.

Home Land, Motherland, Fatherland, Native Land

But what is "home land"? For immigration authorities, it essentially means the nation-state that has the power to issue a valid passport and entry visa. More generally, it is a country where one's ethnic, racial, cultural, national,

---

4. This is the standard definition of a refugee by the Office of UNHCR: www.unhcr.org/en-us/what-is-a-refugee.html.

and even religious identity was formed, because one has lived there for a significant part of one's life. But even this is far from uncontroversial, especially where national identity does not coincide with ethnic and cultural identity. For instance, Kurds might not want to identify themselves as Turk, Iraqi, Iranian, Syrian, Armenian, or Azerbaijani, even if they are citizens of one of these nation-states, which they do not necessarily recognize as their "home lands." The non-identity between the nation-state and the home land is also found in citizens of newly emerging nation-states that have not yet been recognized by the United Nations, of the region of a nation-state that has been illegally annexed by another state (for example, Ukraine's Crimea peninsula), and of island nation-states that have disappeared by being completely submerged underwater. These citizens have a home land but not a nation-state. Furthermore, a person may have more than one home land. For instance, if one's grandfather was born in France, and one's father lived all his life in China, but the person was born in Vietnam and later moved to the United States and became nationalized, that person may claim France, China, Vietnam, and the United States as his or her home lands.

Of course, not every nation or country is a state (nation-state). In international law, a state is a juridical entity that has a defined territory, a permanent population, a government, and the capacity to enter into relations with other sovereign states. Central to the state are the power for self-determination and sovereignty within its territory. Not all nations that are endowed with all the requisites for national identity listed above, albeit administratively autonomous, actually are sovereign nation-states.

For international migrants, their home land is never simply the nation-state they have emigrated from. Home land is not merely a "space" but a "place."[5] It is not merely a land on a map but a "home" land. It is not, to use German vocabulary, simply *das Land* but *die Heimat*. The migrant is not merely *Auswanderer* (emigrant) but *Heimatvertriebener* (expelled from home). Synonyms of home land are native land, motherland, and fatherland. As the birth and familial metaphors suggest, it is the place where one is born, grows up, and dies; where one's ancestors and descendants are gathered together; where one carves out one's own place in society and history; and where one is truly at home, in the literal sense (*heimisch*) and the metaphorical sense (*Gemütlichkeit*). As mentioned above, "home land" is a metonymy for all the things that constitute the context for human existence including but not limited to material and non-material artifacts, economics, politics, culture, society, and religion.

5. For insightful studies of place as distinguished from space, see the many works by Casey, in particular *Getting Back to Place* and *The Fate of Place*.

In a true sense, no one, including migrants, can ever leave the home land behind, even when living outside one's country. Migrants carry indelible memories and personal traces of their home land, and when possible, they recreate, or better, "re-implace," to use Edward Casey's expression, their hometowns in the new countries. So, there are Chinatown, Koreatown, Japantown, Little Saigontown, and so on, where migrants from the same home land tend to settle together and where they can speak their own languages, eat their own foods, preserve their own cultural customs, celebrate their own feasts, and practice their own religions. Also, whenever possible, they name the cities where they settle after those of the "old country" with the adjective "new" added in front, such as New York, New England, New Rochelle, New Mexico, New Tokyo, New Saigon, and so on. In this way, they can feel that they have never left their home land. Moreover, most migrants, especially if they emigrate as adults, often visit their home lands and their families "back home," which today is vastly facilitated by rapid means of travel. Not a few migrants who return home stay permanently ("return migration"); if they cannot do so, they will ask to be buried or have their ashes scattered in their home land, their birth and final resting place.

Despite the migrants' existential inability to leave their home land behind and their manifold attempts to maintain contact with it while living far away from it, even to the point of committing their final remains to its earth, their decision to emigrate, not only in forced and sudden migration but also in premeditated and voluntary migration, is always disruptive, even traumatic, for the migrants and their families. Emigration inevitably means physically moving away from one's home land, forgoing familiarity and security, and facing challenges and risks of all types in a new environment. The host country is not only new and unfamiliar but also foreign and even hostile. Living there as a stranger; looking for jobs, sometimes far below one's professional skills; financially supporting one's family, including the extended family back home through remittances; and lacking mastery of the local language, cultural competence, and societal support—all this produces immense anxiety, fear, confusion, depression, and suffering. Even migrants who have reached the higher rungs of the educational and economic ladder, the so-called "model minorities," are subjected to subtle discrimination and exclusion that undermines their sense of personal identity and self-worth. No wonder migrants remain nostalgic about their home land, in which they believe they can find their rightful "place" and which they not rarely romanticize as their Paradise Lost.

The Migrating Hebrews Leaving Egypt, Their Home Land

To expand this understanding of land in the migrants' lives, it is instructive to examine the role of land in ancient Israel. The Hebrew term 'ereṣ is translated in the RSV as "land" (ca. 1620 times), as "earth" (600 times), as "ground" (107 times), and as "country" (83 times). Another Hebrew term, 'ādāmâ, is also translated in RSV as "land" (105 times), "ground" (67 times), "earth" (37 times), "soil" (6 times) and "country" (2 times). In general, 'ādāmâ is a nonpolitical term designating agricultural land, usually owned by a person, a group, or God, whereas 'ereṣ designates a political geographical area, the rough equivalent of the modern nation-state.[6]

The first mass movement from an 'ereṣ mentioned in the Bible is the migration of the Hebrews from Egypt. It is perhaps anachronistic to name the Israelites' escape from Egypt in the thirteenth century BCE as migration from their home land. Egypt is consistently portrayed in the Bible as a land of oppression and slavery for the Hebrews, and the land of Canaan as the "land flowing with milk and honey" (Exod 3:17; Deut 26:15), which is given them by God and which they would receive as "inheritance," "possession," and "rest." Within this narrative it is easy to forget that Egypt was also the "home land" of the Hebrews; indeed, it was the native land/fatherland/ motherland for all of them since their ancestors had lived there for nearly 500 years, where for a time they prospered economically and politically.[7] Indeed, the book of Exodus notes that "the Israelites were fruitful and prolific; they multiplied and grew exceedingly strong so that the land was filled with them" (1:7).[8] By contemporary standards of "citizenship," such as birthplace, language, political participation, cultural practices, and perhaps even religious affiliation, all the Hebrews at the time of their flight/migration from Egypt were "Egyptians." Like the fictitious person with four home lands imagined above, the descendants of the Hebrew migrants from Egypt could claim Egypt and Palestine their two home lands.

Perhaps an objection might be raised against this view by appealing to Yahweh's frequent admonitions to the Hebrews that they must not oppress a resident alien because they themselves had been "aliens in the land of Egypt" (Exod 22:21). In Leviticus, the Israelites are commanded by God to regard the alien who resides with them in Canaan as "citizens" among them because they themselves were aliens in Egypt: "The alien who resides with

---

6. See Janzen, "Land."

7. The mass migration of the Hebrews to Egypt is conventionally dated to the eighteenth century BCE and the exodus to the middle of the thirteen century BCE (between 1260–1220), under Pharaoh Ramses II.

8. The translation here and throughout the chapter is from the RSV.

you shall be to you as the citizen among you; you shall love the alien as yourself, for you were aliens in the land of Egypt" (Lev 19:34). In response, it may be said that the Hebrews were "aliens" in Egypt not because of their ethnicity as such or their lack of what might be called "citizenship," but because of the Pharaoh Rameses II's fear that due to their historical roots in Canaan and their concentration in Goshen, the Hebrews would ally with invaders from the coast (the Sea Peoples or the Philistines) or the northeastern and northwestern borders.

This situation has parallels in modern history. Examples of violence of citizens against citizens include the Armenian Genocide, in which between 700,000 and 1.5 million Armenians were killed, most of whom were citizens of the Ottoman Empire, like their killers. Of the six million Jews killed during the Holocaust, between 160,000 and 180,000 were German citizens. President Franklin D. Roosevelt's Executive Order 9096 brought about the forced relocation and incarceration in concentration camps of some 120,000 Japanese on the American west coast, 80,000 of whom were *Nisei* (second-generation American-born Japanese with US citizenship). In the Cambodian Genocide, approximately 1.5 to 2 million who were displaced and killed by Pol Pot's government were Cambodian citizens.

In this sense, the Hebrews' flight or exodus from Egypt may be regarded as their forced migration from their home land of which they were citizens, and their "alien" status in Egypt must be seen not as rooted in the lack of "citizenship" and its privileges but in the perceived political threats they posed to the security of the state, not unlike many refugees and migrants of our time. Emigration inevitably meant for the Hebrews physically moving away from their home land, foregoing security and peace, and facing challenges and risks of all types in a new environment. Even if God was with them during their journey, saving them "with an outstretched arm and with mighty acts of judgments" (Exod 6:6), they experienced, no less than today's migrants, immense anxiety, fear, confusion, depression, and suffering before they reached the promised land.

Interestingly, like today's migrants, the Hebrews under the leadership of Moses did not go to Canaan by the "Way of the Land of the Philistines," or the "Way of the Sea," which was the official route under Egyptian jurisdiction. Rather they went by the way of the desert by the Red Sea (Exod 13:17), which was less militarily surveilled but filled with natural dangers, not unlike modern migrants who would travel by a circuitous, perilous route, by land or by sea, risking life and limb rather than traveling by direct routes and exposing themselves to arrest by border patrols.

The Hebrews' flight from Egypt and wandering for forty years in the desert is, therefore, the first biblical mass migration This migration and its surrounding events are presented in Exodus 1–19, which provides a narrative of Egyptian oppression of the Hebrews, the origins and call of Moses as a political and religious leader, the contest with the pharaoh, the ten plagues, the celebration of the Passover, the Hebrews' departure from Egypt to their home land to Canaan (the "land flowing with milk and honey"), the miraculous crossing of the Red Sea / Sea of Reeds, and the establishment of the covenant between God and God's people at Mount Horeb/Sinai.

As with any group of migrants, the fleeing Hebrews experienced doubts about the wisdom of migrating, especially when suffering from hunger, thirst, and physical danger. Then they grew nostalgic about the land of their slavery and fondly recalled sitting by the "fleshpots" and eating "their fill of bread" (Exod 16:3). Such a reaction on the part of migrants is, humanly speaking and apart from the context of faith, fully understandable, especially when facing the possibility of a loss of life and an uncertain and risky future. Without leaders such as Moses and Aaron, the Israelites would have gone back to Egypt, just as today, without the support of others, both fellow migrants and the native-born, migrants would rather return to their miserable lot in their old countries.

THE FOREIGN LAND: THE DESTINATION OF IMMIGRATION

In many cases, like the ancient Hebrews, migrants do not immediately and directly reach the land of their dreams. Like the Hebrews wandering in the wilderness for forty years, they are forced to stay in refugee camps in a country of transit, at times for decades, hoping to be granted entry to the country of their choice after going through multiple vetting processes, and at times plumbing the depth of despair if refused and forced to repatriate. It is not rare that repatriated migrants, especially if their country of emigration is contiguous with the country of destination, such as Mexico and the United States, will try again and again to emigrate, either legally by applying for asylum or illegally, paying exorbitant fees to *coyotes* and embarking on an uncertain journey at the risk of life and limb.

Immigrants Living in the Foreign Land

For migrants who have escaped violence or poverty and have entered the receiving country, once the emotional relief and the novelty and excitement of the new environment have faded, there is the urgent need of facing the challenges of settling down in a foreign country. Unless supported by family and friends and receiving help from state and social organizations, the newcomers find these challenges overwhelming. For those lacking professional skills and language facility, good-paying jobs are out of reach. Most often they can only hope to have the so-called 3-Ds—dirty, danger-ous, demeaning—jobs, susceptible to exploitation, severe physical injury, and mental illness.

Once settled in the receiving countries, immigrants and their descen-dants are confronted with four possibilities. First, assimilation: They can be totally assimilated into the host country, incorporated into the melting pot as it were, a process greatly facilitated if their phenotypical features (e.g., skin and hair color, weight, height, etc.) are similar to those of the natives and if they are willing to abandon their own language, culture, and religion and adopt those of their host country.

Second, separation: If the immigrants are perceived to be a threat to the economic well-being of the nation, the public order of the state, and national identity, they would be regarded as culturally unassimilable and are subjected to discrimination, racism, and xenophobia. In return, to protect themselves and to preserve their language, cultural traditions, and religion, the immigrants tend to form themselves into "ethnic minorities," often lo-cated in separated and poorer neighborhoods, and risk marginalization and exclusion from their host country

Third, integration by means of biculturalism and multiculturalism: If the state enables the immigrants to participate as equals in all spheres of society, without expecting them to renounce all that makes up their ethnic identity, the immigrants constitute "ethnic communities" that are commit-ted to working for the well-being of the nation as a whole, thus espousing the mutually enriching coexistence of two or more cultures.

Fourth, marginalization: The immigrants reject both their own culture and that of the host country. They reject their own culture because it appears backward and incapable of helping them achieve success in the new coun-try. They also reject the host country's culture, because it remains strange, incomprehensible, and unassimilable to them. This occurs especially when the state simply recognizes and accepts ethnic diversity as an unavoidable fact of contemporary society but does not formulate policies and provide programs to help the immigrants understand and integrate the country's culture through social, political, economic, and educational initiatives.[9]

9. On these options—assimilation, separation, integration, and marginalization—see Castles et al., *Age of Migration*, 264–70.

The Foreign Land as Both Host and Enemy

One hard fact in the lives of migrants, especially first-generation migrants, is that despite their successful efforts at integration, and even after they have acquired citizenship, the host country will most often remain a *foreign* land to them. Of course, for those who choose the path of assimilation, and especially their children (second generation), the new country may appear familiar in the long run. However, it is doubtful whether the native-born will accept them as like or equal to them, as insinuated by their disconcerting questions—Where do you come from? When are you going home?—not to mention naked xenophobia and racial discrimination. For those who follow the separation and marginalization options, the host country will remain forever foreign and even hostile, in the double meaning of the Latin *hospes*, namely, host and hostile. For them, the status of "ethnic minority" and marginalization are the unavoidable price.

But even for those who have successfully negotiated integration so that they are now "both this and that," for instance, both American and Vietnamese, there remains the status of being "neither this nor that," that is, not fully Vietnamese and not fully American. When they visit their home land, their former co-nationals would judge them not sufficiently "native," their "Vietnameseness" having been unacceptably diluted. On the other hand, in America, they are deemed as insufficiently "American," especially because they are not white and descendants of Europeans or European migrants.

This existential condition also befell the Hebrews who crossed the Jordan and entered into Canaan, either in one fell swoop by war, as the book of Joshua narrates, or gradually by infiltration, which may be the more likely course of events. It is to be remembered that the Hebrews wandered in the wilderness for forty years and hence, the majority of the generation of the "Hebrews-Egyptians" who migrated from Egypt were already dead. Even Moses could not enter the promised land and died before his people entered Canaan, in his case as a punishment for their rebellion against Yahweh. Most likely the new generation who were born during their wilderness-wandering did not know much about nor had any memory of Egypt as their home land. True, the Hebrew migrants, when faced with thirst and hunger, at first hankered after their former lives in Egypt: "If only we had died by the hand of the LORD in the land of Egypt when we sat by the fleshpots and ate our fill of bread" (Exod 16:3). Like the Hebrews of old, today migrants, too, miss their former way of life in their home land, and romanticize it, as mentioned above, as their Paradise Lost.

The Hebrews who settled in Canaan were reminded by Yahweh of their ancestors' migration out of Egypt and the foreignness of the land they now occupied: "I declare that I will bring you up out of the misery of Egypt, to the land of the Canaanites, the Hittites, the Amorites, the Perrizites, the Hivites, and the Jebusites. A land flowing with milk and honey" (Exod 3:17). The list of the peoples in God's declaration is highly significant for the history of the Hebrews' migration out of Egypt and settlement in the new country since these natives, whose lands the Israelites now occupied, acted toward the newcomers and invaders as both hosts and enemies (*hospes*). The biblical narratives of the twelve tribes and their occupation of these lands, especially as recorded in the Deuteronomistic history of Joshua, Judges, and Kings 1 and 2, are replete of the armed struggles as well as treaties between these natives and the Hebrews, especially regarding territory. The Hebrews themselves both rejected and adopted the natives' cultural practices and even their religious cult, especially that of Baal, thus anticipating the four above-mentioned strategies of contemporary migrants. This ambiguous attitude continued until the destruction and exile of the ten tribes of the Northern Kingdom (Israel) by Assyria in 722 and the destruction and exile of the two remaining tribes in the Southern Kingdom (Judah) by Babylonia in 587. Even for the Hebrews, the land of Canaan, flowing with milk and honey, which they received from God as "inheritance," "possession," and "rest," remained a *foreign* land.[10]

OUR LAND: TOWARD THE KINGDOM OF GOD

Today, for most if not all refugees, one of the much-sought-after goals is citizenship, which guarantees them the rights and privileges enjoyed by all citizens, native as well as foreign-born. Citizenship is of various types and can be obtained in different ways, depending on the prevailing concept of "nation." It can be acquired by birth in the country (*ius soli*), by blood ties with those who are citizens (*ius sanguinis*), by political connections between the origination country and the destination country, by possessing identical ethnicity, or by fulfilling all the requirements for naturalization.[11]

Citizenship, Nation-Sate, National Identity

A most important fact in current migration is that whereas until recently, acquiring a new citizenship required the renunciation of one's former one,

10. Brueggemann, *The Land.*

11. On citizenship and national identity, see Miller, *Citizenship and National Identity.*

there is now in several countries the possibility of dual or multiple citizenships. This represents a major shift in the concept of nationality, since exclusive loyalty to one single state is the central component of the state's sovereignty. Dual citizenship is a form of "internal globalization" by which the destination country acknowledges and legally sanctions the transnational identities of migrants and their descendants and no longer demands the renunciation of former nationalities. Dual citizenship is facilitated by the fact that not only fathers but also mothers are now allowed to transmit their citizenship to their children. Interestingly, many emigration countries have modified their citizenship rules to permit and even encourage emigrants to retain their native citizenship while acquiring new ones, to maintain cultural and religious ties to their mother/fatherlands, to make financial investments there, to participate in electoral politics in their home countries, and even to vote for their own diasporic representatives.

Thus, citizenship is not necessarily and indissolubly tied with the nation-state and by extension, the home land. It is no longer possible to build nationalism on the basis of the dominant home land and exclusive citizenship. The most apparent and unsettling impact of migration on this concept of nationalism is that it undermines the very foundation of nationalism by attacking its core concept of nation and the allied notions of national identity, national spirit, and nationalism. A nation is constituted by a large and stable group of people who are brought into a unified community on the basis of either a historically verified or imagined common origin, race, ethnicity, language, culture, territory, and religion (the "ethnic-genealogical nation," as exemplified by Germany) or by the willingness and commitment of various peoples to live together in harmony in a well-demarcated territory (the "civic-territorial nation," as exemplified by the United States).[12] In both conceptions of nation, the nation is, to use Benedict Anderson's celebrated expression, an "imagined community," formed on the basis of the various presumed shared factors that its members take to be essential for their national identity.[13]

Needless to say, of the two models of nation, the ethnic-genealogical nation runs the greater risk of losing its integrity and even identity because of the presence of immigrants, particularly those who bring with them a set of different attributes of race, ethnicity, language, culture, and religion. The danger is all the more real if the number of immigrants is large and the national fabric is fragile. Furthermore, even the civic-territorial nation, which

12. On the "ethnic-genealogical" and "civic-territorial" notions of nation, see Smith, *National Identity*, 71–84.

13. On national identity, see Verdugo and Milne, eds., *National Identity*.

has fewer natural ties, is not immune from this danger of disintegration if the immigrants, despite their agreement to abide by the political and social norms of the host country, refuse to abandon their cultural heritage and form themselves into ethnic communities gathered in separate enclaves.

Essentially connected with the concept of nation is national identity, which is a social and collective reality constructed from either the shared "facts" of common origin and destiny, language, culture, and religion, or the collective commitment of the members to live together within a territory, or both. It involves a double process: (1) self-categorization by identifying oneself as a member of a national group, and (2) affect-creating by fostering a sense of belonging and emotional attachment to the nation and feelings of pride in and love for the members of the same nation. One of the effects of this national identity formation is the differentiation between the "in-group" composed of the members of the nation and the "out-group" made up of those who do not belong to it. The insiders are said to possess the "national spirit," often romantically and vaguely defined as made up of certain spiritual qualities that permeate their lives exclusively and are allegedly impossible for the outsiders to assimilate.

Just as immigrants undermine the reality of the nation by challenging both its ethnic-genealogical and civic-territorial conceptions, so too, they reject the classification of the inhabitants of the same territory into "in-group" and "out-group" as well as the superiority attributed to the former. They point out that national identity and national spirit are not the product of objective and historically verifiable inborn racial, psychological, sociological, and spiritual traits of the "in-group," but are the highly selective and arbitrary construction of a collective identity by the dominant economic, political, and religious groups within the "imagined community" on the basis of historically multiple, intrinsically contingent, and continuously changing particulars, such as language, blood ties, territory, national symbols, and the manifold and varied elements of culture, to preserve their hegemony within the nation. Thus, the in-groups seek to marginalize the out-groups and perpetuate their stereotypes. Unmasking this invented tradition, immigrants demand the right to have an equal role in the social construction of a new national identity and national spirit by importing their own languages, national traditions and symbols, cultures, and religions into their daily existence. In this way, nationalism will be prevented from degenerating into chauvinism, ethnocentrism, racism, and xenophobia.

It is in this process of national identity construction by both the natives and the immigrants that the *home* land and the *foreign* land are transmuted into *our* land. "Land" here is understood both literally, meaning a geographical area with distinct and defining borders, and metaphorically, signifying all the conditions and common and shared products for human coexistence. The qualifier "our" indicates the common possession and enjoyment of the new land by both the natives and the immigrants, legal and undocumented, on the way to citizenship. In this our land, to reprise the metaphors for migrants used above, the migrants are no longer "either this or that," no longer "neither this nor that," but "both this and that," and now, in "our land," "beyond this and that." The natives too experience this existential transformation, since in "our land" they are no longer "this or that" but can become "both this and that," and "beyond this and that," a personal and national enrichment made possible only by the presence of immigrants.

To give a concrete example of this dynamic of mutual transformation in the process of moving from home land through foreign land to our land: when a group of Vietnamese came to the United States in April 1975 after North Vietnam vanquished South Vietnam, they settled in many states, including California. Because their migration was forced and violent, most of them, especially the older ones, lamented bitterly the loss of their home land and were homesick, physically and psychologically, dreaming of eventually returning to their mother/fatherland. Meanwhile, many settled together, forming cities and giving them the names of cities in Vietnam, with "New" prefixed to them. These cities allowed the Vietnamese to preserve their language, customs, cuisine, ways of life, and as will be shown below, religions. In fact, in Little Saigon in Westminster, California, the Vietnamese can live comfortably there without ever needing to contact a white or black American, with all their needs amply met in terms of foods, healthcare, legal assistance, social media, and all kinds of social services catered by the Vietnamese themselves. Ironically, their needs are better met here than in Vietnam. They are in the United States, but the United States remains in many ways a foreign land for them.

Of course, even living in their "home land" transported to the United States, the Vietnamese still have to confront the many challenges that living in a foreign land presents. Like many other migrants, they have the four options mentioned above open to them: assimilation, separation, integration, and marginalization. Ultimately, they have the choice of transforming their home land and the foreign land into our land. Most of them have become US citizens and some of them have won elections for city council member, mayor, state representative, and member of Congress. Their identity is hyphenated or hybrid: Vietnamese-American or American-Vietnamese. They are both Vietnamese and American (both this and that) but also not purely Vietnamese or purely American (neither this nor that). Eventually, they are more than Vietnamese and more than American (beyond this and that) by transforming the United States into *our* land, literally and metaphorically. In this process, the identity of not only the Vietnamese migrants but also that of the native-born Americans, whose ancestors were themselves migrants, are transformed. It is by no means a pain-free and conflict-free process for both the migrants and the natives, but the outcome—our land—is richer than merely Vietnam and merely America, as both home land and foreign land. But "our land" is never a secure and stable thing; like democracy, it is constantly threatened by the forces of racism, white supremacy, xenophobia, and discrimination of all kinds. And, most tragically, it may disappear altogether, like all past empires, which attempted to turn the home land and the foreign land into a kind of our land by military conquest, colonization, and globalization, on which the sun never sets.

Our Land and the Kingdom of God

It is in this perspective, I submit, that land should be viewed in the Hebrew Scripture/Old Testament. In the history of Israel, from the time of its occupation of Canaan to the exiles of 722 and 587, and the returns from exile to Judah (the Jehud Province of Babylonia) beginning in 538, the land and "landedness" were understood as God's gift to God's people, and correspondingly exile from the land ("landlessness") is understood as God's punishment for the people's infidelity to God's covenant. The reality of land is central in the history of Israel, from the moment of God's promise to Abraham, through the exodus, the occupation of Canaan, the loss of land through the two exiles, the regaining of the land during the return from Babylonia and the restoration in Judah, to the destruction of the Temple in 70 CE and the Diaspora. The land is God's gift and central to the national and religious identity of Israel. But, like our land, it is not a permanent and assured possession, something for the exclusive use of the people of Israel, much less only for the rich and the powerful among them. Rather, it must be equitably distributed to all Israel, including the migrants and sojourners among them (Ezek 47:13–23). Thus, the land becomes our—the Israelites' and the migrants'—land.

In the New Testament, the land-motif (Greek *gē*, *'agros*, and *chōra*) continues to be important; indeed, the third beatitude in Matthew calls the meek blessed "for they will inherit the earth/land (*tēn gēn*)." However, it is also clear that the New Testament introduces new approaches to land and the land motif. At times, the Old Testament theology of land seems to be abrogated, especially in the Letter to the Hebrews, in which even the land promised to Abraham is redirected to "a better country, that is, a heavenly one" (Heb 11:16). God's promise is deterritorialized and located not in a geographical area but in the person of Jesus. At other times, land is given a symbolic meaning, and signifies the eschatological kingdom of God which Jesus has inaugurated, open to both Jews and gentiles. Finally, land is transformed from a limited geographical area to designate the entire world to which the good news of Jesus must be preached, as Luke puts it, "in Jerusalem, in all Judea and Samaria, and to the ends of the earth" (Acts 1:8).[14]

In terms of our reflections here, the transformation of land, from the *home* land to the *foreign* land and finally to *our* land, not only represents the experience of migrants but also invites both natives and immigrants to take part in the transformation of the nation-states with their borders that separate people of different nationalities, races, ethnicities, class, and gender into the universal and all-inclusive kingdom of God. It is, in short, *utopia*, both a good place and no place, God's promise and fulfillment of "a new heaven and a new earth . . . the holy city, the new Jerusalem, coming down out of heaven from God" (Rev 21:1–2).

BIBLIOGRAPHY

Bretell, Caroline B., and James F. Hollifield, eds. *Migration Theory: Talking across Disciplines*. New York: Routledge, 2008.

Brueggemann, Walter. *The Land: Place as Gift, Promise, and Challenge in Biblical Faith*. Philadelphia: Augsburg, 1977.

Carens, Joseph H. *The Ethics of Immigration*. Oxford: Oxford University Press, 2013.

Casey, Edward S. *The Fate of Place: A Philosophical History*. Berkeley: University of California Press, 1998.

———. *Getting Back to Place: Toward a Renewed Understanding of the Place-World*. Bloomington: Indiana University Press, 1993/2009.

Castles, Stephen, et al. *The Age of Migration: International Population Movements in the Modern World*. 65th ed. New York: Guilford, 2020.

Collier, Paul. *Exodus: How Migration Is Changing Our World*. Oxford: Oxford University Press, 2013.

Faist, Thomas, et al. *Transnational Migration*. Malden, MA: Polity, 2013.

Freedman, David Noel, ed. *The Anchor Bible Dictionary*. 6 vols. New York: Doubleday, 1992.

Gutiérrez, David G., and Pierette Hondagneu-Sotelo, eds. *Nation and Migration Past and Future*. Baltimore: Johns Hopkins University Press, 2009.

Janzen, W. "Land." In *The Anchor Bible Dictionary*, edited by David Noel Freedman, 4:143–54. 6 vols. New York: Doubleday, 1992.

King, Russell. *People on the Move: An Atlas of Migration*. Berkeley: University of California Press, 2010.

Miller, David L. *Citizenship and National Identity*. Cambridge: Polity, 2000.

O'Reilly, Karen. *International Migration and Social Theory*. New York: Palgrave Macmillan, 2012.

14. See Janzen, "Land," 151–53.

Portes, Alejandro, and Josh DeWind. *Rethinking Migration: New Theoretical and Empirical Perspectives*. New York: Berghahn, 2007.

Quayson, Ato, and Girish Daswani, eds. *A Companion to Diaspora and Transnationalism*. Oxford: Wiley Blackwell, 2013.

Sarna, Nahum. *Exploring Exodus: The Origins of Biblical Israel*. New York: Schocken, 1986.

Smith, Anthony. *National Identity*. Las Vegas: University of Nevada Press, 1993.

Verdugo, Richard R., and Andrew Milne, eds. *National Identity: Theory and Research*. Charlotte, NC: Information Age, 2016.

The Great Migration

The Incarnation and the Scandal of an Illegal Border Crossing[1]

Daniel G. Groody, CSC

INTRODUCTION

FEW TOPICS ARE AS controversial in our own day and age as migration. More often than not, the conversation hits a wall along dualistic lines of legal/illegal, citizen/foreigner, and native/stranger. By and large most of the literature around the topic is shaped by the social sciences. And while these studies have made important contributions to the conversation, in recent years more theological voices have entered the field and reframed much of the way we think about the debate.[2]

The central focus of this essay is not simply to add more information to this discourse but to offer a new imagination about it from a theological vantage point. My central thesis is that Jesus himself is the migrant Son of God, and his migration to earth in the incarnation and his return migration to the Father after his death and resurrection, is what makes possible our return migration to our heavenly homeland. My hope is that this theological

1. Parts of this chapter are adapted from my forthcoming "Passing Over: Theology, Migration and the Eucharist." For more on this topic, see my *Border of Death*; "Jesus and the Undocumented Immigrant"; "Crossing the Divide"; *Passing Over*; and "Cup of Suffering."

2. Phan, *Christian Theology*; Padilla and Phan, eds. *Contemporary Issues*; and Phan, "Deus Migrator." For an in-depth bibliography on theology and migration, see Campese, "The Irruption of Migrants."

vision cannot only help break down the walls between "us" and "them" but transform the way we think about "the other" as a brother and a sister.

This brief chapter then is about the incarnation of Jesus Christ as the "Great Migration" of salvation history. It raises many questions about the functions of borders, the problem of barriers and the way Jesus crosses them in order to reconcile us to God, others, and even our very selves. Here we want to explore the way Jesus crosses *over* the borders of the cosmos, crosses *into* the borders of human skin, and ultimately crosses *beyond* the borders of life and death. In essence, Jesus' illegal entry into the world helps humanity move away from the land of unlikeness to God (which tradition calls the *regio dissimilitudinis*) and toward the land of likeness to God (*regio similitudinis*).[3] It is a redemptive journey that makes it possible to become "permanent residents" of our native country and "naturalized" citizens of God's kingdom (Eph 2:19).

THE INCARNATION AND THE GREAT BORDER CROSSING

The heart of the New Testament tells the story of God's migration to our world and our return migration to God's kingdom. At the center of this mystery is the person of Jesus of Nazareth. He is the Word made flesh, the incarnate Son, the Divine Migrant who has come from his heavenly home to dwell among us. As he enters into the sinful and broken territory of our human existence, he reveals, in Pope Francis's words, "the face of the Father's mercy."[4] Through the Paschal Mystery, he makes it possible for men and women, lost in their earthly sojourn, to recover their true selves, to cross the borders of this world, and to find their way back home again to God.

When we look at migration from a theological perspective, we see that it is more than a sociopolitical event; it is also a dynamic and spiritual process at work in all of creation. St. Thomas Aquinas, in fact, arranges the whole of his *Summa Theologica*—one of the most significant theological reflections of all time—around the principle that everything comes from God and returns to God (*Exitus et Reditus*).[5] From this vantage point, Jesus'

---

3. The concept of *regio dissimilitudinis* has its origin in Platonic thought, but it has parallels in the Scriptures. Mystics like Bernard of Clairvaux and others in the Middle Ages also used the concept when speaking about the movement of people away from the divine image and likeness toward a state of alienation. For more on this topic, see Gilson, "*Regio dissimilitudinis*."

4. Pope Francis, *Misericordiae Vultus*.

5. St. Thomas Aquinas's *Summa Theologiae*, I-II, question 92. For more on immigration and the Bible, see Carroll R., *Christians at the Border* and *The Bible and Borders*.

migration to the human race and his return migration to the Father can be interpreted as the Great Migration of human history.

CROSSING OVER THE BORDERS OF THE COSMOS

From the beginning of time, God desired that his creatures and all creation live in unity and peace with him. God never intended to build a wall between his kingdom and humankind or to make us wanderers on the earth. When sin entered the world, however, the first man and woman became forced migrants and exiles in this world and were cast out from the garden of Eden (Gen 3:23–24). Consequently, men and women became alienated from their homeland, and divine border guards—in cherubim form—prevented humanity from re-entering paradise.

In eating from the tree, Adam and Eve became the first illegal aliens. They were illegal because they broke God's commands and aliens because they had become estranged from God. But even after their transgression, God did not abandon humanity and leave them hopeless in their displacement. In the first pages of the Scriptures we learn of God's gratuitous and tender care for human beings their material needs, regardless of their worthiness (Gen 3:21). In the fullness of time, God would eventually extend his mercy to the point of sending his Son into the world, who would help people recover what was lost in the first Adam, namely the image and likeness of God (1 Cor 15:22).[6]

Each of the four Gospels begins its account of the Great Migration from different locations. The later the Gospel is written, the earlier the evangelist traces back Jesus' journey. Mark begins with John the Baptist in the desert at the start of his mission, some thirty years into Jesus' earthly sojourn (Mark 1:1–8). Matthew and Luke begin with his divine-human border crossing at his birth in Bethlehem (Matt 1:18–25; Luke 2:1–7). John starts with his residence in his celestial homeland and his cosmic movement to the human race (John 1:1–5).

When God descended to the human race, a star arose in the cosmos (Matt 2:2). It signaled that something powerful has happened in the universe and that a celestial event had connected heaven and earth in an irrevocable way. The first to behold its message were not the scholars, the powerful, nor even the Jewish religious leaders. The initial witnesses were migrant gentiles from the East, who came from afar to pay homage to the infant king of the Jews. Coming from Babylon, Persia, or perhaps the Arabian desert, they

---

6. Irenaeus, *Adversus Haereses*, 3.18.1.

testified to the advent of a boundless love that reaches across all borders to all people, in all lands, and for all generations (Matt 8:11–12; 28:18–20).[7]

The magi traveled from the East to Jerusalem (Matt 2:1–2) and then from Jerusalem to Bethlehem (Matt 2:9). If they were to make this journey today, they would not only have to cross various borders, but they would have run into a number of modern barriers along the way as well. Bethlehem is now part of Palestinian controlled territory, and after the Second Intifada in 2000, the modern state of Israel began constructing a twenty-six-foot-high wall that separated the West Bank territories from Israeli-controlled land. While Israeli leaders today consider these barriers as a necessary security measure to prevent terrorism, Palestinians see it as a racial segregation policy that divides the people of the Holy Land on multiple levels.

Reading these biblical texts in light of the current political geography sets up a striking contrast between the God who migrated to the human race to break down the walls that divide (Eph 2:14) and the present climate, which erects walls in order to separate one people from another. If Jesus were born in Bethlehem today, he would have been born outside the walls of contemporary Israel, at the border, on the margins, in divisive territory, and in the shadow of an imposing barricade. Some local Palestinian merchants in Bethlehem have picked up on this theme by creating nativity sets that include a separation-wall that keeps the migrant magi from paying homage to the Christ child.

The Church of the Nativity in Bethlehem marks the traditional site of Jesus' birth, and to enter one has to pass through what is called the "Door of Humility." It is a small door, only about four feet tall and two feet wide. Some historians argue it was built to prevent horse and camel-riding looters from pillaging the Church at the time of the Crusades, but its figurative renderings offer much material for spiritual reflection.

In what is regarded as one of the church's earliest christological hymns, St. Paul writes,

> Have among yourselves the same attitude that is also yours in Christ Jesus,
> Who, though he was in the form of God,
> did not regard equality with God something to be grasped.
> Rather, he emptied himself,
> taking the form of a slave,
> coming in human likeness;
> and found human in appearance,
> he humbled himself,

7. Harrington, "Matthew," 865.

> becoming obedient to death,
> even death on a cross.
> Because of this, God greatly exalted him
> and bestowed on him the name
> that is above every name,
> that at the name of Jesus
> every knee should bend,
> of those in heaven and on earth and under the earth,
> and every tongue confess that
> Jesus Christ is Lord,
> to the glory of God the Father. (Phil 2:5–11)

The Church of the Nativity reminds us that, in imitation of the God of the Universe who lowered himself when he migrated to the human race, one has to bow down to understand its mystery. The magi were some of the first to grasp the arrival of the One who came for the salvation of the human race. And among the first to cross the borders of their own worlds to greet him. They realized that only by opening themselves in vulnerability could they receive the gift of a promised redemption; and only by sharing their own treasure could they be enriched beyond measure.

When their horizontal migration from the East aligns with the divine migrant's vertical migration from above, and the cosmos responds with a celestial sign, they encounter the child and his mother. In response they bow down and worship to offer their gifts to the giver of all good gifts (Matt 2:9–11). Yet as the wise men opened themselves to this divine epiphany, the powerful closed their hearts to the coming of the divine migrant. They build walls they thought would protect themselves, but instead they erected a prison within themselves that enclosed them in fortresses of disordered desires. Choosing to worship the gifts of creation rather than the God who created them, they mistakenly oriented their lives around the love of power rather than the power of love and lost their souls in the process.

As the biblical drama unfolds, the newborn King of the Jews enters Herod's territory and is laid to rest for the first time in a manger or a live-stock feeding trough. There he empties himself in order to nourish a grace-emaciated humanity and liberate those powerless in bondage. Meanwhile, Herod, resting in luxury, seeks to fulfill his own desires by enslaving oth-ers and using them to nourish his own needs. Refusing to bow down, he takes refuge behind his palace fortress called Herodium and builds walls to protect his possessions, his property, and his power. When he realizes his rule is in jeopardy, he lashes out in fear, hoping to eliminate the threat of divine migrant threat (Matt 2:16–18). Jesus Christ's humble entrance in human estate signals the beginning of a new reign and the end of all human kingdoms, beginning with Herod's.

CROSSING INTO THE BORDERS OF HUMAN SKIN

When God entered our world as a divine migrant, he did not land as if on a spaceship from another planet. Nor did he remain at a distance, as if in some kind of divinely insulated spacesuit that would have shielded him from the sinful elements of our world that could harm him. Rather he moved into the vulnerability of our flesh, took on the absolute "otherness" of our human condition, and allowed himself to be circumscribed by human skin.

The skin is largest border of the human body, and it is essential in regulating the relationship between the inner life of the person and the outside world. To some degree the incarnation validates the value of borders and reveals that they are integral to our very nature. Removing the border of the skin from a human being, for example, would expose a person to outside elements that could be harmful and even fatal. Sealing the border completely and turning the skin into a barrier, however, would cause overheating, toxicity, and eventual death. The skin, as a protective and permeable border, manages a necessary and complex process that helps the human body maintain an internal balance or homeostasis.

In a similar way, borders can play a positive role in the body of society. They are especially important as the human community struggles to attain a global homeostasis, which is another way of speaking about the state of justice and peace. But achieving such a state is dependent upon what St. Augustine referred to as *tranquillitas ordinis*, or "the tranquility of order."[8] While a detailed discussion of this subject is beyond the scope of this section, it highlights that borders must be understood in light of the well-being of the whole body, not just an isolated part of it. In light of our reflection here, we can say that God entered the borders of a human body, but he did so for a specific reason, namely the salvation of the human race. I call this movement the "incarnational principle of migration."

The incarnational principle of migration is not just about God's movement into human skin; it is about God's movement into human skin for the sake of the well-being of others. He became human not his own sake but for

8. "Peace between man and God is the well-ordered obedience of faith to eternal law. Peace between man and man is well-ordered concord. Civil peace is a similar concord among the citizens. The peace of the celestial city is the perfectly ordered and harmonious enjoyment of God, and of one another in God. The peace of all things is the tranquility of order. Order is the distribution which allots things equal and unequal, each to its own place." St. Augustine, *City of God*, 690–91.

the sake of a people who had become alien to him. He became bordered by the human body not to exclude people but to reconcile people to God and to make them a part of his own body, his own kingdom.

In a similar way, the right to construct borders must be viewed not simply in light of the desire to protect a privileged few but especially in view of the need to provide for the neglected many. This involves recognizing a larger responsibility to the whole body and its well-being. This analysis is especially important in light of the socioeconomic disorders of our present age, and without a serious evaluation of the way they contribute to the social ills of the human family, a global homeostasis can never be achieved. In other words, borders have a value and a function, but they also have limitations. They are subject to the dignity of the human person, the common good of all, and their impact on the overall well-being of the entire social body.

CROSSING OVER THE BORDERS OF RELIGION

As we look closer at the Great Migration, however, we see that God in Jesus not only crossed the borders of the cosmos and even the borders of human skin, but he scandalously also crossed the borders of conventional religion too. When we pause, contemplate, and consider the radical initiative of God in the incarnation, we are compelled to ask, why would God choose a plan to save the world through what was, in effect, an illegal border crossing?

Though this initiative of the incarnation was divine, it was at the same time a surprisingly illegal act by the rules of this world. At the center of this drama is the person of Mary of Nazareth. At the time of the Great Migration, she was betrothed to Joseph. Betrothal in biblical times was a year-long, interim period between courtship and marriage, and while it was not exactly the same as a marriage today, it still had legal stipulations. The penalty under the law of Moses for breaking this agreement by adultery, rape, incest or fornication was death by stoning (Num 5:11–31; Deut 22:23–30).[9] Sexual relations during betrothal would have been considered the equivalent to adultery, so to be found pregnant at that time—let alone by someone other than one's partner—would have put Mary's life at risk. If she stayed at home, she would have been subjected to a trial and likely the death penalty.

Although Mary trusted God's promises not to be afraid, the news of receiving the Divine Migrant into "her home" troubled her at the same time (Luke 1:29–45). She knew it would bring judgment from others, who would marginalize her and even criminalize her. In faith she accepts the risks associated with migrant hospitality, but she comes to understand that the path

9. Hatfield, "Betrothal," 199.

forward cannot be worked out through black and white certainties but only by love worked out through faith.

The Jewish law had guided Mary's life up until this point, but her spiritual experience would call her beyond the rules of organized religion to a deeper vision of what God required of her; Mary's life, calling, and destiny would now be worked out principally by God's grace, which will go far beyond a strict and narrow interpretations of the Jewish law and human perception. Because those in Nazareth do not have the eyes to see the deeper mystery at work, she moves in haste from Nazareth and migrates to Ein Karem to see her cousin Elizabeth (Luke 1:39).

Because God's migration into the world put Mary and Joseph at variance with a surface reading of the Jewish law, it meant that Jesus himself in some sense was an "illegal alien." Jesus was illegal in view of his law-breaking conception. And an alien, because he really did come from another world! How perplexing it is that God's plan of salvation would start with God's illegal entry into our world! And how ironic that it would also take shape amid a drama of where Jesus and Mary would be required to report to Bethlehem for political documentation (Luke 2:1–5)!

I would argue here that God's choice of an illegal alien to save the world is in many ways the beginning of the good news. And there is much in this story that can help rescript our operative narratives about legality, justice, and righteousness, especially in regard to those deemed as "undocumented," "illegal," "alien," and "criminal." The gospel reveals to us that the incarnation scandalized some people, but we can only imagine how this news would been received by outcasts, criminals, and the "undocumented" of society. In revealing that no one is walled off from God's mercy, the God of Jesus Christ opens up a pathway to hope for all, beginning with those marginalized from society and deemed illegal by the social, political, and even religious powers of the world. More generally, it reveals that every human being—who without exception have become aliens of God's kingdom through sin (Rom 5:10–11; Eph 2:1–9)—can now have access again to God's kingdom (Rom 3:23)!

Moreover, as we study more closely the life of Jesus, this does not mean that we disregard the valuable role of religion, the legitimate use of the law, and the way these shaped his identity. As a first-century Jewish man, Jesus entered into a particular period of history, and his human identity was significantly shaped by different kinds of religious, geographical, and political borders. The nation of Israel—like other world religions—established borders to protect their community and nurture values central to their life of faith. As a practicing Jew, Jesus would have understood the proximate value and a positive function of borders, especially as they helped form the identity and mission of a people.

Jesus was born into a Jewish family (Luke 2:39), obedient to the Jewish law (Num 18:15; Luke 2:22), circumcised a Jew (Lev 12:2–3; Luke 2:21), studied the Torah (Luke 2:46–47), and celebrated Passover (Luke 22:14–15). He is called Rabbi (John 4:31), the Messiah (Mark 14:61–62; John 1:41; 4:25–26) and even the King of the Jews (Matt 27:37; Mark 15:26). Each of the evangelists brings out Jesus' connection to his Jewish roots, but Matthew in particular is the most Jewish of the four evangelists. Throughout his Gospel he is intent on illuminating different ways that borders of religion shaped Jesus' identity.

As much as Matthew emphasizes Jesus' Jewish roots, however, he also brings out that Jesus refuses to use that identity as a reason for building walls and excluding others.[10] Jesus' Jewish heritage, in fact, is permeated by people outside its ranks. Many of his ancestors mentioned in Matthew's genealogy came from foreign lands or were closely associated with migrants, like Ruth the Moabite, Rahab the Canaanite prostitute, Tamar the proselyte, and Bathsheba, who was married to a Hittite foreigner (Matt 1:1–17). Scholars debate the reason for their inclusion in the descriptions of his family lineage, but some convincingly argue that their presence foreshadows the universal mission of Jesus, which extends beyond the borders of Israel to all nations.[11]

Though he is the image of the invisible God, the church confesses that Jesus was also fully human. And, as a human being, Jesus inevitably underwent a developmental sense of himself and his mission. As he grew in wisdom, understanding and experience, the scope of his own mission expanded (Luke 2:52). Initially, he seems to have circumscribed it within the borders of the nation of Israel, but as he encountered those who suffered—and had the eyes to see those who came to him in faith—his compassion extended beyond these provisional borders. The story of the Syrophoenician woman, in particular, brings out Jesus' evolving consciousness and willingness to go beyond even the borders of religion and to enter the space of "the other:"

> A Canaanite woman of that district came and called out, "Have pity on me, Lord, Son of David! My daughter is tormented by a demon." But he did not say a word in answer to her. His disciples came and asked him, "Send her away, for she keeps calling out after us." He said in reply, "I was sent only to the lost sheep of the house of Israel." But the woman came and did him homage, saying, "Lord, help me." He said in reply, "It is not right to take the

10. Donahue, "'Parable' of the Sheep."

11. Luz, *Matthew 1–7*, 84–85.

food of the children and throw it to the dogs." She said, "Please, Lord, for even the dogs eat the scraps that fall from the table of their masters." Then Jesus said to her in reply, "O woman, great is your faith! Let it be done for you as you wish." And her daughter was healed from that hour. (Matt 15:22–28, NABRE)

Through his encounter with this woman, Jesus realizes that his mission as the messenger of God's love and mercy extends beyond the Jewish nation to everyone in the world.

CROSSING BEYOND THE BORDERS OF LIFE AND DEATH

Whatever arguments can be made about their relative value of borders and the way Jesus related to them, he did not allow his boundless mercy to be constricted by them. He was concerned not only with those protected by borders but even and especially with those excluded and abused by them. To put it another way, he did not allow borders to become barriers.[12] Especially when such barriers justified and legitimated division, Jesus crossed over them or destroyed them entirely.

In crossing these borders, however, Jesus often crossed his adversaries as well. His trans-border ministry was good news to many, but it scandalized others, especially those who used their power, title, wealth, or even moral principles to justify the exclusion of others. Jesus' table fellowship with sinners and with the poor symbolizes the all-inclusiveness of his ministry and the ways he even crossed over the borders created by false religion. As John Meier puts it:

> In the eyes of the stringently pious, Jesus' table fellowship with the ritually or morally unclean communicated uncleanness to Jesus himself. Jesus, of course, saw it the other way round: he was communicating salvation to religious outcasts. His meals with sinners and the disreputable were celebrations of the lost being found, of God's eschatological mercy reaching out and embracing the prodigal son returning home (see, e.g., Mk 2:13–17; Lk 15:1–32). His banquets with sinful Israelites were a preparation and foretaste of the coming banquet in the kingdom of God (see, e.g., Mk 2:19; Lk 13:28–29 par; 14:15–24 par).[13]

12. Heyer, *Kinship across Borders*. For more on a theological perspective from Jesus' social location, and its connection to the US-Mexico border, see Elizondo, *Galilean Journey*; and Rose, *Showdown in the Sonoran Desert*.

13. Meier, *Mentor, Message, and Miracles*, 303.

In place of barriers, Jesus built bridges.[14] He taught his disciples to take up their crosses and follow him and to "cross over" to those vulnerable places that involved tending to a neighbor, a stranger, or even an enemy in need. He understood that while fear erects walls and divides relationships, love crosses borders and creates connections among people.

Throughout the entirety of his life, the central barrier that Jesus sought to annihilate was the barrier of death. But death here not only has to do with what happens when we cease to breathe; death also has to do with defeating the powers in this world that diminish life, such as sickness, poverty, injustice, hunger, inequality, prejudice, rejection, exclusion, division, and other forms of suffering.

Even though Jesus as the divine migrant knew firsthand the struggles of the human journey through this world, he was never meant to set up his "tent" in this world and become a "permanent resident" in this world. His own death on the cross gives testimony to God's desire to destroy the wall that has put enmity with God and divides us from one another (Eph 2:14). The resurrection reveals God's desire to open up in a final and definitive way the road to leads to a place where there will be no more death, mourning, crying, or pain, and where the old order has passed away and all creation is finally made new (Rev 24:1).

SUMMARY AND CONCLUSION: SPIRITUAL "NATURALIZATION" AND KINGDOM CITIZENSHIP

In this chapter we have looked at the journey of the divine migrant in the Gospels, and we have explored some of the ways Jesus crossed over borders and broke down walls in order to reconcile us to God and save sinful people. In many respects this redemptive process is a way of helping an "alien people" become "naturalized citizens" in God's kingdom (Eph 2:19).[15] This road ultimately leads to communion (*com*, with, together; *unus*, oneness, union) with God, with creation, and with one another.

This mystery of the word made flesh cannot be understood from the logic of reason, politics, or economics.[16] The mystery of the Great Migration can only be understood through the economy of grace and the logic of love: a God who became one with us so we could again become one with God. By entering the "otherness" of our condition, he reveals the "oneness" of our

14. US Conference of Catholic Bishops, *Strangers No Longer*.

15. O'Neill, "No Longer Strangers."

16. Hollenbach, *Humanity in Crisis*. See also Christiansen, "Movement, Asylum, Borders"; Hing, *Deporting Our Souls*; and Wilbanks, *Re-creating America*.

created destiny, and through his return journey to the Father, he makes it possible to find our way again to God, to one another and even our inmost selves. As Leonardo Boff summarizes the divine migration, "The God who is revealed in and through Jesus is human. And the human being who emerges in and through Jesus is divine . . . Only a God could be so human!"[17]

BIBLIOGRAPHY

St. Augustine. *The City of God*. Translated by Marcus Dods. New York: Random House, 2017.

Boff, Leonardo. *Jesus Christ Liberator: A Critical Christology for Our Time*. Translated by Patrick Hughes. Maryknoll: Orbis, 1978.

Bergant, Diane, and R. J. Karris, eds. *The Collegeville Bible Commentary: New Testament*. Collegeville: Liturgical, 1989.

Brand, Chad, et al. *Holman Illustrated Bible Dictionary*. Nashville: Holman Bible Publishers, 2003.

Campese, Gioacchino. "The Irruption of Migrants: Theology of Migration in the 21st Century." *Theological Studies* 73 (2012) 3–32.

Carroll R., M. Daniel. *The Bible and Borders: Hearing God's Word on Immigration*. Grand Rapids: Brazos, 2020.

————. *Christians at the Border: Immigration, the Church, and the Bible*. 2nd ed. Grand Rapids: Baker Academic, 2013.

Christiansen, Drew. "Movement, Asylum, Borders: Christian Perspectives." *International Migration Review* 30 (1996) 7–17.

Donahue, John R. "The 'Parable' of the Sheep and the Goats: A Challenge to Christian Ethics." *Theological Studies* 47 (1986) 3–31.

Elizondo, Virgilio P. *Galilean Journey: The Mexican-American Promise*. Rev. ed. Maryknoll: Orbis, 2000.

Francis, Bishop of Rome. *The Face of Mercy: Misericordiae Vultus—Bull of Indiction of the Extraordinary Jubilee of Mercy*. https://w2.vatican.va/content/francesco/en/apost_letters/documents/papa-francesco_bolla_20150411_misericordiae-vultus.html.

Gilson, Etienne. "*Regio dissimilitudinis* de Platon à Saint Bernard de Clairvaux." *MS* 9 (1947) 109–17.

Groody, Daniel G. *Border of Death, Valley of Life: An Immigrant Journey of Heart and Spirit*. Celebrating Faith. Lanham, MD: Rowman & Littlefield, 2002.

————. "Crossing the Divide: Foundations of a Theology of Migration and Refugees." *Theological Studies* 70 (2009) 638–67.

————. "Cup of Suffering, Chalice of Salvation: Refugees, Lampedusa and the Eucharist." *Theological Studies* 78 (2017) 960–87.

————. "Jesus and the Undocumented Immigrant: A Spiritual Geography of a Crucified People." *Theological Studies* 70 (2009) 298–316.

————. "Passing Over: Migration as Conversion." *International Review of Mission* 104 (2015) 46–60.

17. Boff, *Jesus Christ Liberator*, 178.

Harrington, Daniel J. "Matthew." In *The Collegeville Bible Commentary*, edited by Diane Bergant and R. J. Karris, 861–902. Collegeville: Liturgical, 1989.

Hatfield, Lawson G. "Betrothal." In *Holman Illustrated Bible Dictionary*, edited by Chad Brand, et al., 199–200. Nashville: Holman, 2003.

Heyer, Kristin E. *Kinship across Borders: A Christian Ethic of Immigration*. Washington, DC: Georgetown University Press, 2012.

Hing, Bill Ong. *Deporting Our Souls: Values, Morality, and Immigration Policy*. Cambridge: Cambridge University Press, 2006.

Hollenbach, David. *Humanity in Crisis: Ethical and Religious Response to Refugees*. Washington, DC: Georgetown University Press, 2020.

Luz, Ulrich. *Matthew 1–7: A Commentary on Matthew 1–7: A Continental Commentary*. Continental Commentaries. Rev. ed. Minneapolis: Fortress, 2007.

Meier, John P. *Mentor, Message, and Miracles*. A Marginal Jew: Rethinking the Historical Jesus 2. New York: Doubleday, 1994.

O'Neill, William. "No Longer Strangers (Ephesians 2:19): The Ethics of Migration." *Word and World* 29 (2009) 227–33.

Padilla, Elaine, and Peter C. Phan, eds. *Contemporary Issues of Migration and Theology*. Christianities of the World. New York: Palgrave Macmillan, 2013.

Phan, Peter C., ed. *Christian Theology in the Age of Migration: Implications for World Christianity*. Lanham, MD: Lexington, 2020.

———. "Deus Migrator—God the Migrant: Migration of Theology and Theology of Migration." *Theological Studies* 77 (2016) 845–68.

Rose, Ananda. *Showdown in the Sonoran Desert: Religion, Law, and the Immigration Controversy*. New York: Oxford University Press, 2012.

United States Conference of Catholic Bishops. *Strangers No Longer: Together on the Journey of Hope: A Pastoral Letter Concerning Migration*. Washington, DC: United States Conference of Catholic Bishops, 2003.

Wilbanks, Dana W. *Re-creating America: The Ethics of U.S. Immigration and Refugee Policy in a Christian Perspective*. Nashville: Abingdon, 1996.

Ecclesiological and Missiological Challenges

Global Migrations and Climate Refugees

Identity in the Anthropocene

Mark Douglas

COMPLICATED NARRATIVES AND COMPLICATED CAUSES: CLIMATE, VIOLENCE, AND MOVEMENT

LATE IN AUGUST OF 2005, a tropical depression over the Atlantic Ocean began to move westward, intensifying into hurricane status two hours before making landfall near Hallandale Beach on August 25. After weakening to tropical storm status as it passed over Florida, it grew in fury and size, becoming a Category 5 hurricane in the Gulf of Mexico, nearly doubling in size while there and becoming what was, at the time, the strongest hurricane ever recorded in the Gulf of Mexico. Though by the time Hurricane Katrina made landfall for a second time on August 29, and it had been downgraded to a Category 3 hurricane, its impact was, nevertheless, immense. The storm surge associated with the hurricane breached dozens of flood protection structures and submerged some 80 percent of the city of New Orleans, eventually leading to nearly 2,000 deaths along the Gulf Coast and costing around $125 billion, making it one of the deadliest and most costly natural disasters in the history of the United States.

Its immensity and impact—not to mention the failures in preparedness and response that we associate with it—have magnified its impact in American memories. We are left with images of a battered and leaking Superdome; of people on their rooftops awaiting rescue in St. Bernard Parish;

of FEMA trailers and of the Danziger Bridge, where several unarmed African Americans were shot by police while trying to leave the city. We remember phrases like President Bush's "Brownie, you're doing a heckuva job" and Kanye West's "George Bush doesn't care about black people." We compare disasters since then to Katrina, up to the present day: "The coronavirus isn't another Hurricane Katrina. It's worse."[1]

Of greater pertinence to this book were the more than a million Gulf Coast residents displaced by Hurricane Katrina, the largest diaspora of persons in US history. Though many people returned to their homes within days, some 600,000 were still displaced a month later. At their peak, more than a quarter of a million people were living in evacuee shelters; later there were still 114,000 people living in FEMA trailers. The population of New Orleans is still almost 100,000 less than it was immediately prior to Hurricane Katrina.[2] Those who were displaced fled to cities throughout the United States: Houston, Atlanta, Mobile, and even Chicago, where some 6,000 people were living a year after they took up residence there post-Katrina.[3]

A variety of terms were used to describe those who left the Gulf Coast immediately prior to, during, or after Katrina. "Internally displaced persons" was accurate, albeit a mouthful and unlikely to be used in a headline. "Displaced residents" was not uncommon, although quite the oxymoron. "Evacuees" worked immediately after the storm but became strained over time as people were either unable to return for months or never returned at all. One of the terms regularly used to describe such persons was "climate refugees,"[4] although no one fits the legal definition of a refugee, since that definition excludes those who leave their homes because those homes are significantly damaged or destroyed by natural disasters, not to mention the fact that almost none of those who evacuated the Gulf Coast crossed an international border, which is another part of the definition of a refugee. What then should we call them?

A few years after Hurricane Katrina (between 2007 and 2010) Syria suffered a series of the worst droughts in instrumentally recorded history. As noted in the *Proceedings of the National Academy of Sciences*, those droughts caused

> widespread crop failure and a mass migration of farming families to urban centers. Century-long observed trends in precipitation, temperature, and sea-level pressure, supported by climate

1. Gerson, "The Coronavirus Isn't Another."
2. Data from Plyer, "Facts for Features."
3. Avi, "Katrina Evacuees at Home."
4. See, e.g., Milman, "Meet the 'Climate Refugees.'"

model results, strongly suggest that anthropogenic forcing has increased the probability of severe and persistent droughts in this region, and made the occurrence of a 3-year drought as severe as that of 2007–2010 2 to 3 times more likely than by natural variability alone. We conclude that human influences on the climate system are implicated in the current Syrian conflict.[5]

The causes of the Syrian conflict that began in 2011 were manifold:

1. An oppressive regime engaging a restive population that was disproportionately young and male.

2. Regional unrest that was an outgrowth of the US-led invasion of Iraq in the century's first decade.

3. The advent of the Arab spring, especially as manifest in uprisings in Tunisia, Egypt, and Libya leavened uprisings throughout the Middle East and northern Africa.

4. The pretensions and reconfigurations of global powers like the United States of America and the Russian Federation as they exerted political muscle in the region.

5. Growing populist resentments toward global economic interdependence and increasing economic inequalities.

6. Tensions between the majority Sunni population and the Alawite/Shi'a ruling minority.

The war's manifestations were distressing:

1. The use of chemical weapons against civilian populations.

2. The arrival of ISIS as a player on the world political stage, filling a power void in the region.

3. The genocide of Yazidis and persecution of Christians by ISIS in Iraq.

4. Attacking United Nations peacekeepers.

5. Shifting and unstable political alliances within and between Western powers that undermined coherent responses and long-standing treaties.

And the war's consequences—diffused and partial though they have been—have been far-reaching:

---

5. Kelley et al., "Climate Change," 3241.

1. The empowering of far-right politicians and political platforms giving voice to xenophobia.

2. The stalling out of some social reforms in the Middle East.

3. The growth of religious animosities and extremist behavior throughout the world.

4. And, above all, millions of refugees streaming into surrounding countries, Europe and, to a lesser extent, North America.[6]

Though the numbers continue to change as the conflict in Syria persists and as people move into and out of Syria, estimates now put the total number of refugees at over five and a half million, with another six-plus million persons who have been internally displaced. Certainly, those who left Syria fit the accepted definition of refugees: they have crossed an international and recognized border due to war, violence, or a well-founded fear of persecution for reasons of political opinion or membership in a particular social group. Almost but perhaps not quite as certainly, they would not have left Syria were it not for the way droughts in the first decade of the twenty-first century helped to precipitate the events that led to the violence they were fleeing. So maybe they weren't "climate refugees," per se, but to ignore the way their status turned on both climatic and political events is not only to fail to understand the intersecting forces that shaped the conditions for their flight but to ignore the degree to which such intersecting forces are likely to play increasingly significant roles in the wars of the twenty-first century, as we face the political and social upheavals shaped by the impact of climate change, the catastrophic loss of biodiversity, the exponential growth in pollutants around the world, etc. Events in Syria demonstrate that the climatic events that lead to displacement can't be wholly separated from the political events that lead to it—or, more accurately, that the political events that lead to displacement should increasingly be linked to climatic events. That we are not well-situated to understand these links is something I will take up momentarily.

Next, a trip to yet another part of the world and another series of events. In eastern Africa, in an area composed of northwestern Kenya, South Sudan, southern Ethiopia, and northeastern Uganda, the Turkana and the Potok have been carrying out a low-level war against each other for decades. Both peoples are semi-nomadic pastoralists who share a great

6. It is important to note that most Syrian refugees went to other countries in the Middle East like Jordan and Turkey (and some then moved on from those places). I name their movement into Europe and North America, because it was in those places that the entrance of Syrian refugees caused the most political upheaval.

deal in common: their origins in Uganda, diets, social structures, economic systems, and some religious practices mirror each other's even though they speak different languages and tell different stories about themselves. They do not share the land with each other, though. Inter-ethnic conflict between the two groups has been ongoing since the late 1960s, and even though both the Kenyan government and the Roman Catholic Church have intervened at various points in the recent history of the conflict, it not only continues; it is growing.

The causes for this conflict are multiple and the source of much theoretical reflection, but among them are the impact of violence and corruption within early postcolonial political systems in the area, the ready availability of small arms, the aggravations of ethnic differences, long-standing competition for grazing areas, the loss of political authority among tribal elders, and economic instability exacerbated by these causes. None of these, by themselves, drive conflict and, to be clear, even their combination does not make conflict inevitable. They do make it more likely though. And, over the past several years, the escalation of the conflict between the Potok and the Turkana is at least partly being driven by climate change.

Surface temperatures in the area are rising, the rains of the Intertropical Convergence Zone are becoming more intermittent, and the glaciers of Mount Kenya that feed the water sources in the area are disappearing. Desertification in the region is intensifying and, with it, shortages of water and grasses for grazing cattle herds. As reported in Christian Parenti's book *Tropic of Chaos: Climate Change and the New Geography of Violence*, droughts that used to come every ten years are now coming almost every year, driving increasingly desperate and violent actions between the Turkana and Potok.[7] The Potok, who live mainly in the hills of eastern Uganda, cross the border into Kenya on cattle- camel- and goat- raids in which they also engage in murder and kidnapping. The Turkana respond in kind. Both groups are moving their herds around the area in increasingly desperate attempts to find enough food and water for them and to protect them from the other group.

How should we think about those movements? They are driven partly—but not exclusively—by climate change—but, again, not exclusively—by violence, and by the life that comes with being semi-nomadic pastoralists. Members of both groups cross back and forth over internationally-recognized borders. Both the changing climatic conditions and the violent skirmishes between the two groups further destabilize the political systems in the area and further inhibit economic stability.

7. Parenti, *Tropic of Chaos*, 40.

And, as a related question, how should we think about those who are moving, especially if the Turkana and Potok represent an increasing number of people groups around the world? Nomads? Yes, but the shape and seasons of their nomadism is changing. Climate refugees? The term hardly fits when the borders they cross are already simply incidental to their movements. Climate migrants? Using that term would involve parsing out important differences between migrants and nomads. Maybe we might develop a neologism like "climate nomads"? If so, how do we signal the degree to which their movements are also driven by political violence and economic vulnerability? Questions multiply.

Finally, one last trip—briefly—to another part of the world and another series of events. In 1946, the United States government "asked"[8] the 167 residents living on Bikini Atoll to leave their homes so that it could begin testing nuclear weapons there. They left and it did: over the next twelve years, the United States detonated twenty-three nuclear devices on or near the island. Initially, the residents of this small atoll in the Marshall Island chain were resettled on nearby Rongerik Atoll, where they continued to hope that they would be able to return to their home soon. Unable to sustain themselves on the smaller Rongerik Atoll and threatened with starvation and unable to return to their homes on Bikini Island, they then moved to Kwajalein Atoll before eventually settling on Kili Island, an island one-sixth the size of their home island. Twelve years after the last nuclear detonation, about 150 Bikini Islanders returned to their homes, having been told that it was safe to live there. They remained there for about ten years, until studies showed dangerously high levels of Cesium-137 and Strontium-90 in their bodies and they were, once again, removed. Most of them settled Majuro, the capital of the Marshall Islands. Several trusts were established to cover medical and other costs associated with their exposure and relocations; as of 2013, each individual affected was paid about $550 annually. Since then, a few caretakers live on the island, including the descendant of one of the original Bikini Islanders, but the island is otherwise uninhabited.[9]

Each of these four examples offers insight into only some of the many ways that the vectors of violence, changing environmental conditions, and the movement of peoples intersect with each other. Sometimes climatic events drive the movement of persons, which leads to violence. Sometimes climatic events lead to violence that drives the movement of persons. Sometimes violence induces changing environmental conditions, which drives

---

8. The word *asked* regularly appears in the literature, though the verb hardly conveys the range of forces, powers, and threats that came with such a request.

9. Data about Bikini Atoll and its inhabitants taken from Wikipedia, "Bikini Atoll."

the movement of persons. Sometimes the movement of peoples shapes the conditions for environmental crises that then lead to violence. And, in a highly mobile, fossil-fuel-driven world, the movement of peoples contributes to the conditions that shape climate change and, therein, violence.

Taken collectively, these four examples also start to reveal some of the limits of contemporary definitions about displaced persons; the strains on domestic and international law that are shaped, in part, by those definitional limits; the confusions about the connections between violence, environment, and displacement;[10] and questions about the origins and implications of such limits, strains, and confusions as we make our way further into the Anthropocene.[11]

DEFINITIONAL UNCLARITY AS A SIGN WORTH INTERPRETING

I am mostly a Wittgensteinian on matters of definitions. *Migrant, refugee, nomad, exile, asylum-seeker, internally-displaced person*: show me how you are using the term in context if you want me to understand what you mean

10. It is worth noting in this context that climate change can also inhibit the movement of persons by removing from them the very resources that migrants need in order to feel prepared to move, by increasing the amount of work needed to survive in an area, and/or by increasing in-group cohesion among otherwise disparate but similarly affected persons. Even by themselves, environmental changes simply do not shape the movement of persons in uniform ways.

11. *The Anthropocene* is a term popularized by chemist Paul Crutzen at the beginning of the twenty-first century to describe the epoch in which human beings gained the capacity to fundamentally alter the earth's geological and ecological systems. While start dates for the Anthropocene vary—from the dawn of agriculture and animal domestication to the dawn of the widespread use of fossil fuels to the first explosion of a nuclear weapon on July 16, 1945—most people use the term to describe the time period that human beings are now entering, which will be defined by environmental concerns. Meant to convey the idea of a human-influenced time period that can be measured on a geological scale, the term is used informally in scientific and popular culture, and neither a firm starting point nor an agreed upon definition exists for it. When I use the term in this chapter, I mean it to convey the time period that we are now entering in which environmental concerns are so severe, so widespread, so dramatic, and so impactful of human existence that human beings will increasingly make sense of the world around them through environmental lenses: not only will climate change, the catastrophic loss of biodiversity, growing human populations, the proliferation of waste, and other environmental concerns become problems to which we must attend; they will shape the way we understand and address other problems. As such, I will use the terms *Anthropocene* and *Environmental Age* as near-synonyms, recognizing that *environmental* is also a politically fraught term within the literatures of those who engage matters having to do with the interactions and interconnectedness of the natural world and human beings.

by it. There are, though, important ramifications that come with which terms we use: admission into some well-defined groups that comes with the application of a noun like *refugee* or *asylum-seeker* also offers access to a range of goods and services (e.g., financial grants, food, tools, shelter, schools, medical care) as determined by the agreements of international law. Adjectives used to qualify the terms associated with such groups (like *climate* before *refugee*) can have the effect of preventing such access[12] and doubled adjectives (like *forced climate* before *migrant*) are no better. Short of an as yet unshaped set of international agreements about how to define such persons that can also drive work toward establishing the benefits that those who fit such a definition receive, there is little reason to think that we will get any clarity about what to call such persons. Partly because of the costs that would come with such an agreement, there is little international will toward establishing a widely acceptable definition of those whose displacement is driven by climatic events. Even major international organizations that deal with the movement of peoples struggle with language. The International Organization for Migration settles—with some hemming and hawing—on "forced climate migrant,"[13] the entry on climate change and migration in *The Oxford Research Encyclopedia of Climate Science* uses "environmental migrant,"[14] and Lauren Nishimura uses "climate change migrant."[15] Among the failings of any of these terms—a failing highlighted above—is that each definition relies on the ability to separate out a range of causes for displacement (climate change, violence, politics, economics, etc.) that may be inseparable in practice. And here, I am no help: Wittgensteinians don't necessarily make good lawyers and they certainly don't make good encyclopedists.[16]

Rather than attempting to arrive at a definition and then pursue implications, perhaps it is worth treating the difficulty of arriving at a definition as a sign worth interpreting in order to understand its implications. There are a variety of reasons for this definitional unclarity. As late as it was in coming into existence compared to other parts of international law, the development

12. See, e.g., Brown, "Migration and Climate Change," esp. 36–40.

13. Brown, "Migration and Climate Change," 13–15.

14. Klepp, "Climate Change and Migration."

15. See Nishimura, "'Climate Change Migrants.'"

16. For further explorations of questions about whether "climate refugees" should be accorded the status of refugees (and, therein, whether the term *climate refugee* is functional), see Mukuki, "Re-imagining the Concept." For more on the failings of the international community to deal with persons whose displacement is linked to environmental changes due, in part, to definitional unclarity, see Marshall, "Politicizing Environmental Displacement."

of international laws around refugees still preceded by decades the recognition of anthropogenic climate change. Likewise, environmental security studies are fairly late on to the scene, arriving only in the last decades of the twentieth century and growing in prominence only in the first decades of the twenty-first. The prioritization of neoliberal economic policies for shaping globalization over the past forty years have not only oriented international bodies around trade but have undermined the coherence and strength of such bodies to address environmental and humanitarian crises. Concomitantly, a world order based around the Westphalian sovereignty of nation-states[17] makes it difficult for those who are displaced—and especially those crossing international borders—to get much standing for addressing the problems they face. Climate migrants do not garner the attention that refugees fleeing war do. And those who do study climate change and migration do so from a wide range of disciplines within Western academic frameworks that tend to be unhelpfully insular.[18]

At least one further cause for such definitional unclarity is worth exploring: its genealogy. Perhaps if we can get a sense of its DNA, we might be better located not only to understand the sources of its unclarity but also of thinking our way past it toward shaping moral and functional structural responses to those whose movements are linked to environmental and political causes. Toward developing such a genealogy, I turn to one of the founders of international law, Hugo Grotius.

THE ORIGINS OF INTERNATIONAL LAW AND THE LACUNAE OF DISPLACED PERSONS[19]

Hugo Grotius (or Huig de Groot) was born in Delft on Easter in 1583, the oldest child of Jan de Groot and Alida van Overschie. At the time, the Dutch Republic was in its second decade of a war intended to free it of Hapsburg rule, and the Republic's economic power—particularly on the seas—was growing rapidly. Trained in humanist and Aristotelian thought by Protestant (Calvinist) parents during his childhood, Grotius's prodigious intellectual abilities soon revealed themselves: he entered Leiden University at

17. The sovereignty of nation-states has been the sine qua non of modern nation states (so, e.g., international law is premised on it, and it is central to the charter of the United Nations) and is associated in history with the Peace of Westphalia (1648). See Croxton, "Peace of Westphalia."

18. See, again, Klepp, "Climate Change and Migration."

19. Portions of this section come from my forthcoming book, *Modernity, the Environment, and the Just War Tradition* (currently under review).

eleven, accompanied leading Dutch politician Johan van Oldenbarnevelt to Paris on a diplomatic mission at fifteen, published his first book at sixteen, was appointed as an advocate to the Hague at about that same time, and was selected as the official Latin historiographer of the United Provinces at eighteen.

As an adult, Grotius continued the ambitious and intellectually prodigious path he began in childhood. He worked as a lawyer, politician, diplomat, historian, philologist, classicist, poet, and theologian. His passions in these areas are visible in his writings and his life. As the Pensionary of Rotterdam (akin to its governor), his pursuit of ecclesial moderation in the Netherlands led him to write both *Ordinum Hollandiae ac Westfrisiae pietas* (1613) and *Resolution for Peace in the Church* (1614), thereby incurring the wrath of Prince Maurice of Nassau. These works offered Arminian responses to conflicts with harder-core Calvinists. The prince's wrath at those works, especially when linked to Grotius's long friendship with the prince's opponent, Oldenbarnevelt, led to Grotius's imprisonment in the castle at Loevestein. After escaping prison hidden in a box of books, Grotius settled in Paris, where he would expand a book begun in prison, *De Veritate Religionis Christianae* (published in Dutch in 1622 and Latin in 1627) and write *De Jure Belli ac Pacis* (1625).

After further adventures in Sweden and Paris, the ship he was sailing on foundered off the coast of Germany, and Grotius became gravely ill as a result. He died at Rostock on August 28, 1645, and his body was returned to Delft to be buried shortly thereafter.

While he wrote widely and engaged in an epic life, Grotius would be best known for two things: among Protestants, he would be known for his defense of Arminianism against Calvinism and his pursuit of unity across Roman Catholic/Protestant divisions; within the wider world, he would be known for *De Jure Belli ac Pacis*, the first great text of international law. Both pursuits reveal a scholar who was imagining (and inventing) a new understanding of the self: the sovereign citizen who shaped the sovereign state. So, for instance, his Arminian self can will the creation of a peaceful church through the power of free choice; his political self can will the creation of a peaceful nation through the power of humanist thought; and his juridical self can will the creation of peace between nations by emphasizing the sovereignty of persons and states.

It isn't simply that a new way of thinking about the self leads to a new way of thinking about the state and the rules that will govern its interactions with other states; it's that selves create states that mirror their vision of themselves (hence the language of "sovereign" applied to both state and individual) and advance the authority of those selves to make their own distinct ways in the world. As Grotius shaped modern international law through his advocacy for such a self, he also shaped modernity and the modern self: an agent capable of making decisions and acting on them apart from undue external forces whose voluntaristic engagement with religion, the market, and the state shapes a religion that prioritizes personal choice, a market that favors free trade, and a state capable of seeing its members as citizens.

One of the paradoxes of Grotius's thought emerges here: in spite of the fact that he was, himself, at various times a refugee and even though Europe was awash in refugees as he was writing, Grotius gave almost no attention to them. In the whole of his three-volume *Jure Belli ac Pacis*, they warranted barely a few paragraphs. Why?

One reason for Grotius's lack of attention to refugees in his developing international law is that refugees constitute a problematic category for any sort of international law premised on state sovereignty while recognizing the rights of persons. Not only are refugees crossing borders; they're doing so to escape their treatment at the hands of one sovereign country by entering another. When they cross those borders, they carry their beliefs and cultures with them, and it is an open question as to whether such beliefs and cultures fit much better in their new space than their old one. Their commitments to whatever state they find themselves in are treated with suspicion, given the fact that those very commitments didn't seem to fit in whatever state they had left. They are dependent on others for aid and support and can threaten to swamp the social services that are available in their new location. In sufficient numbers, they reinforce the very distinction between being part of a state and being part of a nation that the notion of the modern nation-state attempts to erase. Four hundred years into the development of international law, not only the status but even basic conceptions of refugees remain a thicket of competing values, opinions, and political possibilities.[20] One wonders how refugees would be understood and their conditions addressed in international law had Grotius paid more attention to his own

20. "The refugee in international law occupies a legal space characterized, on the one hand, by the principle of State sovereignty and the related principles of territorial supremacy and self-preservation; and, on the other hand, by competing humanitarian principles deriving from general international law (including the purposes and principles of the United Nations) and from treaty. Refugee law nevertheless remains an incomplete legal regime of protection, imperfectly covering what ought to be a situation of exception. It goes some way to alleviate the plight of those affected by breaches of human rights standards or by the collapse of an existing social order in the wake of revolution, civil strife, or aggression; but it is incomplete so far as refugees and asylum seekers may still be denied even temporary protection, safe return to their homes, or compensation." Goodwin-Gill and McAdam, *The Refugee*, 1.

situation in shaping early international law. Almost undoubtedly, the trajectory of international law toward state sovereignty would be different.

More fundamentally, refugees also create a problem for modern identity. Refugees clearly have the capacity to make choices, but those choices are not framed by identification with their own state; indeed, they regularly make choices to identify with a non-state community as they decide where to go. Their choices simultaneously reveal their independence from others and put them in situations where they are likely to be dependent on others. Flight from state-sanctioned violence is tantamount to a rejection of the modern nation state's claim of a monopoly on the legitimate use of force and flight from non-state actors (e.g., religious groups, gangs, tribes, families) is tantamount to an accusation that the modern nation-state does not have such a monopoly. And their claims to rights (for, e.g., economic and political support) come not because they are citizens, but because they are human beings, therein separating out modern existential goods from the political systems that undergird and sustain those goods.

The problems that refugees create within the framework of modern identity are exacerbated when the forces driving displacement are linked to events in the natural world. And, again, Grotius both exemplifies and shapes these problems. One manifestation of the way Grotius emphasizes the power and voluntarism of the modern self is to locate that self's relation to the non-human natural world as a relation of owner to property.[21] Throughout his disparate works, Grotius advanced three foundational claims: that in the beginning, when human beings exist in a state of nature, all things are free, shared, and seemingly abundant; that by seizing particular things and occupying particular spaces, those things and spaces become our own; and that once things are owned, we have the right to fight to keep them as an expression of justice. These claims undergirded his arguments for using force to protect property in his just war thinking, for distributing resources in his broader development of international law, and for his humanism in his religious writings.

Note, though, what follows from these claims: the non-human natural world sits as object to be controlled more than a force capable of shaping human activities. It is inert rather than dynamic; a mechanism to be harnessed more than a partner in development; the stage upon which human beings perform rather than an actor in their dramas. While Grotius was not the sole progenitor of such a vision (one thinks of the impact of Francis Bacon's similar sensibility) and while this vision has funded an explosion

21. On Hugo Grotius and his understanding of human relations to the non-human natural world, see, among others, Mancilla, "What We Own Before Property"; Salter, "Hugo Grotius"; and Porras, "Appropriating Nature."

on scientific and technological advancement since the seventeenth century, it has also complicated human recognition of our enmeshment with the non-human natural world by simplifying the way human beings relate to that world.

A CONCEPTUAL DISPLACEMENT
DRIVEN BY DISPLACED PERSONS

One consequence of this vision is that it shaped a conceptual framework—a modern social imaginary, to use Charles Taylor's term[22]—in which political matters are exclusively intra-human affairs. For much of modern history, such a framework has been mostly adequate for framing large political questions. Yet at the beginning of Anthropocene, such a framework increasingly falters, especially when human and non-human natural forces interact in shaping and reshaping political systems and sensibilities.

It follows that when climatic events force people to move—even when climatic events are the only drivers of that movement—they face at least two obstacles. First, they encounter a comparatively underdeveloped version of international law which is unlikely to be further developed because their very existence and actions sit in tension with modern understandings of the self and the state. And, second, they lack recourse to the resources of international law because that law provides almost no way to recognize or respond to the force that the non-human natural world exerts on them.

But as my examples at the beginning of this chapter reveal, climatic changes are seldom the only drivers of the movement of peoples. Climatic changes mix with political and economic drivers (including those that shape patterns and/or explosions of violence) in complex and multivariable ways such that even adequately naming all the forces at work in driving such movement still will not be adequate to shape appropriate responses to that movement, whether at individual, corporate, or structural levels. The modern vision given voice to by Hugo Grotius (among others) has shaped a way of relating politics and violence that has long been ill-equipped to respond to violence that isn't primarily inter-state violence. Refugees have endured such an ill-equipped version of politics within international law. That same vision has separated the political realm from the realm of the non-human natural world, making it difficult to see and respond to their interactions in driving displacement. Climate refugees thus face not only an ill-equipped version of politics within natural law but an unhelpfully framed understanding of the interactions between political forces and those of the

22. Taylor, *Modern Social Imaginaries.*

non-human natural world. And, commutatively, that same vision has all but prevented us from naming the connections between climate change and violence.[23] Refugees fleeing the toxic mix of violence and climate change have, at this point, no effective language by which to advocate for either rights or repair. And their numbers are only likely to grow exponentially in the coming years.

These are concerns that the international community needs to address, and to do so with some urgency. Doing so, though, will mean moving away from the modern social imaginary that has structured international law regarding displaced persons. And as it shapes new forms of address, it will inevitably have to rethink questions of identity, agency, and the relations between politics, violence, and human interactions with the non-human natural world. The displacements of climate migrants may well drive our own displacement from a modern social imaginary into an environmental one.[24]

BIBLIOGRAPHY

Avi, Mema. "Katrina Evacuees at Home in Chicago." *Chicago Defender*, August 30, 2006. https://web.archive.org/web/20071212040739/http:/chicagodefender.com/page/local.cfm?ArticleID=6776.

Brown, Oli. "Migration and Climate Change." *IOM Migration Research Series* 31. Geneva: International Organization for Migration, 2008.

Croxton, Derek. "The Peace of Westphalia of 1648 and the Origins of Sovereignty." *International History Review* 21 (1999) 569–91.

Gerson, Michael. "The Coronavirus Isn't Another Hurricane Katrina. It's Worse." *Washington Post*, March 9, 2020. https://nu.aeon.co/images/3f59683d-9895-4acc-82f6-d506470a2890/header_essay-sk-a-1718.jpg.

Goodwin-Gill, Guy S., and Jane McAdam. *The Refugee in International Law*. 3rd ed. New York: Oxford University Press, 2007.

Hsiang, Solomon M., et al. "Civil Conflicts Are Associated with the Global Climate." *Nature* 476 (2011) 438–41.

Kelley, Colin P. et al., "Climate Change in the Fertile Crescent and Implications of the Recent Syrian Drought." *Proceedings of the National Academy of Sciences* 112 (2015) 3241–46.

23. Solomon Hsiang and his colleagues were the first to establish a clear causative relationship between changes in climate and violence; they did so in 2011. See Hsiang et al., "Civil Conflicts."

24. As I write this piece, the SARS-CoV-2 pandemic has swept the globe and is ravaging countries around the world. It is, in its own way, an apocalypse for us: a revelation about human interconnectedness with the non-human natural world that is, itself, shaping conditions for violence and the movement of peoples. Had I a greater word limit and more wisdom, exploring the revelation that COVID-19 is could be an important next focal point.

Klepp, Silja. "Climate Change and Migration." In *Oxford Research Encyclopedia of Climate Science*. New York: Oxford University Press, 2016. https://oxfordre.com/climatescience/view/10.1093/acrefore/9780190228620.001.0001/acrefore-9780190228620-e-42?rskey=SaHgVn&result=6.

Mancilla, Alejandra. "What We Own Before Property: Hugo Grotius and the *Suum*." *Grotiana* 36 (2015) 63–77.

Marshall, Nicole. "Politicizing Environmental Displacement: A Four-Category Approach to Defining Environmentally Displaced People." *Refugee Review* 2 (2015) 96–112.

Milman, Oliver. "Meet the 'Climate Refugees' Who Already Had to Leave Their Homes." *Guardian*, September 24, 2018. https://www.theguardian.com/environment/2018/sep/24/climate-refugees-new-orleans-houston-hurricane-katrina-hurricane-harvey.

Mukuki, Allan M. "Re-imagining the Concept of Forced Migration in the Face of Climate Change." *Groningen Journal of International Law* 70 (2019) 73–98.

Nishimura, Lauren. "'Climate Change Migrants': Impediments to a Protection Framework and the Need to Incorporate Migration into Climate Change Adaptation Strategies." *International Journal of Refugee Law* 27 (2015) 107–34.

Parenti, Christian. *Tropic of Chaos: Climate Change and the New Geography of Violence*. New York City: Nation, 2011.

Plyer, Allison. "Facts for Features: Hurricane Katrina." *Data Center*, August 26, 2016. https://www.datacenterresearch.org/data-resources/katrina/facts-for-impact/.

Porras, Ileana. "Appropriating Nature: Commerce, Property, and the Commodification of Nature in the Law of Nations." *Leiden Journal of International Law* 27 (2014) 641–60.

Salter, John. "Hugo Grotius: Property and Consent." *Political Theory* 29 (2001) 537–55.

Taylor, Charles. *Modern Social Imaginaries*. Durham, NC: Duke University Press, 2003.

Wikipedia. "Bikini Atoll." https://en.wikipedia.org/wiki/Bikini_Atoll#Resident_and_non-resident_population.

"The Sea Has Betrayed Me"

Broken Journeys and Restoring Survivors to the Image of God

George Kalantzis

"Love your neighbor as yourself."

—JESUS OF NAZARETH (MARK 12:31; MATT 22:39)

"THE WORST REFUGEE CAMP ON EARTH"

IN 2018–2019 I WAS on sabbatical leave from teaching,[1] engaging in research on the Greek response to the most recent refugee crisis, the one that made the news in the summer of 2015, when 85 percent of the more than a million migrants who crossed by sea into Europe came through Greece. My research concentrated on the response of the local Christian communities, focusing primarily (but not exclusively) on the various expressions of the evangelical churches. Moria Refugee Camp is Europe's largest refugee camp and is contained within the Greek island of Lesbos, known since antiquity for its natural beauty and welcoming inhabitants. As we were getting ready to visit the refugee camp in August 2018, BBC reporter and producer Catrin Nye produced a fourteen-minute film of her own recent visit to the

1. The leave was supported by the John Stott Global Faculty Study and Research Leave at Wheaton College and the John Stott Faculty Grant in Human Needs and Global Resources, for which I am deeply thankful. I am also grateful to Dr. Laura S. Meitzner Yoder, the John Stott Chair of Human Needs and Global Resources and director of the program at Wheaton College, for her friendship and encouragement throughout the years.

camp. The film described the conditions at one of the so-called "hotspots" of the refugee crisis for the last five years under the title: "The Worst Refugee Camp on Earth."[2] "At Moria camp on the Greek island of Lesbos," wrote Nye, "there is deadly violence, overcrowding, appalling sanitary conditions and now a charity says children as young as 10 are attempting suicide."

The camp in Moria was never meant to be what it has become. In order to reduce the number of people arriving into Europe from Turkey, in March 2016 the EU and Turkey reached a landmark agreement under which refugees seeking asylum on Greek islands[3] have been forbidden from leaving what are called "hotspot" camps to travel to the mainland until their status had been established.[4] Established originally to provide temporary housing for 2,000–3,000 asylum seekers as they initiated their registration processes and movement into Europe, Moria Refugee Camp is overflowing with over 9,000 refugees and asylum seekers from some 50 countries and ethnic groups.

Conditions at the camp were so appalling that charities like Médecins Sans Frontières (MSF) had actually left in protest. "The place smells of raw sewage, and there are around 70 people per toilet," narrated Nye. "The violence in the camp is extreme. In May, hundreds of Kurdish people fled because of a huge battle largely between Arab and Kurdish men." Nye spent a considerable amount of time listening to Luca Fontana, an epidemiologist and the coordinator of MSF in Lesbos, who had previously worked in war-refugee camps and Ebola outbreaks in Africa. "People, even if infected by Ebola, they still have the hope to survive or the support of their family, their society, their village, their relatives," Fontana said. "Here, no, here the hope is taken away by the system."

Toward the end of the film, Nye sat at a picnic table outside the camp with Ali, a Kurd from Afrin in Syria, who fled his country because his home, like most of his city, was destroyed during the civil war that is still raging. Next to Ali sat his young daughter, looking at her father as he narrated their journey. Ali spoke of the three years he and his family spent in Turkey as they tried to gather the money necessary to pay the smugglers for the sea journey across to Europe, in Greece. "When we first got to Moria it was a very violent surprise," Ali stated in a matter-of-fact tone. "We found that there was already existing sectarianism and racism. Whether it was between Sunni and Shia Muslims or Kurds, Arabs and Afghans." To the surprise of

2. Nye, *Worst Refugee Camp on Earth*. See also Nye's written report, "Children 'Attempting Suicide.'"

3. The Greek islands of Chios, Lesbos, and Samos comprised one of the two main routes of migration for the approximately 1.7 million refugees who crossed over into Europe in 2015–2016; Italy being the second route. BBC News, "Migrant Crisis."

4. Boffey and Smith, "Oxfam."

no one who has ever worked at a war refugee camp, the conflict between rebel groups in Syria had also come into the camp in Europe. Tribal identities and conflict follow people even as they flee. "The political problems that were happening in Syria also played out in Moria," said Ali. "The same problems of the YPG, Qasads, Al-Nursa, Free Syrian Army and Daesh [(ISIS)]. It moved here." And then Ali's affect changed. He strained to contain the tears running down his cheeks: "No matter what someone might say, if you don't live through it you don't understand. It's like the war in Syria, and even uglier." Nye asked, "What did you expect when you came here, to Europe?" Visibly beaten, Ali hesitated for a moment, but then he gave voice to the thousands who took the journey with him: "For three years I have trusted the sea would take me somewhere better. But the sea has betrayed me."

A REFUGEE CAMP DOES NOT EXIST IN A VACUUM[5]

In spite of the realities experienced by the refugees housed in Moria and other camps in Greece and northern Europe, the harshness of their experience does not exist in a vacuum.

Humanitarian crises range from the Syrian war to the Botswana drought and the Venezuelan collapse. The numbers are staggering. In 2020, the UN estimates that approximately 1 percent of the world's population is displaced. The United Nations High Commissioner for Refugees, the UN refugee agency, estimates the number of forcibly displaced persons (FDP) worldwide at the end of 2019 to be in excess of 79.5 million—26 million of whom are refugees. Sixty-eight per cent of FDP came from just five countries: Syria, 6.6 million; Venezuela 3.7 million; Afghanistan, 2.7 million; South Sudan, 2.2 million; and Myanmar, 1.1 million. The UN reports that 30,000 people were uprooted every day in 2019 alone, bringing the total number of newly displaced persons to 11 million for 2019. Of those, 8.6 million were newly internally displaced persons (IDP) (bringing the total number of IDP to 45.7 million), while 2.4 million were new refugees and asylum seekers. The total of those seeking asylum was estimated to be 45.7 million persons.[6] To these, one should add the 4.2 million stateless persons who are in an indefinite state of displacement without hope of redress. Eighty percent of the world's displaced persons are hosted by developing countries or territories affected by acute food insecurity and malnutrition. Forty-eight percent of the world's refugees are women and girls, and 50 percent of the world's refugees

5. McAuliffe and Bhadria, eds., *World Migration Report 2020,* by the International Organization for Migration, is the most comprehensive report on migration to date.

6. Albinson, *Refugee Realities.*

are under 18 years old. Of the over 2 million asylum applicants in 2019, only 107,800 (5.39 percent) were resettled in 26 countries.[7]

Like most of Europe, Greece was completely unprepared for the realities of 2015–2017. In 2015, of the 1,011,700 people who reached Europe across the Mediterranean, 856,723 came through Greece. The landmark figure, "which was reached late on December 29, also indicated that 84 percent of those arriving in Europe came from the world's top 10 refugee producing countries, fleeing war and persecution."[8] Of those attempting the arduous journey into Europe by sea, 3,735 persons were missing in 2015, believed drowned. For the period 2015–2020, UNHCR calculates the total number of those missing at sea to over 19,500.

In spite of its aspirational policies on migration/immigration, Greece could not have been prepared for this reality. Since the middle of the first decade of the twenty-first century, the country has faced chronic unemployment and economic stagnation. Oxford Analytica records that in the period 2012–2017 the unemployment rate ranged between 21.5–27.5 percent.[9] In an in-depth review of the response to the refugee crisis by the Greek State, political scientist Dimitris Skleparis of Glasgow University concluded, "The Greek state's response to the migration challenge in the 1990s and 2000s was characterised by unpreparedness, inconsistencies and short-termism. [Because of this new reality,] migration to Greece was reflexively understood and governed in security terms."[10] The relocation of asylum seekers into the EU is painfully slow and inefficient. The European Commission reports that by mid-2017 only 15 percent (9,610) of the total number of 63,302 relocation petitions from Greece have been filled, "leaving thousands in limbo in the country."[11] Those waiting for their applications to be processed are hosted in the mainland, either in official and informal camps run by the state, NGOs and volunteers, or in apartments and hotels run by municipal authorities and NGOs. "Those living in camps are currently in need of health care, education, services for survivors of gender-based violence, and mental health and psychosocial support services. Some access to the aforementioned services is available, but the quality varies greatly across camps. Food security and accommodation conditions also need to be improved for many of those living in the camps."[12]

7. "Figures at a Glance."
8. Clayton and Holland, "Over One Million Sea Arrivals."
9. *Oxford Analytica*, "Greece Will Struggle to Reverse 'Brain Drain.'"
10. Skleparis, "Greek Response," 2.
11. Skleparis, "Greek Response," 5.
12. Skleparis, "Greek Response," 6.

COMMUNITIES OF FAITH AND RECOVERY

In most of our discussions about displaced persons, our language (even in Christian circles) tends to veer toward legal descriptors and terminology to describe persons: *Refugee, Migrant, Immigrant, Asylum Seeker*, etc. That is understandable as we seek to engage each other clearly, with identifiable terms across disciplines and legal systems. Yet, throughout the years there has been another term that seems to me to be a far better descriptor, for it shifts the focus from *status* to *person*, from legal description for purposes of registration and accommodation to the real subject; and that term is *survivor*.

As one watches the face of Ali change from stoic recounting of a journey to the shattered reality of his family's experiences, as one follows the quiet eyes of his young daughter listening to her father trying hard to maintain his dignity through the tears, *survivors* is the only descriptor that seems to capture their reality. These are not simply entries in legal categories and bureaucratic debates. They are *survivors* of war and famine, extortion, exploitation, and rape. These are women and men who have endured. They have survived. Yet, in the process, they have also been *dehumanized*. They have become numbers. Attention has shifted from who they are to the legal status under which they can be categorized. Thus, the trauma of the circumstances that forced people from their homes, families, and communities is compounded daily. Study after study, for example, reveals the stark reality that the number one fear among migrants of all categories is sexual violence—and those who work with survivors bear witness to that throughout the world. Whether during the journey from one's homeland or as they wait for transport from one region to another or even at the refugee camps and relocation centers, sexual assault and rape are common experiences affecting refugees of both sexes, of all ages, throughout the migratory journey.[13]

The International Association for Refugees (IAFR) has identified the continuum of trauma and recovery common in humanitarian disasters, including the unique role communities of faith have in the long-term process of recovery for the survivors. The continuum is represented in figure 1.

---

13. E.g., Araujo, "Prevalence of Sexual Violence."

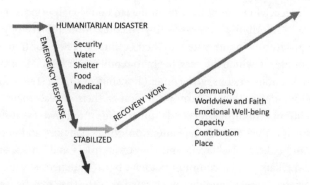

FIGURE 1. IAFR CONTINUUM OF RECOVERY

Thomas Albinson, the president of the IAFR, has remarked often, "When humanitarian disaster strikes, disaster response agencies need to rush in and stop the free fall of those directly affected by providing security, water, shelter, food, and medical care." The original, short horizontal line represents the level of "normalcy" in which each situation or person is in as the acute humanitarian event (or series of events) erupts. The emergency response to the humanitarian disaster is usually the task of large state and non-state actors with adequate resources who can intervene en masse to address the crisis and stop it from causing further harm. Otherwise people continue to die. During this acute phase of the humanitarian disaster, persons are most traumatized and in need of assistance, dependent on outside agents for survival. Survival is paramount during this phase, and all other elements of what we usually consider as contributing to one's well-being, personhood, and humanity, whether intellectual, professional, artistic, relational, or even spiritual are pushed aside for the sake of survival. This is also the most acute phase of *dehumanizing*; people lose their own agency and are most often completely dependent on the agency of others for survival.

The second phase in this continuum is that of stabilization. Refugee and resettlement camps and other such expressions of post-event stabilization are usually the purview of non-state actors such as the UN, NGOs, etc., and even though state actors may be involved in this phase, it is most often other relief and care organizations that work with the survivors of humanitarian disasters for the long term. What is evident during this phase, however, is that even though a basic level of stability may have been achieved, where security, water, shelter, food, and medical care have been established at one level or another, survivors experience a deep sense of brokenness and of being dehumanized further, for they still have not regained agency. "All too often, refugees find themselves viewed only as people in need. They are confined to the receiving end of the humanitarian and social services that keep them alive."[14] As Albinson notes, "A tiny fraction of the refugee population is given opportunity to integrate into their country of refuge or to resettle to another country in which they can begin to rebuild their lives. Most languish in camps, detention centers, government housing, or on the streets for years and even decades as they wait on a solution to their displacement. Life in such conditions is nothing short of dehumanizing."[15] Survivors may be (relatively) safe, but they are still dependent on others. Doctors and engineers, teachers and bakers, bricklayers and lawyers, farmers and artists, spiritual leaders and pillars of their communities have been "flattened" to the status of "disempowered refugee," and they are treated as such. They may be "safe," but they are far from recovered. Often, they are far from being seen as human.

The last, and perhaps longest and most difficult phase of the continuum is that of recovery and *rehumanizing*. This, we argue at IAFR, is where communities of faith have a central role, for no NGO or state agency can walk with a survivor through the processing of one's trauma with the patience, care, and affection a community of faith can. No state program or humanitarian organization can reintroduce the sense of belonging, of "being seen," of being recognized as human again; not in a holistic sense. It is at this juncture of recovery, however, that communities of faith are uniquely situated to be places of long-term recovery. Christian churches and communities of faith, who recognize every person as an *image-bearer* of God, have the unique responsibility in this continuum of recovery to assist in the long and arduous work of *rehumanizing* survivors and restoring hope by being places of safety and healing, strengthening community, faith, emotional well-being, and personal capacity. Christian communities ought to recognize their unique role to *not* be limited to relief and aid work akin to that of the NGOs, but rather to "invest in the [survivor's] resilience and seek to strengthen their sense of personal worth and belonging as they work to regain a sense of normalcy in life."[16] And this begins with the stories we tell.

---

14. IAFR, "IAFR Continuum of Recovery." At the Fall 2019 Human Needs and Global Resources held at Wheaton College, Dr. Myrto Theocharous argued, "When God made humans in his image, he placed us on a path of becoming increasingly humane . . . The path of justice is the path of Jesus Christ and being the church means being placed on this path, the *only* path there is. Learning it, failing, repenting and continuously returning to it. No other path exists for the church."

15. Albinson, "Stand Up, Speak Out," 2.

16. IAFR, "Unique Role."

POWER, STORIES, AND THE RE-HUMANIZING COMMUNITY

When we, in positions of power, tell the stories of migrants, how do we narrate them? Whose stories are they? To what end?[17] Language matters. Stories matter. Stories are not "innocent." They are system-formative. We know this instinctively. We know it from experience; we know that the language we use in the telling of our own stories and those of others provides the structure of our experience, understanding, and perspectives. Language shapes our humanity and the communities of discourses and practices in which we participate. Narratives are identity-formative. As we narrate, language relates others to us and us to others. Through stories we enter into a social and psychological transaction of power that forms us into the people we are and the people we wish to be. Because storytelling forms the teller, the hearer, and the very story itself, *how* we tell stories is equally as important as *which* stories we choose to tell.[18]

In *I Saw Ramallah*, Palestinian poet Mourid Barghouti reminds us that stories also have the power to dispossess people:

> It is easy to blur the truth with a simple linguistic trick: start your story from "Secondly" . . . and the world will be turned upside-down. Start your story with "Secondly," and the arrows of the Red Indians are the original criminals and the guns of the white men are entirely the victims. It is enough to start with "Secondly," for the anger of the black man against the white to be barbarous. Start with "Secondly," and Gandhi becomes responsible for the tragedies of the British.[19]

Start the story of people on their migratory journey with the crossing of immigrants, migrants, asylum-seekers, or refugees from Turkey into Europe, and we lose the war-torn cities, the collapsed apartment buildings that have buried their tenants, the famine that killed thousands, or the generational oppression and war that disinherited the rest. Start with the powerlessness of the survivors and arms stretching for help to come out of the sinking dingy that brought them across the waters, and we will never see anything else. Start with "secondly," and we miss the beauty, the goodness, the eloquence, the artistry, the intellect, the capacity, the faith, love, and hope. Start with "secondly," and we lose our culpability in the economic, political, religious, and social systems that have created and continue to contribute to the global

17. See, e.g., Pittaway et al., "'Stop Stealing Our Stories.'"
18. I have argued this previously in Kalantzis, "Bodies Transgressing Boundaries."
19. Barghouti, *Ra'aytu Ram Allah*, 178.

nexus of oppression and exploitation causing hunger, conflict, and disease, the manifest causes of displacement throughout the globe. Start with "secondly," and we lose the fact that poverty and hunger are the result of our own choices, that neither is unavoidable, and that both can be reversed and resolved in our lifetime. Start with "secondly," and people become a single story; they are dispossessed and they become "other." The Nigerian writer Chimamanda Ngozi Adichie speaks of the danger of "single stories" and the markers of power operative in them. "Power is the ability not just to tell the story of another person, but to make it the definitive story of that person," says Adichie. "The consequence of the single story is this: It robs people of dignity. It makes our recognition of our equal humanity difficult. It emphasizes how we are different rather than how we are similar. . . . Stories matter. Many stories matter. Stories have been used to dispossess and to malign, but stories can also be used to empower and to humanize. Stories can break the dignity of a people, but stories can also repair that broken dignity."[20]

The gospel restores the dignity of people as image-bearers of God. From beginning to end, that is the Christian story. Christian communities have the unique responsibility to reverse this "othering," this dispossessing, to restore broken dignity and become the welcoming communities within which persons can move on the path of regaining the humanity that has been stripped from them. For the gospel to bear its social significance, however, it also "requires the recognition of the narrative structure of Christian convictions for the life of the church."[21] That means Christian communities need to be continuously reexamining the narratives we tell about ourselves, others, the good news, and God. Christians recognize that their story begins with "Firstly," not "Secondly." "In the beginning" is the God who is love (1 John 4:7), the God who loves (John 3:16), the God who creates human beings to be bearers of God's own image (Gen 1:26–27). These matters are indeed good news to the survivors, the dispossessed, to all who continue to be dehumanized by the power of the powerful.

WHY DO WE DO WHAT WE DO?

The stories we tell also guide our actions and our understanding of why we behave in certain ways and not others, of why we do what we do and not act otherwise. The importance of understanding the "narrative structure of Christian convictions" Stanley Hauerwas refers to also helps Christian communities, churches especially, to understand how they differ from relief

20. Adichie, "Danger of the Single Story."
21. Hauerwas, Community of Character, 9.

and other humanitarian organizations. The distinction lies in what I term a difference between *etiology* and *teleology*. The former refers to the *source* (not the motive) from which an action originates, the latter to its *aims* and *purposes*. When Christians tell the story of the gospel truthfully, we come to recognize that unlike relief and charitable organizations, Christians do not clothe the naked, feed the hungry, shelter the homeless, or protect the orphan and the widow so that the naked may be clothed, the hungry fed, the homeless sheltered, and the orphan and the widow be protected. That is what humanitarian organizations do. That is a *teleologically* driven relationship: one does something so that a desirable outcome might be accomplished. Such work is necessary; it is desirable and laudable, but *teleology* is not the operative principle for Christians. For it is when actions driven by *teleologies* come face-to-face with the enormity of the task that burn-out happens, and despair sets in (both are exceedingly common among relief workers throughout the world). When measured against the immensity of the situation, one's actions seem small and insignificant: "What difference does my involvement actually make?" is a question asked in exasperation.

Because the Christian story begins with "in the beginning God" (Gen 1:1), and ends again with God, who is "all in all" (1 Cor 15:28), Christians know that the *telos* is not in their own hands but rather in God's, and therefore do not seek to be in control of either systems or history itself. Christians clothe the naked, feed the hungry, shelter the homeless, and protect the orphan and the widow simply because that is what Christians do. This is what it means to be *Christlike*, it is the Christian's *etiological raison d'être*. While non-Christians may well aspire to and even achieve acts of love and kindness and acts of mercy and justice, these are *not* optional for the Christian, but rather they are the phenotypical expression of our genotype. For as Michael Gorman has shown, from the very beginning Christians have been called "not merely to *believe* the gospel but to *become* the gospel and in so doing to participate in the very life and mission of God,"[22] here and now. Such an understanding can navigate well both the enormity of the situation and the perceived insignificance of one's actions, because the question, "What difference does my involvement actually make?" does not arise. Christians do what they do *not* so as to make a difference, but rather Christians do what they do *because* that is what it means to be Christians. It's called faithfulness, πιστότης, and it leads to שלום, shalom.

God's promise of shalom is much more than an absence of war or conflict. Shalom is wholeness, completeness, balance, well-being, tranquility, security, and justice. Shalom speaks of the inherently *relational* nature of

---

22. Gorman, *Becoming the Gospel*, 2.

God's intention for creation as it points to the perfect unity God intended to exist between God, humans, and creation.[23] Shalom is *wholistic*.[24] God's shalom does not allow for an exploitative attitude toward each other or creation. God is making all things new (Isa 43:19, Rev 21:5), here and now.

"All Christians approach their faith from within a particular cultural context," Todd Billings reminds us. "This fact is inescapable. Yet, one of the peculiar things about culture is that it involves many assumptions that we didn't recognize we had—until we encounter something different."[25] For Christian communities to be bearers of God's good news, we need to jettison those teleological narratives that are driven by utility and power. Otherwise we may succumb to what N. T. Wright calls *Platonized* eschatologies, escapist theologies that "substitut[e] 'souls going to heaven' for the promised new creation."[26] The danger is that when our hope for the future is that "our souls would go to heaven" and we escape this world, when our attention is so "other-worldly" oriented, we miss what God is doing in this world, here, and now. We miss the new order of things God has established through the resurrection of Jesus here, and now. We miss how God's promise to bring heaven and earth together in a great act of new creation here, now. Soteriological escapism becomes the operative motif and kerygmatic proclamation from church pulpits and youth camps to evangelistic campaigns and prayer groups (especially when coupled with one form or another of twentieth century apocalyptic theologies of end-times conflagrations),[27] the earth becomes expendable, and so does everything in it, including its inhabitants, especially those who are not like or think like us.[28] Moreover, such narratives

23. See Evans and Gower, "Restorative Economy."

24. I am using the older form of the word, *wholistic*, rather than Smuts's 1920 alteration to *holistic*, to emphasize that *shalom* pertains to the whole.

25. Billings, *Union with Christ*, 3.

26. Wright, *Day the Revolution Began*, 145–67.

27. A profound misreading of 2 Pet 3:10 and the book of Revelation.

28. Such transformations of societies facing overwhelming external pressures are not unique to Christian communities. A cursory look at the primarily monocultural societies of Europe reveals the results of increased economic, political, cultural, and religious pressures. Even in countries with secular pluralities and polyvalent ideological traditions fears of non-integration of migrants and immigrants highlight cultural pressures that are perceived as threat, as cancellation of local culture and customs, and lead to conscious or subconscious racist responses. All this is evident in the movements of heightened nationalism erupting in Europe and North America over the past ten years, resulting in closed borders and rejection of those seeking refuge. It has been well documented that since 2016, the wave of refugees seeking refuge in Europe has been met by another wave, a tsunami of nationalism that rose to "protect European economy and culture, national identity and religious coherence" from what was caricatured as invading hordes of brown and black, Arab-speaking, Muslims who attempt to conquer Europe again, now

often fuel intense incurvation meant to guarantee the community's purity and participation in the blessedness of "the time to come." The result often is either a self-imposed separation in the pursuit of theological and liturgical purity, or the equally incurvated attempt of assuming eschatological control of history through political power, an attempt to hasten "the coming of God's kingdom." Because such ecclesiologies are teleologically driven and are based on an "us vs. them" paradigm, they rarely allow for the "stranger in our midst" to be received as an image-bearer of God.

COMMUNITIES OF FAITH AND PRACTICAL PRESENCE

A number of years ago, my friend and colleague David Boan,[29] a clinical psychologist and the cofounder of Wheaton College's Humanitarian Disaster Institute (HDI) invited me to embark on a multiyear project of training pastors at one of the world's largest and diverse refugee camps in Kakuma, in Northwest Kenya.[30] Our goal was to provide pastors and church leaders with a combination of basic training in trauma-care coupled with coherent, in-depth biblical and theological training that would aid refugee and host community pastors as they navigated their own and their community's experiences.

Throughout the world, as long-term refugees have been trained to be on the receiving end of charity, they have learned through the many years of suffering what to say, how to act, at which camera to look so as to receive aid. Promises of biblical (rarely theological) training abound, but they usually come with strings attached that perpetuate colonial paradigms and reinforce theological dependence. Cognizant of the overwhelming power differential between our US-based organizations and the communities of refugees and local Turkana, our commitment from the very beginning was that we would follow the lead of the local United Refugee and Host Churches (URHC) and would work *under* their leadership to develop local voices, empowering African Christians to speak of God using their own voices and experiences. We never imposed a curriculum from the outside.

---

disguised as refugees. Countries led by nationalist governments closed the borders to refugees—first Hungary, then Austria, Northern Macedonia, Croatia, and Slovenia, effectively stranding thousands of migrants and refugees at the borders of Greece and Italy.

29. David Boan is currently the Director of Relief and Development for the World Evangelical Alliance (WEA).

30. The International Association for Refugees (IAFR) and the National Council of Churches of Kenya (NCCK) invited us, opened the way, and have been indispensable partners since the beginning. For the work of IAFR at the Kakuma Refugee Camp, including descriptions of the training we provide, see IAFR, "Kakuma," https://www.iafr.org/kakuma.

Rather, at every step we asked for the URHC leadership to tell us how we could assist in their training and development, and we followed through. The road was hard, and it took a very long time because trust has to be earned. This is trust in the ones who claim to come in peace, but also trust in one's own experiences and ability to articulate who God is from within *those* experiences, apart from the language and structures of the European and North American teachers. That, too, takes time.

The reversal of the power dynamic built on long-term trust relationships is not easy to accomplish. Survivors have learned to be dependent "guests," while the power resides with the "host." This is the "danger of the single story" in real time, where survivors continue to be dispossessed and dehumanized by the power of the powerful. In order to improve the trajectories of survivors into recovery and healing, Christian communities, and churches in particular, must be *safe* places where the dominant guest/host paradigm is not the operative motif. In the *Spiritual First Aid* manual, HDI identifies fourteen principles that combine to create a safe space, especially for survivors of the trauma of migration.[31]

Communities that aim to be safe places recognize the power imbalance and operative dynamics, they respect individual differences, accept survivors without imposing conditions or judgment, respect the wishes of the survivors, do not impose themselves or their culture those who seek safety, and they align with survivors where they are spiritually, that is, they do not *impose* spiritual conversions. For some Christian communities this last principle might sound peculiar, but, as Tom Albinson reminded me as we were walking among the "temporary" dwellings of Kakuma to visit a Muslim Somali refugee family, "The last piece of their homeland is their religious identity. Be careful how you shake this. Be gentle and careful." Survivors have been lied to, lied about, used, traumatized, and isolated throughout their migratory journey. Our goal is to "be consistent and trustworthy," as Tom told me, "so as to become the new center of stability."

Welcoming communities are places where survivors can truly be treated as persons, as image-bearers of God. Faithful Christian communities become places of such *practical presence* when trust and humility prevail, for they create the space necessary for survivors to regain the rehumanizing

31. These are: (1) confidentiality, (2) trust, (3) reciprocity, (4) relation, (5) shared experience, (6) sensitivity, (7) being aware of the level and types of trauma, (8) being able to receive help, (9) avoid giving unsolicited advice (it highlights the power imbalance), (10) learn from the survivor (listen to their stories), (11) avoid taking an expert stance, (12) do not get defensive, (13) remember you are here to help, not to be right, (14) apologize quickly when survivors react negatively to something you say or do (it restores power balance). See Aten and Boan, *Spiritual First Aid.*

power of being hosts themselves. By "practical presence" I mean a wholistic way of being and a strategy of engaging the spiritual needs of survivors by attending to their human needs, on the one hand, and by allowing the wholeness of the community, as a beloved community, to be engaged, on the other.

Practical presence also means that we are willing to *be* with the survivors in their suffering and lament rather than trying to fix or "rescue." Survivors know how to bake, how to sing, how to build, how to teach. Being given the opportunity to do so is part of the rehumanizing process. Lastly, faithful Christian communities are places where members of the dominant culture are willing—slowly—to become "guests" and allow survivors to assume the place of the "host." Survivors have gifts and talents, experiences, affections, ideas that are true gifts to the "host" communities, and we ought to recognize them as such. Practical presence cannot be rushed, for it is the outflow of a radical inner transformation that takes time. It is the patient work of becoming *for* the other.

FINAL THOUGHTS

A young student of mine had become wonderfully sensitive to the plight of the homeless in the affluent suburbs of Chicago. As a result, she always walked about with coupons from a chain restaurant, the kind one could exchange for a meal. One day, between classes, our paths crossed and we were walking together for block or two toward the local coffee shop. On our way, we met a person asking for charity. Having been raised in a family that practiced Christlike engagement with the poor, Kerryn sat down, on the pavement, and she started talking to him: "Hi, I'm Kerryn. What's your name? I'd like to help you with these two coupons. Will you take them to buy some food?" It is safer to walk by. It is easier not to notice. It appeases the conscience to toss two coins in the can or the hand. The disciple of Jesus is called to *see* those in need and *do* something about it. Until one *sees*, there is nothing one can *do*. It begins by offering one's name and welcoming the name of the other.

For Christian communities to become places of such openness and vulnerability it requires a robust theology of community and body politics, and a commitment to live out the faith conviction that God is the Lord of history. It requires intentionality. Such a transformation often requires a complete reorientation of self and community toward a posture of vulnerability not usually fostered by dominant ecclesiological narratives. It requires a willingness to listen to the voices of survivors rather than our own. It requires a willingness to recognize the voice of God when it comes to us in an accent that strains our ear, from the lips of one who does not look or speak or think like us.

To become such communities requires that we relax our grip on our attempt to secure our provisions, in whatever form we imagine them—food, health, safety, relationships, happiness, love, or the ever-elusive "future"—and learn that abundance, not scarcity, is the mark of God's care for creation. Only then are we freed from the crippling fear that there is never enough. Then we learn to live in God's economy of plentitude and abundance. Only then can Christian communities become safe communities that recognize the stranger as a welcomed gift. Until then, we will continue to be habituated by the economies of scarcity and live in alienation from God and one another.

At the end, "Love your neighbor" (Mark 12:31, Matt 22:39) is not an idiosyncratic peculiarity for the few; it is a dominical command. The church is God's declaratory statement to the world of who God is, of what hope is, of what life without fear looks like. As James K. A. Smith has remarked, "The church doesn't *have* an apologetic; it *is* an apologetic."[32] When the world asks, "Is there a God?" God's first and only response is: "Look at my people, called by my name."

BIBLIOGRAPHY

Adiche, Chimamanda Ngozi. "The Danger of a Single Story." TEDGlobal 2009. https://www.ted.com/talks/chimamanda_ngozi_adichie_the_danger_of_a_single_story?language=en.

Albinson, Thomas P. *Refugee Realities* 2020, IAFR. https://global-uploads.webflow.com/5e753e90e64659ba51ecd6ad/5eecf09bfb8f07009ef02de1_2020_Refugee Realities FAQ-IAFR.pdf.

———. "Stand Up, Speak Out, and Take Action: An Open Letter to the Church at Large On World Refugee Day 2020." June 19, 2020. https://global-uploads.webflow.com/5e753e90e64659ba51ecd6ad/5eecf9ac0aad890f5cdc5b7b_Stand Up Speak Out Take Action—An Open Letter to the Church At Large.pdf.

Araujo, Juliana de Oliveira, et al. "Prevalence of Sexual Violence among Refugees: A Systematic Review." *Revista de saude publica* 53 (September 2019). doi:10.11606/s1518-8787.2019053001081.

Aten, Jamie, and David Boan. *Spiritual First Aid: Disaster Chaplain Guide*. Wheaton, IL: Humanitarian Disaster Institute, Wheaton College, 2013.

Barghouti, Mourid. *Ra'aytu Ram Allah (I Saw Ramallah)*. Translated by Ahdaf Soueif. New York: American University of Cairo, 2000; Anchor repr. ed., 2003.

BBC News. "Migrant Crisis: Migration to Europe Explained in Seven Charts." March 4, 2016. https://www.bbc.com/news/world-europe-34131911.

Billings, J. Todd. *Union with Christ: Reframing Theology and Ministry for the Church*. Grand Rapids: Baker Academic, 2011.

Boffey, Daniel, and Helena Smith. "Oxfam Condemns EU over 'Inhumane' Lesbos Refugee Camp." *Guardian*, January 8, 2019. https://www.theguardian.com/world/2019/jan/09/oxfam-criticises-eu-inhumane-lesbos-refugee-camp-moria.

32. Smith, *Who's Afraid?*, 29.

Clayton, Jonathan, and Hereward Holland. "Over One Million Sea Arrivals Reach Europe in 2015." *UNHCR|USA*, December 30, 2015. https://www.unhcr.org/news/latest/2015/12/5683d0b56/million-sea-arrivals-reach-europe-2015.html.

Evans, Alex, and Richard Gower. "The Restorative Economy: Completing Our Unfinished Millennium Jubilee." Tearfund, 2015. http://www.micahnetwork.org/sites/default/files/doc/page/the_restorative_economy_weaver.pdf.

"Figures at a Glance: UNHCR|USA." https://www.unhcr.org/en-us/data.html.

Gorman, Michael J. *Becoming the Gospel: Paul, Participation, and Mission.* Grand Rapids: Eerdmans, 2015.

"Greece Will Struggle to Reverse 'Brain Drain.'" *Oxford Analytica*, August 2, 2018. https://dailybrief.oxan.com/Analysis/GA236556/Greece-will-struggle-to-reverse-brain-drain.

Hauerwas, Stanley. *A Community of Character: Toward a Constructive Christian Social Ethic.* Notre Dame: University of Notre Dame Press, 1981.

IAFR (International Association for Refugees). https://www.iafr.org/learn.

———. "Kakuma." https://www.iafr.org/kakuma.

———. "The Unique Role of IAFR on the Refugee Highway." https://global-uploads.webflow.com/5e753e90e64659ba51ecd6ad/5f207c5b2a08dee5e9f47e4e_IAFR%27s%20Unique%20Role%20on%20the%20Refugee%20Highway.pdf.

Kalantzis, George, et al., eds. *Who Do You Say I Am? On the Humanity of Jesus.* Eugene, OR: Cascade, 2020.

———. "Bodies Transgressing Boundaries: In *Imitatio Christi*." In *Who Do You Say I Am? On the Humanity of Jesus*, edited by George Kalantzis et al., 113–22. Eugene, OR: Cascade, 2020.

McAuliffe, Marie, and Binod Khadria, eds. *World Migration Report 2020.* International Organization for Migration, Geneva. https://publications.iom.int/wystem/files/pdf/wmr_2020.pdf.

Nye, Catrin. "Children Are 'Attempting Suicide' at Greek Refugee Camp." Victoria Derbyshire Programme, August 28, 2018. https://www.bbc.com/news/world-europe-45271194.

———, producer. "The Worst Refugee Camp on Earth." https://www.youtube.com/watch?v=8v-0Hi3iG01.

Pittaway, Eileen, et al. "'Stop Stealing Our Stories': The Ethics of Research with Vulnerable Groups." *Journal of Human Rights Practice* 2 (2010) 229–51.

Skleparis, Dimitris. "The Greek Response to the Migration Challenge: 2015–2017." KAS-Κάτοπτρον, 5. Athens: Konrad-Adenauer-Stiftung Greece (2017), 2. https://www.kas.de/c/document_library/get_file?uuid=9ca070c8-b546-01ac-e85a-df93ea2e5297&groupId=252038.

Smith, James K. A. *Who's Afraid of Postmodernism? Taking Derrida, Lyotard, and Foucault to Church.* The Church and Postmodern Culture. Grand Rapids: Baker Academic, 2006.

Wright, N. T. *The Day the Revolution Began: Reconsidering the Meaning of Jesus's Crucifixion.* San Francisco: HarperOne, 2016.

Motus Dei (The Move of God)

A Theology and Missiology for a Moving World

Sam George

INTRODUCTION

GOD IS ON THE move. God is moving in the lives of men and women across the street and around the world. The message of the kingdom of God is going forth in a remarkable manner in these days and God's reign is advancing in unexpected ways. God is powerfully moving among the people who are on the move. The migrants, displaced peoples, and diaspora communities are at the forefront of God's mission in the world today. The migration is one of the mega-themes of the Biblical narratives and the trajectory of the salvation history and church worldwide have been reshaped repeatedly by the people on the move.

This chapter delves into the Christian doctrines to introduce (to some) and develop the concept of *motus dei* by arguing that God of the Bible is one who is continually on the move and one who beckons his followers to come alongside to see what God is doing in the world. Thus, the mission is all about moving with God to see all things made new as we harmonize our wandering steps to be in sync with a moving God. The mission is following God, moving in, and catching up with God in many different cultural and geographical spaces all over the world to grow in our appreciation of God's work in, through, and around us as we move about. Within the confines of this brief chapter, I venture into the domains of theology (proper), anthropology, soteriology, pneumatology, and eschatology, while constructing a new theology and missiology for a world in motion. It hopes to draw from the rich resources of the faith to understand God and God's work in a world of unprecedented human mobility and consequent societal and global transformations wrought by what is now considered an age of migration.

MOVING GOD: CREATION AND TRINITY

The God of the Bible is a missionary God[1] because God is always on the move, and God is on the move because God is a living being. The divine attributes of omnipresence, immutability, and impassibility should not lead us in the direction of viewing God as rigid, static, immovable, and stationary. God cannot be confined in space or time, yet he is sovereign over spatial and chronological realms. After closely examining the history of Israel given in the sermon of the first Christian martyr Stephen in the book of Acts, John Stott concluded that "God of the Old Testament was the living God, a God on the move and on the march, who was always calling his people out to fresh adventures, and always accompanying and directing them as they went."[2]

First of all, in the very beginning, in the Creation account immediately after the opening statement about God creating the cosmos, we read "the Spirit of God was hovering over the waters" (Gen 1:2); we observe God's movement over the earth that is without form, empty and dark. Even before God spoke creation commands in Genesis 1:3 and thereafter, we see God moving over the earth. Before the illuminating, life-creating, and order-making creative work of God, we see a moving God. Some translations use words such as *blowing, soaring, sweeping over,* or *moving* in place of *hovering* and could be compared with the word mentioned in Deuteronomy 32:10, which renders imagery of an eagle hovering over its nest. The Hebrew noun for God in Genesis 1:1 is plural, which establishes the Trinitarian foundations from the very beginning, and Pentecostal theologians have affirmed the role the Spirit in the creation using Genesis 1:2.[3] One may argue that the divine utterances of creation resulted from divine movement and in response to it.

Moreover, in the creation account, the formless and empty earth (Gen 1:2) that God "separated" and "gathered" on days one to three to establish a form. And God's "making" and "filling" in days four to six remove the emptiness. Likewise, scattering and gathering could be seen as mega-themes

1. Stott, "Living God Is a Missionary God"; Wright, *Mission of God*, 71–74.

2. Stott, *Message of Acts*, 132.

3. Yong, *Missiological Spirit*; Ma and Ma, *Mission in the Spirit*; Keener, *Spirit Hermeneutics*.

of divine action throughout to establish God's reign in the created order. The creation mandate to be "Be fruitful and multiply, and fill the earth and subdue it" (Gen 1: 28) charges the human beings to be co-rulers over the creation on God's behalf and its scope covers the whole earth, requiring humanity to move from place to place. Unlike the creator who is not confined by space and is sovereign, and yet found moving about, the creatures have to navigate beyond their spatial subjectivities to establish the divine reign on the earth. This mandate encompasses the human destiny to be a relational and communal being in order to inhabit and shape social life as well as the natural world. The fall is portrayed as alienation and expulsion from the Garden, a form of forced displacement, and it sets the stage for eventual redemption that could be conceived as moving back to a state of restored communion and proximity to the divine being, thus requiring soteriology to be articulated afresh in locational and relational terms.

God moves within Godself and outside of Godself. The Trinitarian nomenclature of the three persons of the Godhead as co-indwelling, co-in-hering, and mutual interpenetration "allows the individuality of the person to be maintained while each person shares in the life of the other two."[4] God moves because God is Trinity, since both strictly monotheistic as well as tri-theistic ideation will make Godhead motionless, while the polytheistic notion of gods makes them territorial. The conceptualization of Trinitarian relationality and the dance of perichōrēsis requires kinematic imagination as it cannot be grasped solely in a static state. The Trinity provides the basis of ontological foundations for understanding the human personhood and interpersonal relations.[5]

The relationality of Trinity allows Godself to move toward each other and together move into the created order and the entire cosmos. "God goes forth from God, God creates the world, God suffuses its history and dwells within it, redeeming the world from within."[6] Such a model of Trinitarian God has many implications on theological anthropology and, for this chapter's purposes, such intrinsic sociality of human beings requires mobility, without which the creature is not fully alive or social. Another important manner how humans relate is through language and being in communication with other human beings, which is closely tied to the idea of being in motion. The etymology of the word *migrate* is instructive and it is linked to *commute, communication, commune,* and other words. "Humans are like God in their capacity to go out of themselves and enter into personal

4. McGrath, *Christian Theology*, 325.

5. See Zizioulas, *Being as Communion*; Volf, *After Our Likeness*.

6. LaCugna, *God for Us*, 353.

relations through communicative agency."[7] The history and innovations in transportation, communication, and trade have a symbiotic relationship with the history of human migrations.

In contrast to a living and moving God, idols cannot move about and need to be carried from place to place (Jer 10:5). Idols and territorial spirits are bound within geographical confines and keep devotees chained to a locale. Calvin expounded the second commandment that representing God in images was forbidden because people are bound by physical surroundings when they create an image of a deity, they are distracted from God's true spiritual being, and to some degree the deity is conceived in some corporeal way.[8] In developing a theology of idolatry, Beale asserted that we become what we worship as without mouths, eyes, ears, hands or feet based on the psalmist's claim "those who make them [idols] will become like them" (Ps 115:8) and we resemble what we revere, either for ruin or restoration.[9] In other words, idolatry makes us lifeless and fastened to geography like a dead person. The insular nature of idolatrous societies stems from their provincialism, which in turn makes their religions less transportable and missionary. The parochial tendencies restrict the territorial dominion of evil and demonic spirits as they are not omnipresent or omniscient like God of the Bible. The beliefs of ancestral worship and mediation to guardian spirits point to territorial bondage and ethnic elitism while people remain imprisoned to a locality. These gods, spirits, and ancestors reside in a particular object or territory and protect people who reside within its vicinity. Their powers do not extend beyond those areas and when people travel to distant places, they are no longer under the protection of their gods and expected to change their allegiance to a stronger god of the new region and serve him. In contrast to tribal spirit deities, "Jehovah declared himself not to be a territorial god but the God of the universe."[10]

When the physicality of the Temple occupied a more overbearing place for Israelites and considerable superficiality, corruption and ritualism took over, God allowed it to be destroyed by invading armies, resulting in the exile of the Israelites. The Tabernacle was more archetypal of a moving God than a sedentary God of the Jerusalem Temple. The response of the disciples at the transfiguration of Jesus was to "Let us put up three shelters" (Mark 9:5) as they wanted to erect tents to memorialize or establish a shrine at that place. The divine corrective to disciples affirmed the Sonship of Jesus and

7. Vanhoozer, "Human Beings," 177.

8. Calvin, *Commentaries on Last Four Books*, 116–17.

9. Beale, *We Become What We Worship*, 44–49.

10. Hiebert, *Transforming Worldviews*, 117.

called them to obey him. Likewise, Jesus resolved the dilemma faced by the Samaritan women about the true place of worship between Mount Gerizim for Samaritans and Jerusalem for Jews, by exhorting her that it is neither here nor there but "true worshipers will worship in truth and spirit." (John 4:24). The place has been deemed inconsequential and Jesus broke through the human tendency to domesticate God and bind infinite boundless Spirit within cultural and geographical particularity.

Japanese theologian Kosuke Koyama compared Mount Fuji, the cosmological center of the world according to the Japanese imperial ideology, with Mount Sinai, the place of divine epiphany and where the Law was given to the Israelites. The image of the mobile God did not concede Mount Sinai to become a place of worship and their imagination of God to be bound to a place. Instead, God himself "symbolizes the center of salvation. The center symbolism travels with the people."[11] He further contends that centrality, whether that of an individual, a race, an institution, a nation, or an empire, is always open to abuse and exploitation by a destructive ideology.

CREATED TO MOVE: BEING AND FALL

Secondly, a doctrine of humanity needs to be articulated in motile terms to understand our innate propensity toward peripatetic wanderings. Here, I contend that human movability is a characteristic feature since we are created "in the likeness of God" (Gen 1:26), similar to the notions of human rationality, relationality, dignity, identity, solidarity, freedom, worth, and other dominant interpretations of the image of God in the classical theological texts. We are created to move because we bear the image of a moving God and it is high time to reimagine theological anthropology and mission theology kinesiologically.

"I move, therefore I am" (*moveo ergo sum*) is more pertinent in the age of migration than Descartes's dictum. Augustine spoke of human life as ever on the move: "You have made us *toward* yourself, and our hearts are restless until they rest in you."[12] Walls argued that the history of humanity was "determined by the movements of peoples"[13] and Groody claimed that the theme of migration is intrinsic to our biological and spiritual genes.[14] We are created to move about and only when we move, are we fully alive and exhibiting our likeness to our Creator. The inability to move denies the

11. Koyama, *Mount Fuji*, 88.
12. Augustine, *Confessions*. 1.
13. Walls, "Towards a Theology."
14. Groody, "Homebound."

personhood and utterly dehumanizes the person. Being created in the image of God is not a state or condition, but a movement with a goal.[15] Such a directional teleology can aid the development of a more nuanced construal of the doctrine of the fall as alienation or falling away, using biblical narratives of expulsion from the Garden, the call of Abraham, the exodus, the exile, and other texts. This will help to reconceive the soteriological task as a moving experience "passing over from death to life" and "out of the Kingdom of darkness into his marvelous light" (1 Pet 2:9; Acts 26:17). The contemporary urban nomadism and migration across national borders only prove that we are truly *homo mobilis*.

In his Areopagus sermon, the Apostle Paul quoted the Cretan poet and philosopher Epimenides, of the seventh century BCE, from his work *Cretica*—"In him we live and move and have our being" (Acts 17:28) and used it to talk about a God who made the world and everything in it, in contrast to pantheistic Stoicism. He went on to confront the idolatry of the Athenians, introduce Jesus, and call his listeners to repentance. At the heart of this comparison is the belief that human existence and our very being are intricately linked to our capacity for motion and all of it is derived from the divine being who is not a mere lifeless and immotile idol crafted by human hands. We move in response to God, who is on the move incessantly. And this moving nature is not only a sign of being alive but lies at the very core of our identity. This also presents that the created human being is in total and continual dependence on the creator for its existence, sustenance, abilities, and activities. All living creatures, especially human beings, are brought to life by the divine breath (Gen 2:7) and in the second of the four speeches Elihu makes to Job, he states, "If he [God] would take back his spirit to himself, and gather to himself his breath, all flesh would perish together and man would return to dust" (Job 34:14–15). Paul believed that "he himself gives all men life and breath and everything else" (Acts 17:25). Jesus told his disciples that "Son can do nothing of his own accord, but only what he sees the Father doing" (John 5:19) and "apart from me you can do nothing" (John 15:5).

Later in the same sermon, Paul cited the Cilician poet Aratus (ca. 315–240 BCE) from his writings called *Phaenomena*—"We are God's offspring" (Acts 17:28b)—and found a common anthropological and theological ground with the audience using pagan literature. Paul suggested that the unknown god of Athenians was the God of Jesus Christ and found a mutually tenable platform to engage his heathen listeners evangelistically without alienating them. He was more inclusive and tried to identify with

15. Migliore, *Faith Seeking Understanding*, 128.

his interlocutors without creating division of "us versus them." Earlier he had claimed that from one man God had made every nation inhabiting the whole Earth and thus argued that whole of humanity has a common ancestry. Amos Yong used this passage to renew his vision for pneumatological missiology of the Spirit for the pluralistic context of the twenty-first century.[16] As migration brings people closer to others who are unlike themselves and hold different belief systems, a theological anthropology understood in terms of mobile, familial kinship and mutuality of human diversity without compromising core convictions is required that does not undermine a credible witness of the gospel.

In the Athenian discourse, the Apostle Paul also claimed the sovereignty of God over human dispersion, saying God "determined the times set for them and the exact places where they should live" (Acts 17:26). Beyond the economic, sociological, legal, and political dimensions of human migration, we see a divine origin at work as people change their domiciles across borders. Paul explicates the reason why God moves people and underscores the spiritual consequences of migration. God moves people so that they would seek after him. Though God is not distant from them, the migrants come near to God after moving to a new place. Displacement makes people seek after God in new ways by testing the validity of their past beliefs in new contexts, while keeping them open to other alternatives and spiritual experiences. They compare and contrast between the worlds they are exposed to while striving to seek the ultimate truth claims. No wonder migration is considered "a theologizing experience."[17]

Christians are more likely to travel beyond places of their birth since they are not bound to any locale and their peripatetic encounter with foreign cultures and languages leads to new endeavors in adapting the tenets of their faith and practices into new contexts. Some opine that "if you are a Christian, you will travel, and if you travel, you will become a Christian." On the contrary, Hinduism is considered as a rooted religion because of its prohibition to traverse large expanses of water in its Scriptures, dietary restrictions, pollution taboos, purification rituals, demotion in the social hierarchy, and the fear of dying in a foreign land. Hindus are expected to live and die in a place close to where they were born and most remain largely bound within a specific land and culture.[18] Likewise, Islam is also a rooted religion on account of its pilgrimage, prayers uttered facing a particular

16. Yong, *Missiological Spirit*, 129–31.

17. Smith, "Religion and Ethnicity."

18. George, "Crossing *Kala Pani*."

place, and untranslatable scriptures.[19] Lamin Sanneh succinctly juxtaposed Islam and Christianity by alleging "Muslim *hijrah* bequeathed a legacy of geographical and linguistic orthodoxy while the Christian Pentecost created the reverse, an abandonment of the idea of divine territoriality."[20]

MOVING TO SAVE: INCARNATION AND SALVATION

Thirdly, incarnation means take on, become, or enter into flesh. It refers to the Christian doctrine that the pre-existent Son of God became a man in Jesus.[21] The birth of Jesus can be understood as a move of God into an alien world to become a human being within a particular sociocultural and historical setting, yet without losing his divinity. Thus, by incarnation God in the person of Jesus crosses the divide between the divine self and the created order. The New Testament does not use static or metaphysical concepts to explain the mystery of the incarnation, rather it is seen in terms of a dynamic movement. The Johannine Gospel describes the enfleshment of incarnation as the "Word became flesh and made his dwelling among us" (John 1:14), where God is portrayed as moving into our neighborhood or pitching his tent next door. The imagery is closely linked to the Old Testament idea of the Tent of Meeting, which was filled by the glory of God (Exod 40:34–35) and the portable sanctuary of God during the wilderness period that later becomes the model for the Temple in Jerusalem (Exod 25). God was moving with his people and a visible presence of God in the form of cloud by day and fire by night assured the people on their journey to their promised land.

Likewise, the Apostle Paul speaks of the incarnation of Jesus, the second person of the Trinity, in terms of emptying (kenosis) of himself in becoming a human being and finally of exaltation in the resurrection (Phil 2:6–11). This hymn depicted incarnation as descent and lowering to become nothing. The mystery of the incarnation of Jesus who did not give up his deity but laid aside his glory, being fully man and fully God, was explained using kinetic terms such as being poured out, lowered, exalted, highest place, above all, etc. Such a Christology starts from above, descends to the level of a human being, and ascends again to the divine plane. In contrast, in the Acts of the Apostles, we have a Christology from below, starting with the human life of Jesus Christ and the ascension and angelic assurance to the disciples about the second coming of Jesus (Acts 1:10–11).

19. George, "Diaspora Mission," 36.
20. Sanneh, *Translating the Message*, 262.
21. Reymond, "Incarnation," 555.

These verses are loaded with directional and motional words such as *look up, sky, stood beside, here, above, going, taken from, come back, go into*, etc. The New Testament accounts focused on the functional aspect of Christ, his life, teaching, and redemptive activities while in later centuries theologians took a metaphysical approach to understand his being as two natures (divine and human) united in one person.

The Aristotelian concept of "unmoved Mover" had a significant influence on Christian metaphysics and the notion of the attributes of God's divinity such as God's immutability and impassibility. However, Moltmann believes that the biblical experience of God would more likely correspond to a "self-moved Mover" because "God moves out of Godself and loves the being God has created."[22] The belief that what is divine is not subjected to change over time or change brought about by an external force. The attribute of immutability deprives a divine being of its vitality and the unchangeableness and immovability make God dead rather than a living and active being. In "coming down to deliver" his people, we see God moved by compassion after "seeing the affliction of my people and hav[ing] heard their cry" (Exod 3:8). God descends for the sake of his people, to liberate them from their bondage and suffering in Egypt, and leads them to the promised land by going before them. The view of these as anthropomorphisms does not take the human subject's likeness to God seriously and viewing God as immovable and incapable of love or suffering makes Godhead less divine.

Soteriology cannot only be conceived as acquittal, expiation, justification, atonement, and redemption from sin and death, as commonly done in Western theological writings, but also in relational, religious, and motile terms such as reversal of estrangement, alienation, ostracization, and contamination, using conceptual ideations such as brought near, reconciliation, purification, and restoration. Generally, the effect of the fall is traced as the inherited guilt or corruption of humanity for which salvation is presented as a gift of grace through Christ's death. The finished work of Jesus on the cross offers not only substitutionary atonement but also wholeness and fullness through soul cleansing, adoption into the family of God, and restoration of a broken relationship.[23] In shame and honor-based communitarian cultures, a more holistic and multidimensional stance of Christian salvation is required.

The ultimate aspect of salvation for Christians is their eschatological vision of the future that helps them recast their present predicaments in light of eternity and live with their eyes set on the savior and eternal life. The eschatological kingdom is the ultimate goal of all missionary work and

22. Moltman, *Living God*, 26. See also his *Crucified God*.
23. George, "Shaming the Shame."

mission is all about witness to the reign of God that *has come* in Jesus Christ and one *yet coming*.[24] Christians move, whether in the form of missionaries or migrants, across the cultural and geographical boundaries, and in the process of uprooting and transplantation they become strangely aware of the moving of God in their lives and the new locations. Many become Christians after moving to new places, whether the migration was for economic opportunities, educational prospects, or due to forcible displacement because of famine, wars, or persecution. Faith in a moving God becomes an indispensable resource for people on the move and they become natural evangelists and cultural translators over time, exerting missional influence on their places of origin, sojourn, and settlement. During their earthly peregrine life, the pilgrim people of God have no abiding city on earth, but look forward to the city with a foundation whose maker and builder is God (Heb 11:10). They have no fixed abode on earth; earthly home is *paroikia* (dwell beside or among), a temporary residence with eyes fixed on their eternal abode.[25] Their eschatological hope propels them to live each day faithfully with a divine sense of a grander purpose for their transitory lives to participate in the mission of God. Thus, the displaced immigrants serve a missionary function just as the functional missionaries are culturally displaced migrants.

MISSION IN MOTION: MIGRATION AND MOVEMENTS

Finally, at its core, Christian faith is a diasporic missionary faith. If it remains captive to a culture, people, or geography, it will turn into a religion like any other and be deprived of its innate dynamism. Much of the Bible is written in diasporic contexts and a common thread that runs throughout its pages are the select people and nation that God displaced in the different epoch of history to advance God's reign in the world. Salvation history is framed within migratory wanderings and much of Christian expansion and transformation over the last two millennia have ensued in diverse diasporic contexts. The expansion of Christianity has occurred along the trajectories of human dispersions as they become a conduit for the reinvigoration and cultural diffusion of the gospel from one group of people to another group of people. Consequently, Christianity has now reached every geopolitical entity in the world while becoming the most global, dispersed, and diverse faith in the world.

24. Ott et al., *Encountering Theology*, 90.
25. See Moltmann, *Theology of Hope*.

In developing a radically new Christian theological framework by reversing the order of theological formulation for the increasingly charismatic form of spirituality, diversity of global Christianity, and its missionary character since its beginning, Yong concluded that "Christianity was a transportable religion. Arguably its mobility lay in its capacity to accommodate itself to many different cultures, languages and people groups."[26] It is the mobility of its adherents that took early Christians to the fringes of the Roman Empire, on account of religious persecution as well as the socioeconomic conditions stemming from *Pax Romana* that spread Christianity throughout the Mediterranean rim and beyond. About the early history of Christianity, Harnack noted that "the apostles as well as many of the prophets traveled unceasingly in the interest of their mission. Paul . . . [and] his fellow workers and companions were also continually on move."[27] Christians are mobile people since they get unhinged from the geographical, sociocultural, fiscal, and political bondages of a particular locality. The anonymous *Epistle to Diognetus*, written in 124 CE, states, "The difference between Christians and the rest of mankind is not a matter of language, customs, or nationality. For them, any country is a motherland, and any motherland is a foreign country."

The nature of Christian faith is that its center lies outside the circle and continually pivots itself with new people and new centers. In establishing the nature of the church for the reign of God, Gutierrez contended "Its [the church's] existence is not 'for itself' but rather 'for others.' Its center is outside itself; it is in the work of Christ and his Spirit."[28] Mission, thus, is pivoting its message of the gospel of the risen Jesus outside the walls of the church with an eschatological orientation and pneumatological empowerment. No wonder the ancient Greek mathematician came out with the principle of lever and fulcrum that is widely used in common gadgets and engineering applications, who claimed that he could move the Earth, if he had a place to stand outside of it and lever long enough. Christian faith is translatable and continually engaged in tweaking its Scripture and practices for others. Lamin Sanneh claimed that vernacular translation of the Bible has played a central catalytic role in the spread of the Christian faith.[29] The Christian message can be expressed in any language and interpreted into any culture. Christian faith can be at home in any culture and it cannot be bound within any culture or geography, for its very nature makes it diffuse

26. Yong, *Renewing Christian Theology*, 2.

27. Harnack, *Expansion of Christianity*, 463.

28. Gutierrez, *Theology of Liberation*, 260.

29. Sanneh, *Translating the Message*.

across cultural lines. This translatability helped the spread of Christianity to new cultures across many regions of Africa, Asia, and Latin America in the last few centuries. I argue that it is the mobility that results in its translatability, as displacement creates the need to bridge the linguistic divide. Moreover, it is evident from the great European migration and the modern missionary movement that people who had richly benefited from the translation of the Scripture became champions for the cause of Bible translation into the vernacular languages in places where they went.

Several new theologies of the mission have taken journey, sojourner, pilgrim, hospitality, migration, alien, and exile as major theological motifs to understand the contemporary Christian mission for a world that is in perpetual motion.[30] Some have maintained that "journey" does not offer a helpful analytical concept for describing Paul's missionary praxis, since he lived and worked in Corinth and Ephesus for two years each.[31] However, I argue that the detailed account of Paul's travels, ministry and writings have emerged as a result of his being a product of the Jewish diaspora; his work began with diasporic settlers, and his distinctive conceptualization of the gospel from a diasporic vantage point liberated it beyond Jewish captivity into the broader Gentile world.[32] An apt metaphor about doing mission in the age of migration is "shooting a moving target." Our theologies and strategies for mission engagement have to be completely reinvented in the context of global migration. Many unreached people groups are no longer confined within a window or a geographical region but have relocated to other nations. As in archery, strategies to shoot a fixed target and moving target are poles apart and archers are to be trained not to shoot where the target is at present but where it will be when the arrow reaches that place. This requires anticipating where the target is going, creative and quick thinking, mastery over equipment, take into account the environment, and being prepared for high failure rates.

A major development at the turn of the twenty-first century is the move (or shift) of "the center of gravity of Christianity" in the world from the Global North to the Global South, first noted by Andrew Walls and subsequently examined it at length by many others, only to confirm the trend and its far-reaching repercussions.[33] Christianity has a universal savior and is now more global, geographically dispersed, and more diverse than it has

30. See Van Engen, *Mission on the Way*; Frost, *Exiles*; Cruz, *Intercultural Theology*; Pohl, *Making Room*; Stroope, *Transcending Mission*; Flett, *Witness of God*; and others.

31. Schnabel, *Paul and The Early Church*, 1445.

32. See Barclay, *Pauline Churches*, 1–34.

33. Walls, *Cross Cultural Process*, 45–47.

ever been in its entire history, closer to "the full stature of Christ" (Eph 4:13). This Ephesian Moment holds tremendous potential for much increased momentum in mission while it also poses many new challenges. Christians from other cultures and regions of the world can enrich our understanding of the faith, remedy our mistakes, enlarge our parochial perspectives, and help us gain a fuller perspective of God's moving work among all peoples of the world.

Undoubtedly one of the major theological innovations of the last century is the notion of *missio dei*, understanding mission as God's mission.[34] Based upon Barthian conceptualization, the mission was no more perceived as an activity of the church but an attribute of God derived from the very nature of God and framed within the context of the doctrine of the Trinity, not based on ecclesiology or soteriology. Mission is seen as a movement from God to the world and the church is viewed as an instrument of that mission. Such movement is not limited to a particular incident or age, but God is continually moving toward the world and his creation, to recreate it and establish his reign. The development of missional ecclesiology further emphasized the sending nature of God and the church.[35] However, it fortified the critical role of the sending bodies, the sociocultural and economic disparity between senders and receivers, reproduction of sending institutional cultures, unhealthy dependencies, lopsided power structures, and a form of neo-colonialism.[36] The sending model is incongruous for reimagining the work of God in a postcolonial, post-Western, post-Enlightenment, post-Christendom, and post-mission era.[37] The contemporary mission praxis is from everywhere to everywhere, multilateral, multidirectional, sending as well as receiving, with a polycentric global network requiring it to be conceived as polycentrifugal and polycentripetal flow. A multidirectional scattering and gathering are helpful motifs to understand the contemporary moving of God in the world.

---

34. Bosch, *Transforming Mission*, 390. Also, Kirk, *What Is Mission?*; Wrogemann, *Theologies of Mission*; Ott et al., *Encountering the Theology*; and Van Engen, *Transforming Mission Theology*.

35. Guder, *Missional Church*, 2009.

36. See Stroope, *Transcending Mission*; Flett, *Witness of God*; Flett and Congdon, eds., *Converting Witness*; and Gittins, *Ministry at the Margins*.

37. Yong, *Mission after Pentecost*; Escobar, *New Global Mission*; and Stroope, *Transcending Mission*.

CONCLUSION

Christianity is a missionary faith par excellence since it is a faith that was born to travel. In fact, the mobility of its adherents and the moving nature of God is what makes Christian faith a transportable and translatable faith as it continually transcends borders of all kinds over time. The movement of people is of utmost significance to Christian faith as displaced people have reconfigured the contours of its growth and expansion throughout its history. Since its inception, Christianity has diffused across cultural and geographical lines repeatedly, and many different people in varied places have been the chief representatives of Christianity. Christian faith cannot be bound to a location or domesticated by any people because its nature is to break free of the prisons in which we enshrine it. It is constrained to move from one place to another continually because it is a quintessential missionary, translatable, and mobile faith. Seeing God as a moving being and his ongoing work as a result of the moving of God are a helpful way to develop a theology and missiology for a moving world. A fresh formulation using *motus dei* can help in this regard and it is consistent with biblical, historical, and ongoing work of God in the world.

BIBLIOGRAPHY

Augustine. *Confessions.* Translated by Rex Warner. New York: Mentor, 1963.

Barclay, John M. G. *Pauline Churches and Diaspora Jews.* Grand Rapids: Eerdmans, 2016.

Beale, G. K. *We Become What We Worship: A Biblical Theology of Idolatry.* Downers Grove: InterVarsity, 2008.

Bosch, David. *Transforming Mission: Paradigm Shifts in Theology of Mission.* Maryknoll: Orbis, 2001.

Calvin, John. *Commentaries on the Last Four Books of Moses.* Grand Rapids: Eerdmans, 1964.

Cruz, Gemma Tulud. *An Intercultural Theology of Migration: Pilgrims in Wilderness.* Leiden: Brill, 2010.

Elwell, Walter A., ed. *Evangelical Dictionary of Theology.* Grand Rapids: Baker, 1984.

Escobar, Samuel. *The New Global Mission: The Gospel from Everywhere to Everyone.* Downers Grove: IVP Academic, 2003.

Flett, John. *The Witness of God: Missio Dei, Karl Barth, and the Nature of Christian Community.* Grand Rapids: Eerdmans, 2001.

Flett, John, and David Congdon, eds. *Converting Witness: The Future of the Christian Mission in New Millennium.* Lanham, MD: Lexington, 2017.

Frost, Michael. *Exiles: Living Missionally in a Post-Christian Culture.* Grand Rapids: Baker, 2006.

George, Sam. "Crossing *Kala Pani*: Overcoming Religious Barriers to Migration." In *Diaspora Christianities: Global Scattering and Gathering of South Asian Christians*, edited by Sam George, 69–83. Minneapolis: Fortress, 2019.

——. "Diaspora Mission and North American Muslims." *EMQ* 56 (2020) 35–37.

——. "Shaming the Shame: Healing Inner Wounds through Loving Relationships" In *Caring for a South Asian Soul: Counseling South Asians in the Western Word*, edited by Thomas Kulanjiyil and T. V. Thomas, 171–87. Bangalore: Primalogue, 2010.

Gittins, Anthony. *Ministry at the Margins: Strategy and Spirituality for Mission*. Maryknoll: Orbis, 2002.

Groody, Daniel. "Homebound: A Theology of Migration." *Journal of Catholic Social Thought* 9 (2012) 409–24.

Guder, Darrell. *Missional Church: A Vision for the Sending of the Church in North America*. Grand Rapids: Eerdmans, 1998.

Gutierrez, Gustavo. *A Theology of Liberation: History, Politics, and Salvation*. Translated by Caridad Inda and John Eagleson. Maryknoll: Orbis, 1973.

Hanciles, Jehu. *Beyond Christendom: Globalization, African Migration, and the Transformation of the West*. Maryknoll: Orbis, 2008.

Harnack, Adolf. *The Expansion of Christianity in the First Three Centuries*. London: Williams and Norgate, 1904.

Hiebert, Paul. G. *Transforming Worldviews: An Anthropological Understanding of How People Change*. Grand Rapids: Baker Academic, 2008.

Jenkins, Philip. *The Next Christendom: The Coming of Global Christianity*. New York: Oxford University Press, 2002.

Keener, Craig. *Spirit Hermeneutics: Reading Scripture in Light of Pentecost*. Grand Rapids: Eerdmans, 2017.

Kirk, J. Andrew. *What Is Mission? Theological Exploration*. Minneapolis: Fortress, 2000.

Koyama, Kosuke. *Mount Fuji and Mount Sinai: A Critique of Idols*. Maryknoll: Orbis, 1985.

LaCugna, Catherine M. *God for Us: The Trinity and Christian Life*. San Francisco: HarperSanFrancisco, 1993.

Ma, Wonsuk, and Julia Ma. *Mission in the Spirit: Toward a Pentecostal/Charismatic Missiology*. Oxford: Regnum, 2011.

Martinez, Juan F., et al., eds. *The Global Dictionary of Theology*. Downers Grove: InterVarsity, 2009.

McGrath, Alister. *Christian Theology: An Introduction*. Malden, NJ: Blackwell, 2011.

Migliore, Daniel. *Faith Seeking Understanding: An Introduction to Christian Theology*. Grand Rapids: Eerdmans, 1991.

Moltmann, Jürgen. *The Crucified God*. Translated by R. A. Wilson and John Bowden. 40th anniv. ed. Minneapolis: Fortress, 2015.

——. *The Living God and the Fullness of Life*. Geneva: WCC, 2015.

——. *Theology of Hope*. New York: Harper & Row, 1967.

Ott, Craig, et al. *Encountering the Theology of Mission*. Grand Rapids: Baker Academic, 2010.

Pohl, Christine D. *Making Room: Recovering Hospitality as Christian Tradition*. Grand Rapids: Eerdmans, 1999.

Reymond, R. L. "Incarnation." In *Evangelical Dictionary of Theology*, edited by Walter A. Elwell, 555–57. Grand Rapids: Baker, 1984.

Sanneh, Lamin. *Translating the Message: The Missionary Impact on Culture*. 2d ed. Maryknoll: Orbis, 2009.

Schnabel, Eckhard. *Paul and The Early Church*. Vol. 2 of *Early Christian Mission*. Downers Grove: IVP Academic, 2004.

Smith, Timothy L. "Religion and Ethnicity in America." *American Historical Review* 83 (1978) 1155–85.

Stott, John. "Living God Is a Missionary God." In *Perspectives on World Mission Movement: A Reader*, edited by Ralph Winter and Steve Hawthorn, 10–18. Pasadena, CA: William Carey, 1981.

———. *The Message of Acts*. The Bible Speaks Today Series. Downers Grove: IVP Academic, 1994.

Stroope, Michael. *Transcending Mission: The Eclipse of a Modern Tradition*. Downers Grove: IVP Academic, 2017.

Thomas, Norman, ed. *Classical Texts in Mission and World Christianity*. Maryknoll: Orbis, 1994.

Van Engen, Charles. *Mission on the Way: Issues in Mission Theology*. Grand Rapids: Baker, 1996.

Vanhoozer, Kevin. "Human Beings: Individual and Social" In *Cambridge Companion to Christian Doctrine*, edited by Colin Gunter, 158–88. New York: Cambridge University Press, 1997.

Volf, Mirolsav. *After Our Likeness: The Church as the Image of the Trinity*. Grand Rapids: Eerdmans, 1988.

Walls, Andrew F. "Towards a Theology of Migration." In *African Christian Presence in the West: New Immigrant Congregations and Transnational Networks in North America and Europe*, edited by Frieder Ludwig and Kwabena Asamoah-Gyadu, 407–17. Trenton, NJ: Africa World, 2011.

Walls, Andrew F. *The Cross Cultural Process in Christian History: Studies in the Transmission and Appropriation of Faith*. Maryknoll: Orbis, 2002.

———. "Culture and Coherence in Christian History." *Scottish Bulletin of Evangelical Theology* 3 (1985) 1–9.

Wright, Christopher. *The Mission of God: Unlocking the Bible's Grand Narrative*. Downers Grove: IVP Academic, 2006.

———. *The Mission of God's People: A Biblical Theology of the Church's Mission*. Grand Rapids: Zondervan Academic, 2010.

Wrogemann, Henning. *Theologies of Mission*. Vol. 2. Downers Grove: IVP Academic, 2018.

Yeh, Allen. *Polycentric Missiology: Twenty-First Century Mission from Everyone to Everywhere*. Downers Grove: IVP Academic, 2016.

Yong, Amos. *The Missiological Spirit: The Christian Mission Theology in the Third Millennium Global Context*. Eugene, OR: Cascade, 2014.

———. *Mission after Pentecost: The Witness of the Spirit from Genesis to Revelation* Grand Rapids: Baker Academic, 2019.

———. *Renewing Christian Theology: Systematics for a Global Christianity*. Waco, TX: Baylor University Press, 2014.

Zizioulas, John D. *Being as Communion: Studies in Personhood and the Church*. London: Darton, Longman and Todd, 1985.

Name Index

Scripture Index